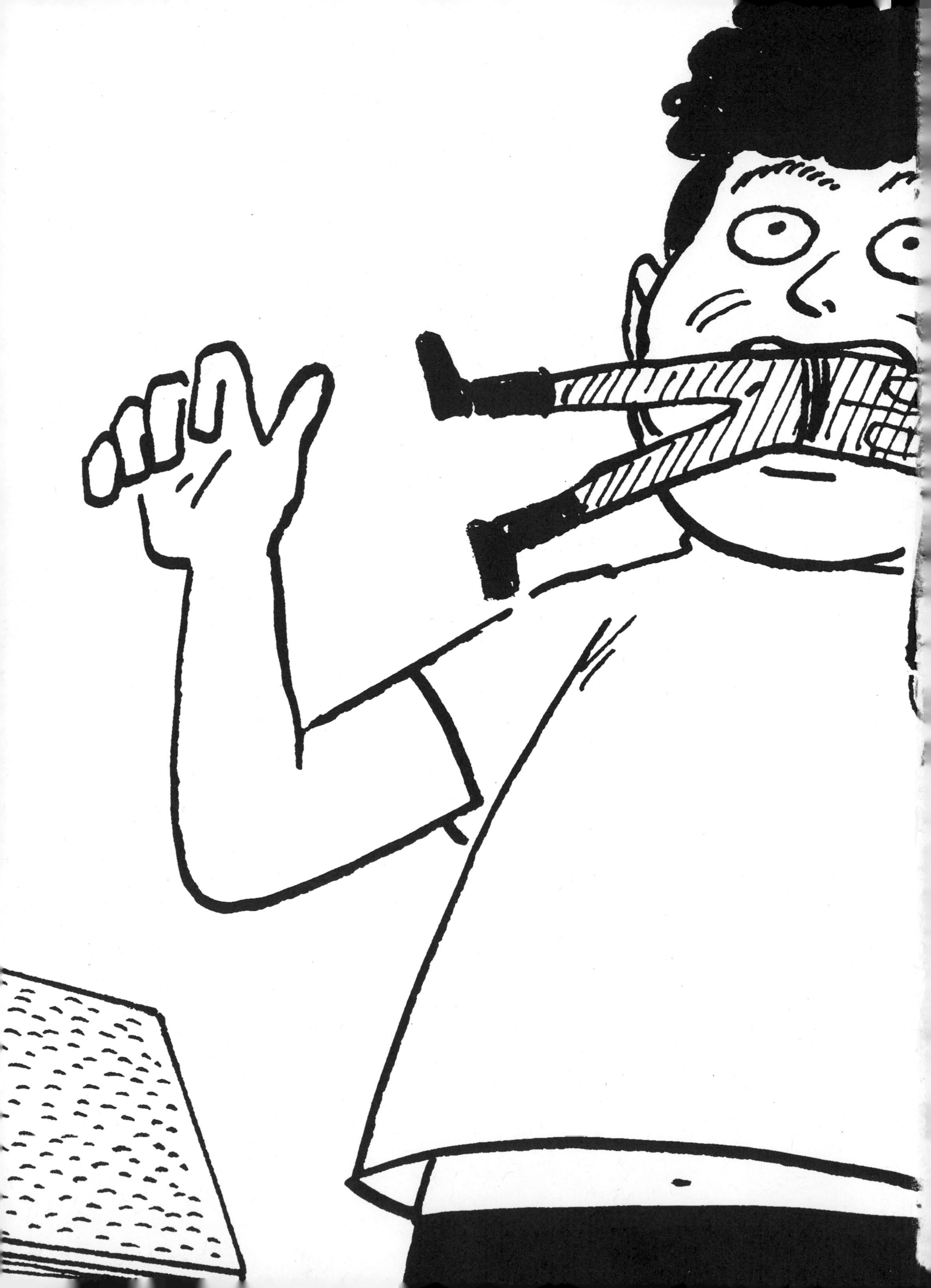

Marble Season

by GILBERT HERNANDEZ

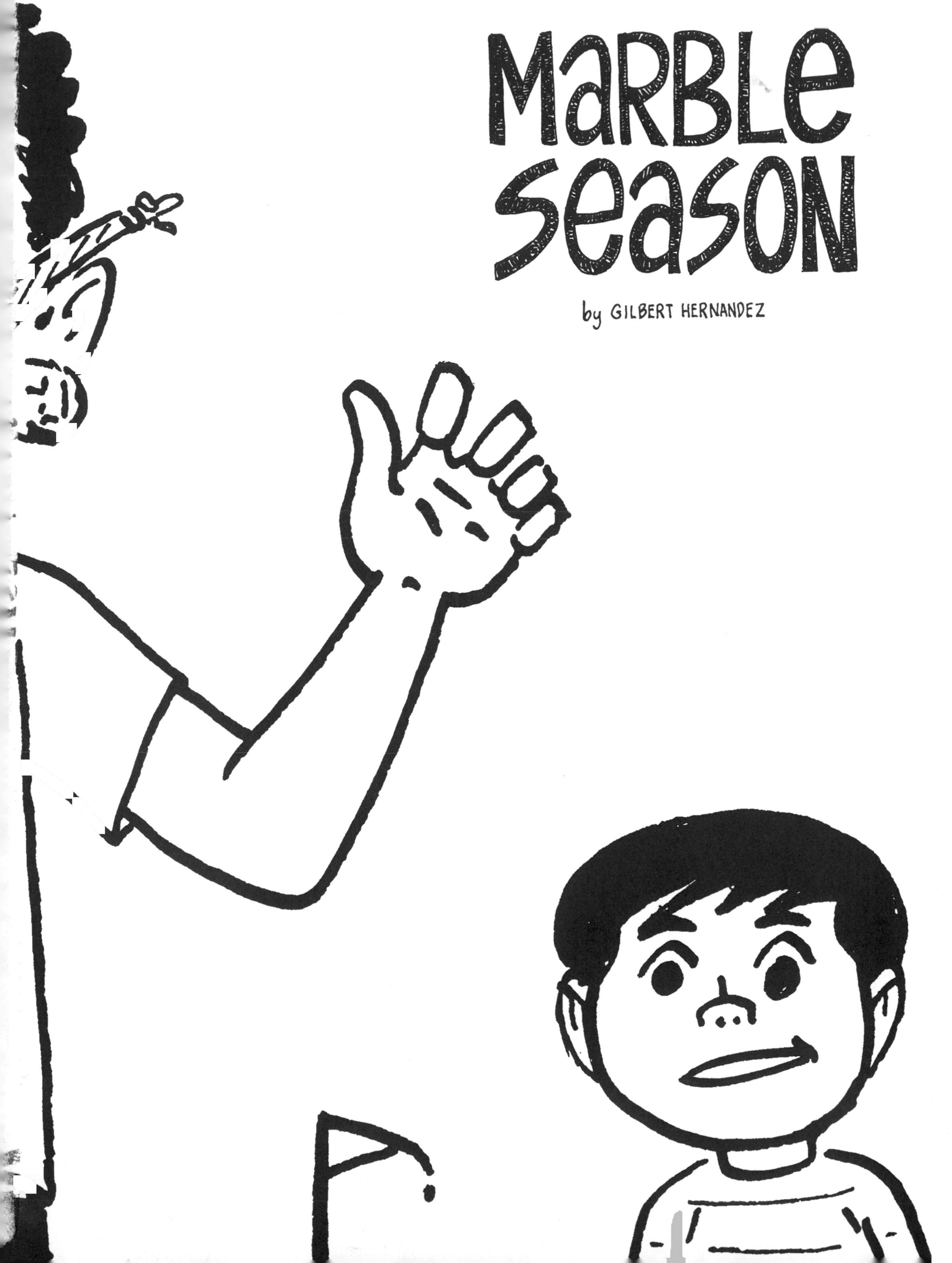

Entire contents © 2013 by Gilbert Hernandez. All rights reserved. No part of this book (except small portions for review purposes) may be reproduced in any form without written permission from Gilbert Hernandez or Drawn & Quarterly. "What it Feels Like: Childhood in Gilbert Hernandez's *Marble Season*" © 2013 by Corey K. Creekmur. www.drawnandquarterly.com. First hardcover edition: April 2013. Printed in Canada. 10 9 8 7 6 5 4 3 2 1. Library and Archives Canada Cataloguing in Publication: Hernandez, Gilbert Marble Season / Gilbert Hernandez. ISBN 978-1-77046-086-7 1. Graphic novels. I. Title. PN6727.H47M37 2013   741.5'973   C2012-907116-1. Published in the USA by Drawn & Quarterly, a client publisher of Farrar, Straus and Giroux, 18 West 18th Street, New York, NY 10011; Orders: 888.330.8477. Published in Canada by Drawn & Quarterly, a client publisher of Raincoast Books, 2440 Viking Way, Richmond BC V6V 1N2; Orders: 800.663.5714.

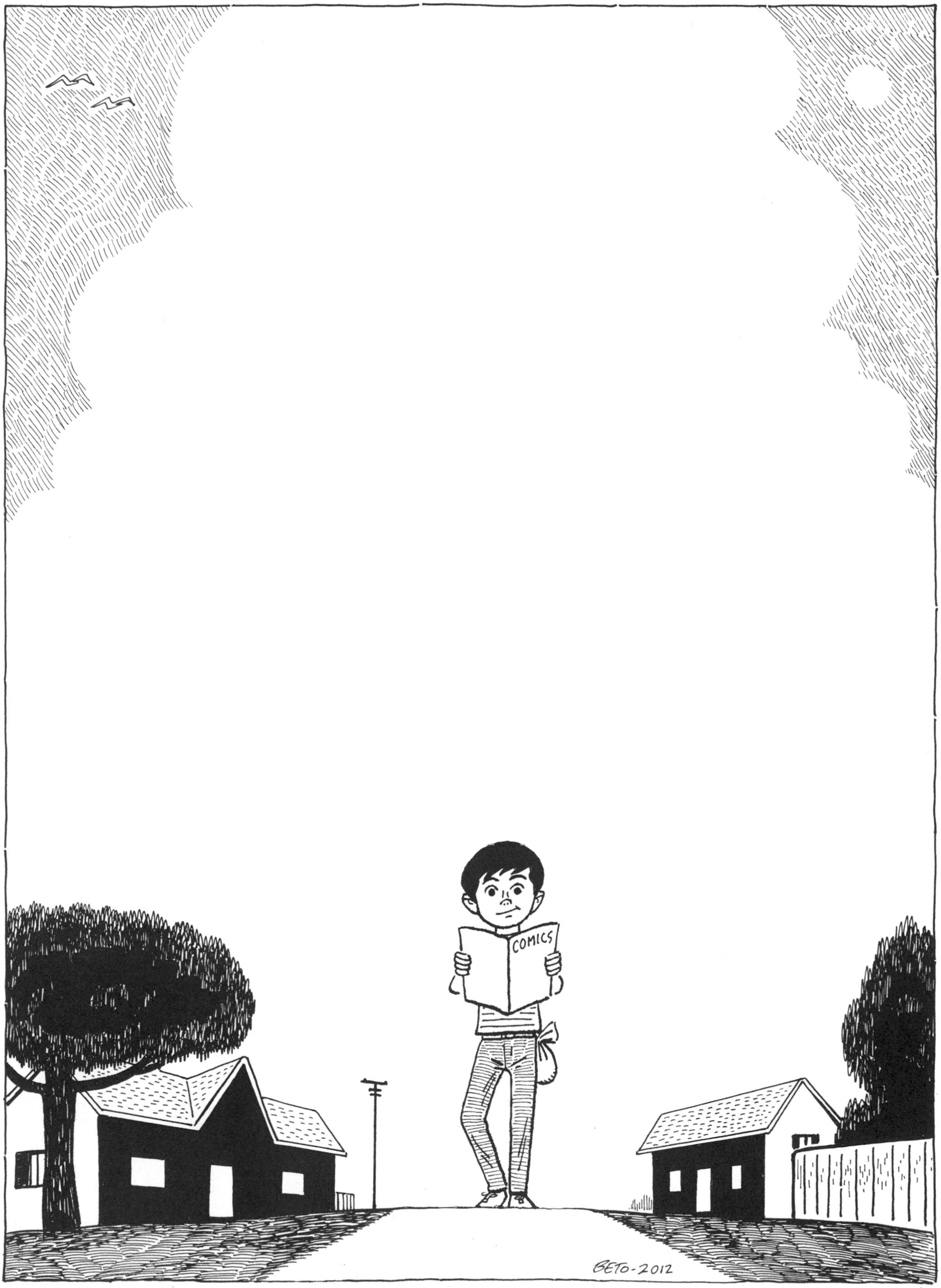
COMICS
BETO-2012

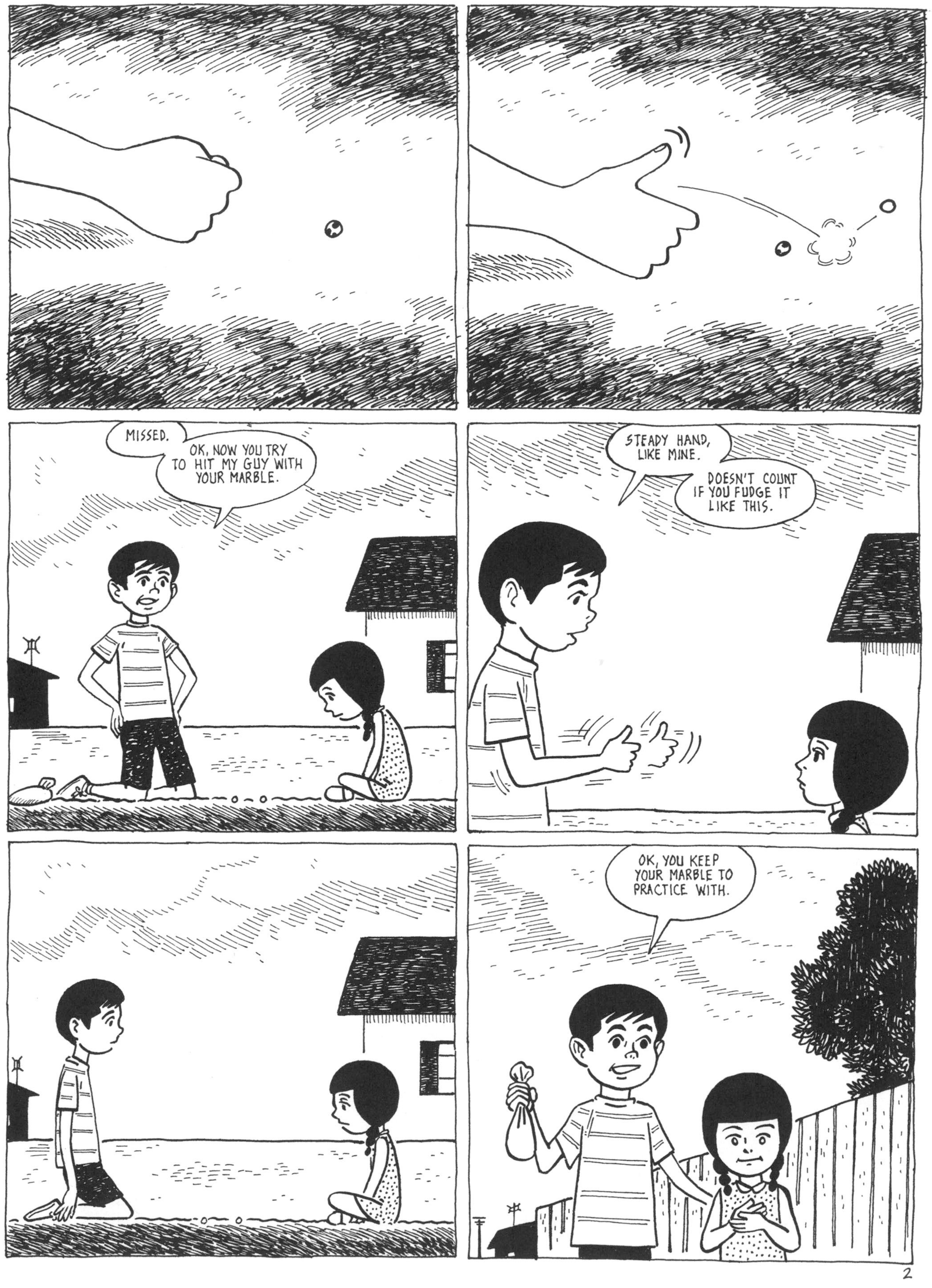
MISSED.
OK, NOW YOU TRY TO HIT MY GUY WITH YOUR MARBLE.
STEADY HAND, LIKE MINE.
DOESN'T COUNT IF YOU FUDGE IT LIKE THIS.
OK, YOU KEEP YOUR MARBLE TO PRACTICE WITH.

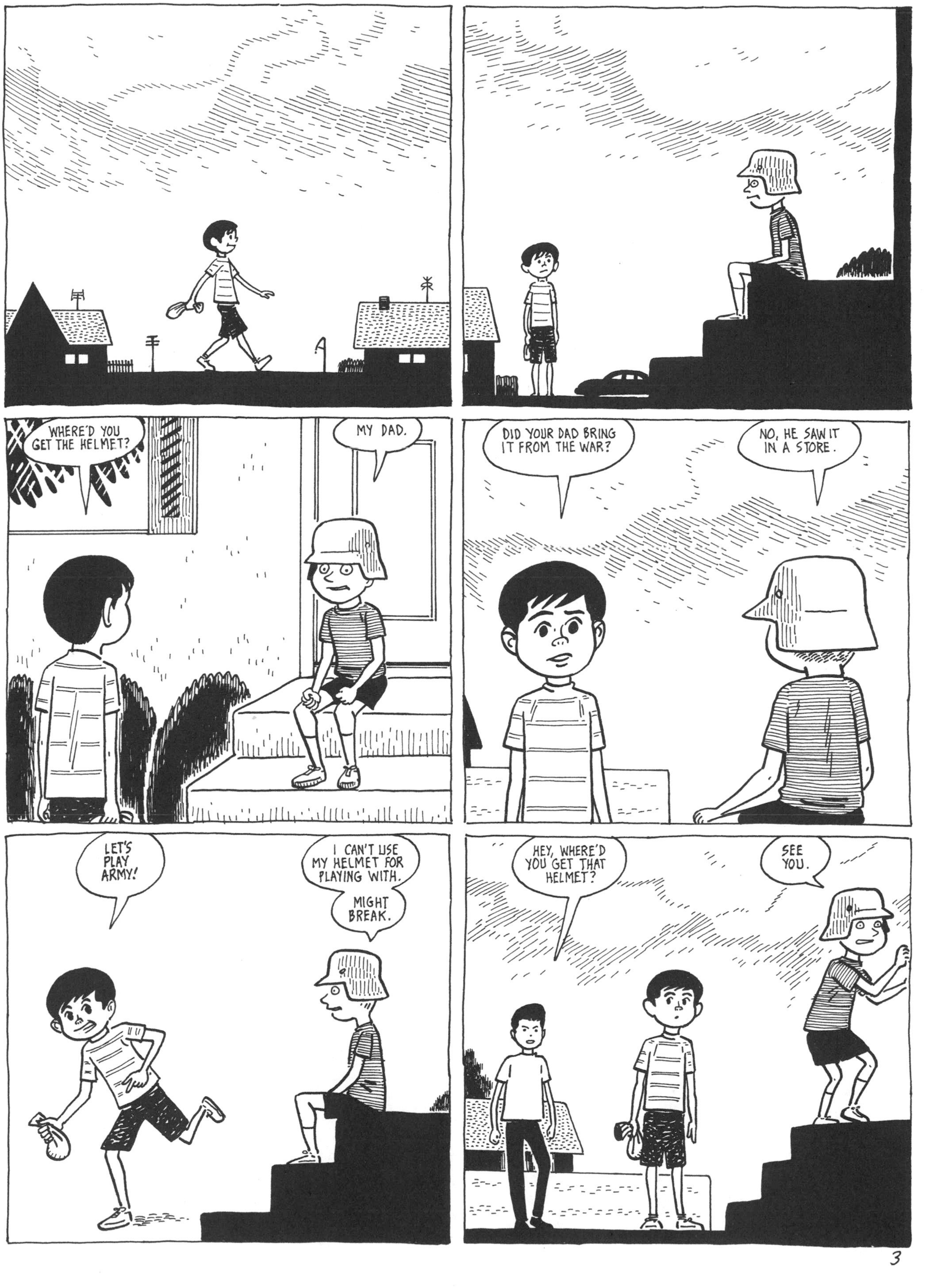
WHERE'D YOU GET THE HELMET?
MY DAD.
DID YOUR DAD BRING IT FROM THE WAR?
NO, HE SAW IT IN A STORE.
LET'S PLAY ARMY!
I CAN'T USE MY HELMET FOR PLAYING WITH.
MIGHT BREAK.
HEY, WHERE'D YOU GET THAT HELMET?
SEE YOU.

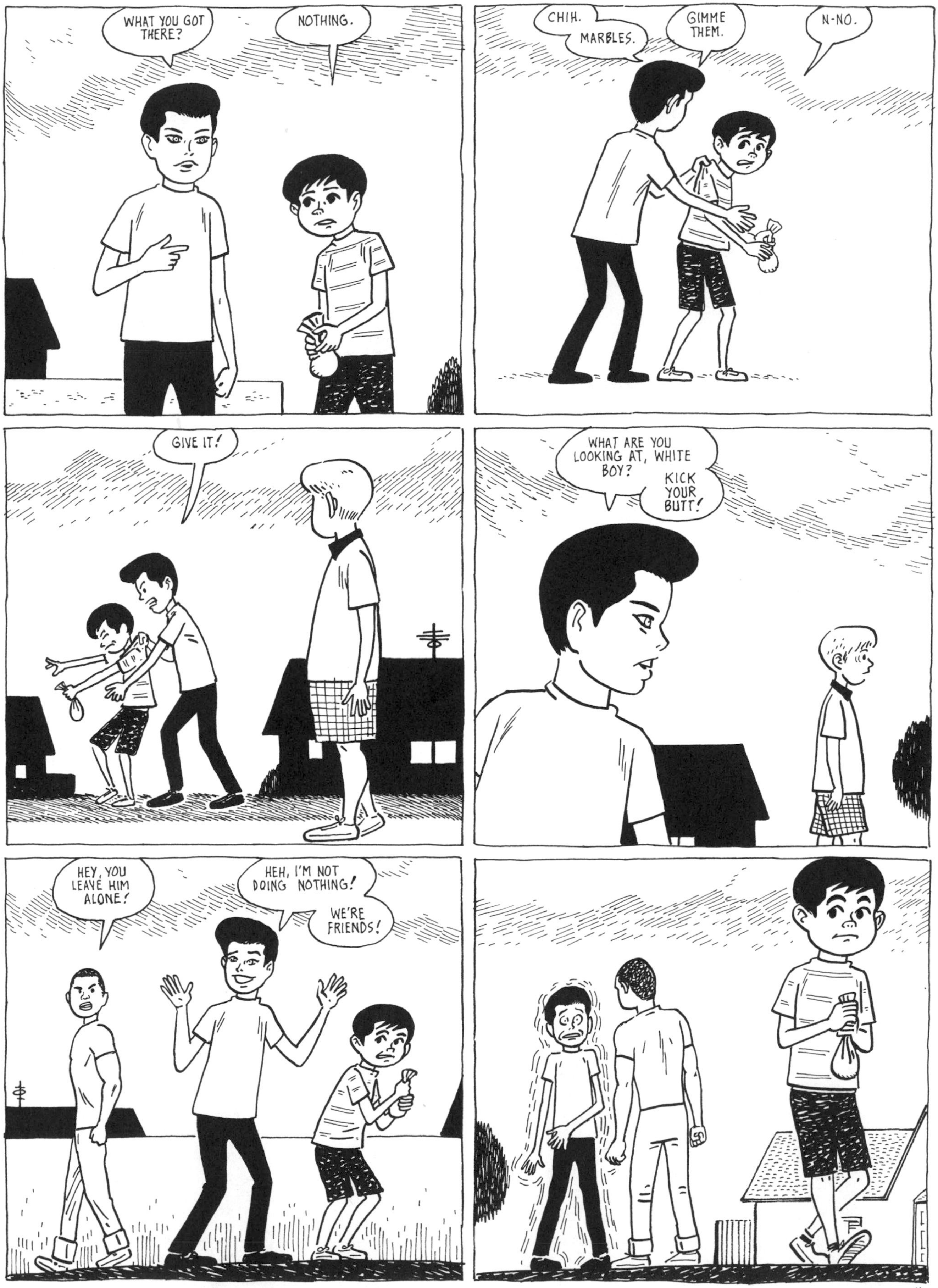
WHAT YOU GOT THERE?
NOTHING.
CHIH.
MARBLES.
GIMME THEM.
N-NO.
GIVE IT!
WHAT ARE YOU LOOKING AT, WHITE BOY?
KICK YOUR BUTT!
HEY, YOU LEAVE HIM ALONE!
HEH, I'M NOT DOING NOTHING!
WE'RE FRIENDS!

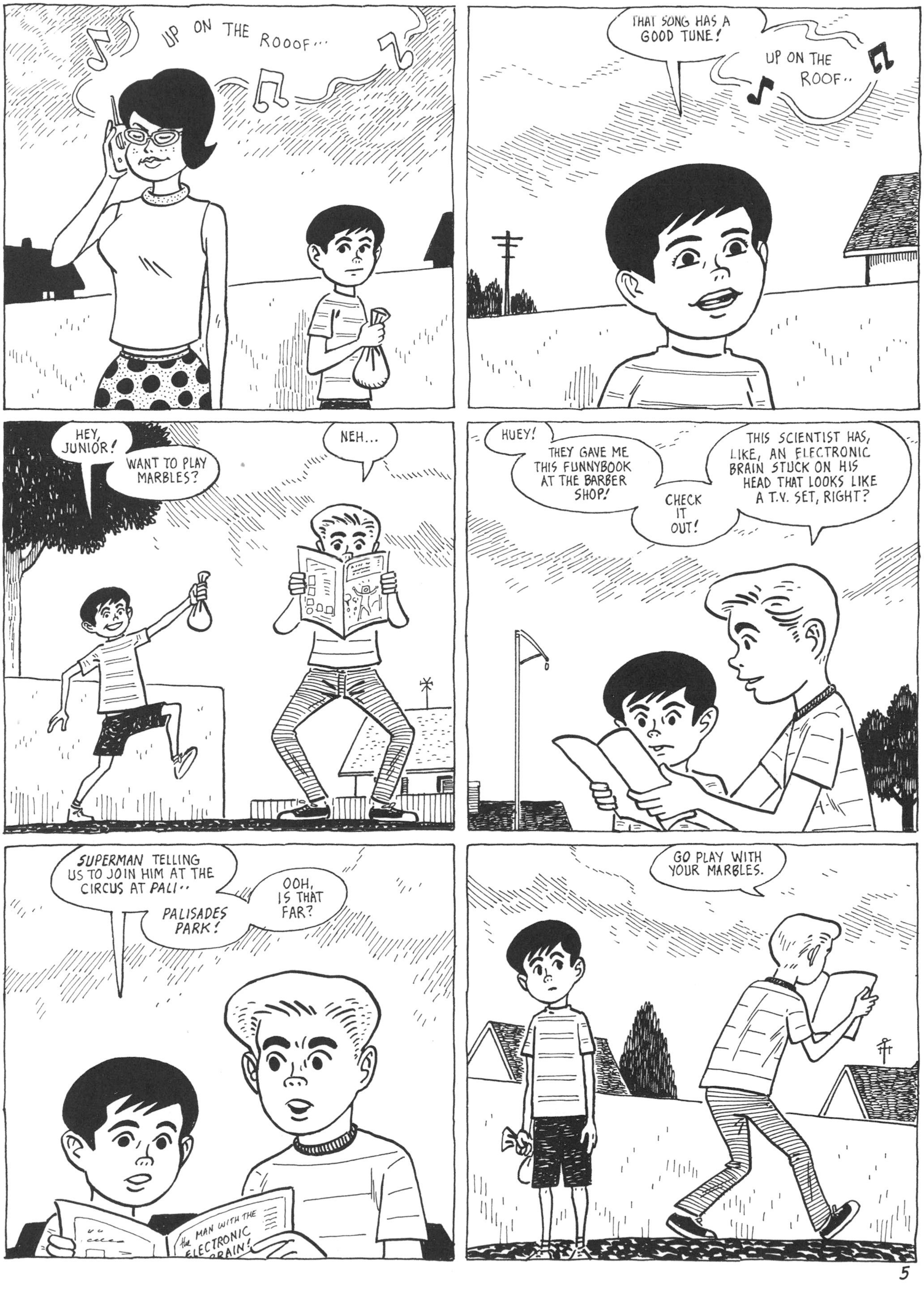
UP ON THE ROOOF...
THAT SONG HAS A GOOD TUNE!
UP ON THE ROOF..
HEY, JUNIOR!
WANT TO PLAY MARBLES?
NEH...
HUEY!
THEY GAVE ME THIS FUNNYBOOK AT THE BARBER SHOP!
CHECK IT OUT!
THIS SCIENTIST HAS, LIKE, AN ELECTRONIC BRAIN STUCK ON HIS HEAD THAT LOOKS LIKE A T.V. SET, RIGHT?
SUPERMAN TELLING US TO JOIN HIM AT THE CIRCUS AT PALI..
PALISADES PARK!
OOH, IS THAT FAR?
the MAN WITH THE ELECTRONIC BRAIN!
GO PLAY WITH YOUR MARBLES.

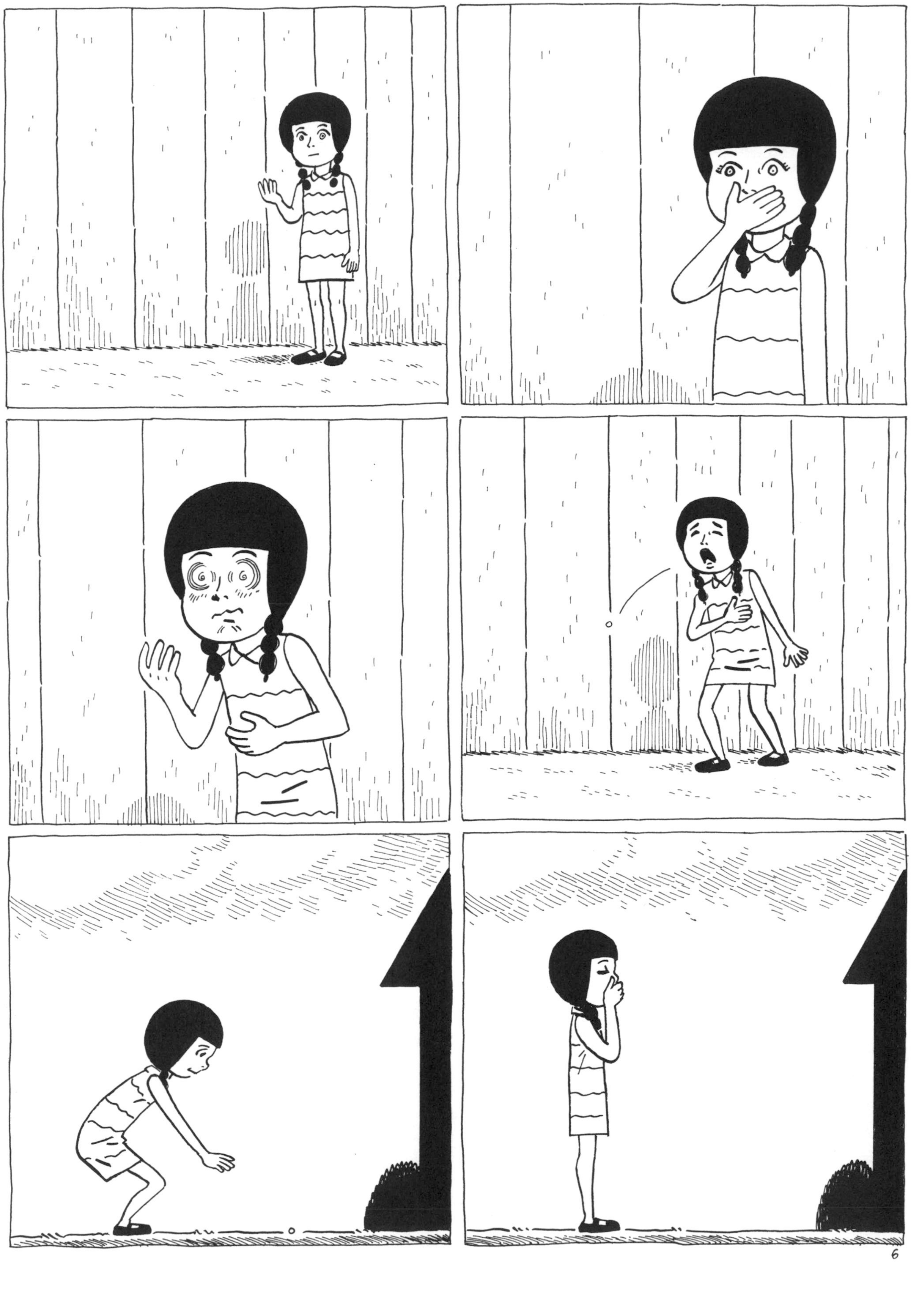

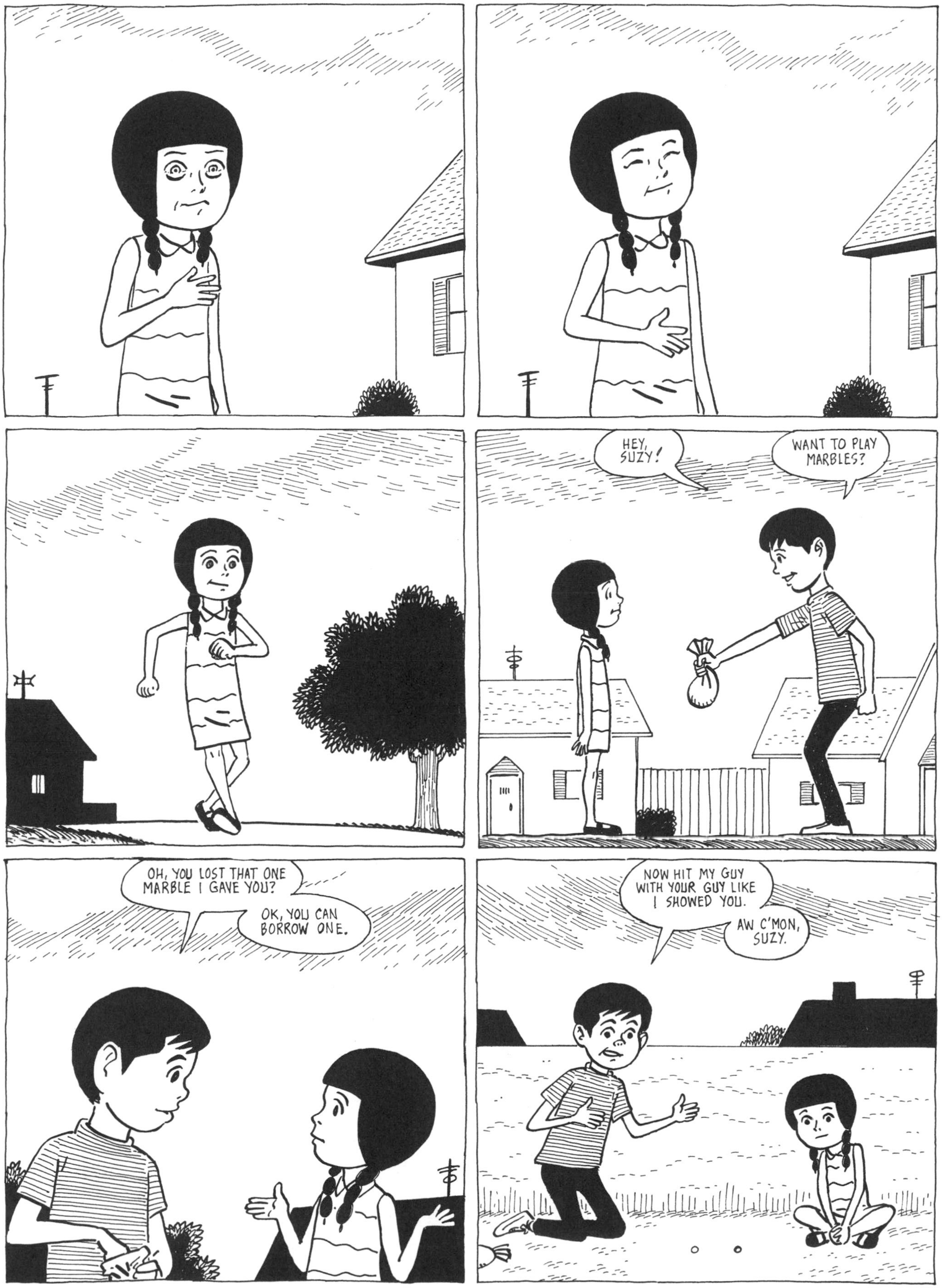
HEY, SUZY!
WANT TO PLAY MARBLES?
OH, YOU LOST THAT ONE MARBLE I GAVE YOU?
OK, YOU CAN BORROW ONE.
NOW HIT MY GUY WITH YOUR GUY LIKE I SHOWED YOU.
AW C'MON, SUZY.

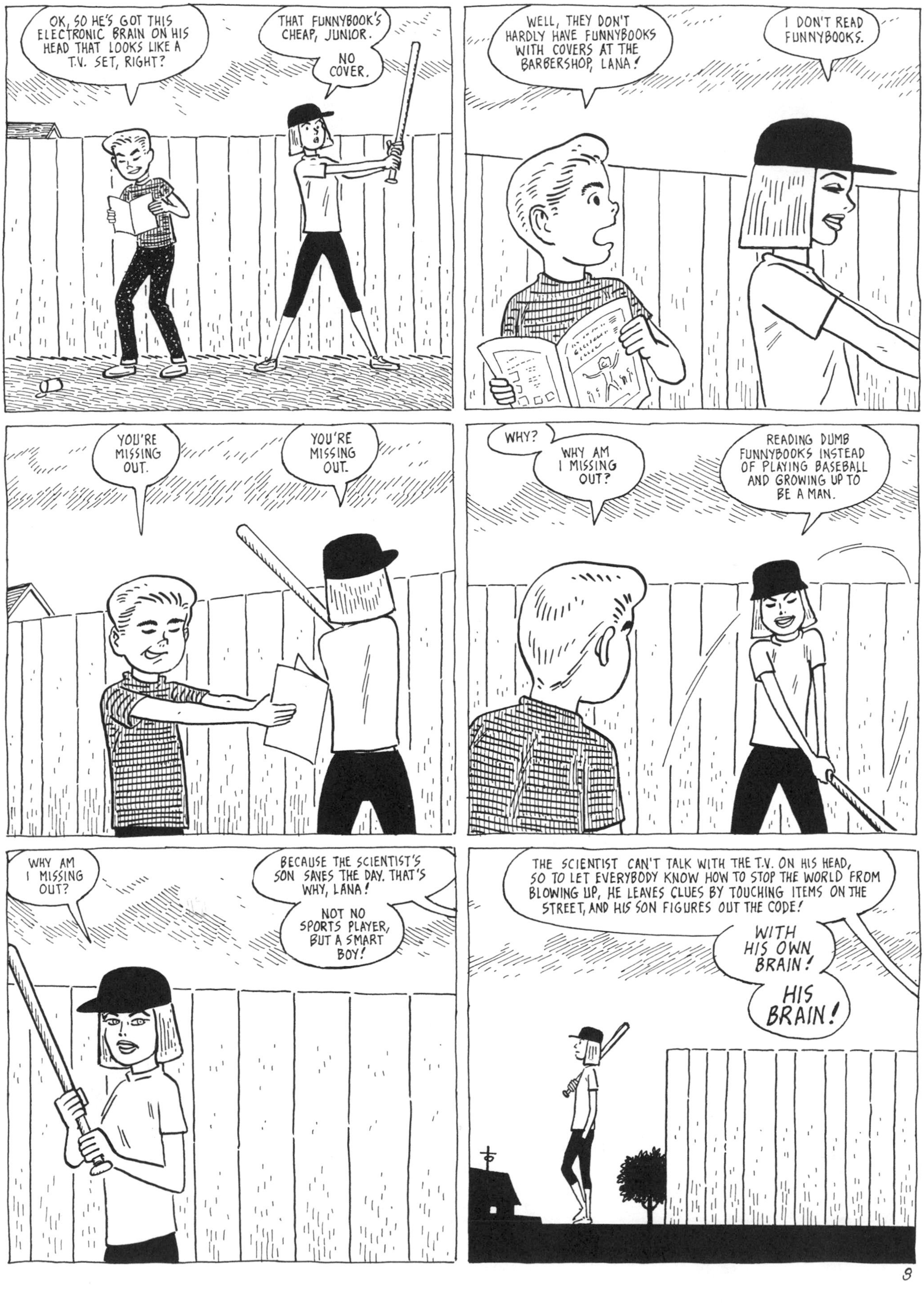
OK, SO HE'S GOT THIS ELECTRONIC BRAIN ON HIS HEAD THAT LOOKS LIKE A T.V. SET, RIGHT?
THAT FUNNYBOOK'S CHEAP, JUNIOR.
NO COVER.
WELL, THEY DON'T HARDLY HAVE FUNNYBOOKS WITH COVERS AT THE BARBERSHOP, LANA!
I DON'T READ FUNNYBOOKS.
YOU'RE MISSING OUT.
YOU'RE MISSING OUT.
WHY?
WHY AM I MISSING OUT?
READING DUMB FUNNYBOOKS INSTEAD OF PLAYING BASEBALL AND GROWING UP TO BE A MAN.
WHY AM I MISSING OUT?
BECAUSE THE SCIENTIST'S SON SAVES THE DAY. THAT'S WHY, LANA!
NOT NO SPORTS PLAYER, BUT A SMART BOY!
THE SCIENTIST CAN'T TALK WITH THE T.V. ON HIS HEAD, SO TO LET EVERYBODY KNOW HOW TO STOP THE WORLD FROM BLOWING UP, HE LEAVES CLUES BY TOUCHING ITEMS ON THE STREET, AND HIS SON FIGURES OUT THE CODE!
WITH HIS OWN BRAIN!
HIS BRAIN!

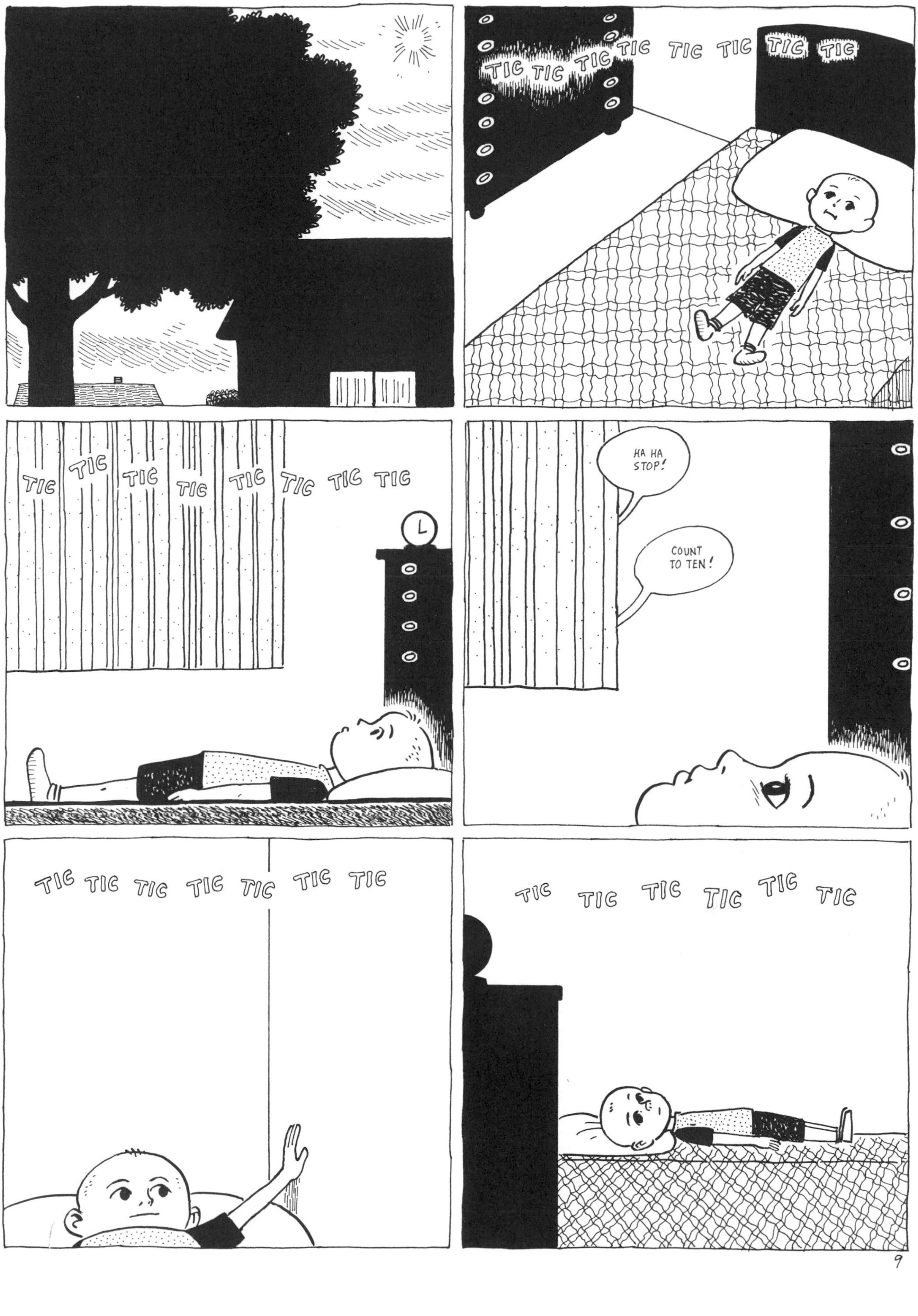
TIC TIC TIC TIC TIC TIC TIC TIC
TIC TIC TIC TIC TIC TIC TIC TIC
HA HA STOP!
COUNT TO TEN!
TIC TIC TIC TIC TIC TIC TIC
TIC TIC TIC TIC TIC TIC

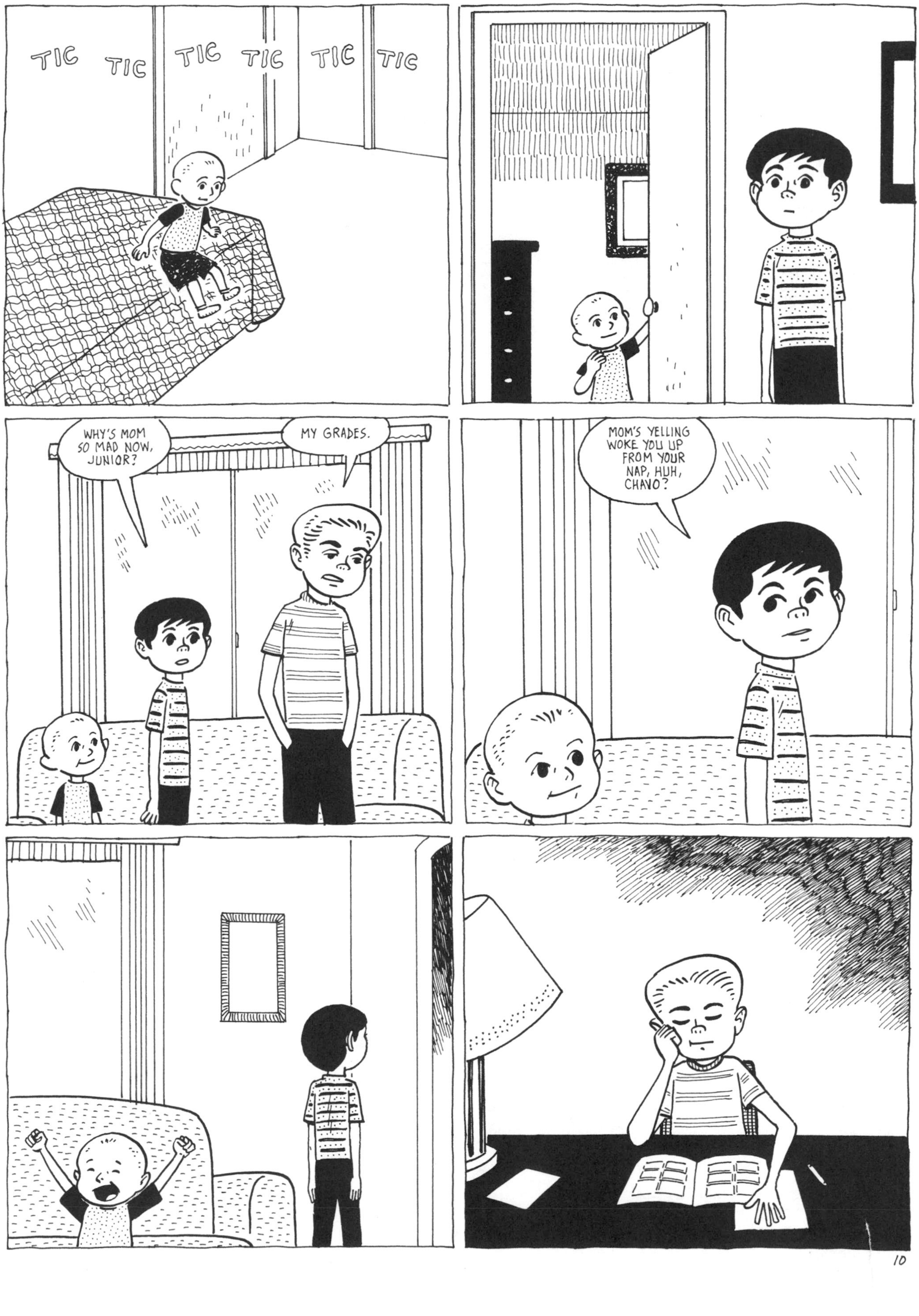
TIC TIC TIC TIC TIC TIC
WHY'S MOM SO MAD NOW, JUNIOR?
MY GRADES.
MOM'S YELLING WOKE YOU UP FROM YOUR NAP, HUH, CHAVO?

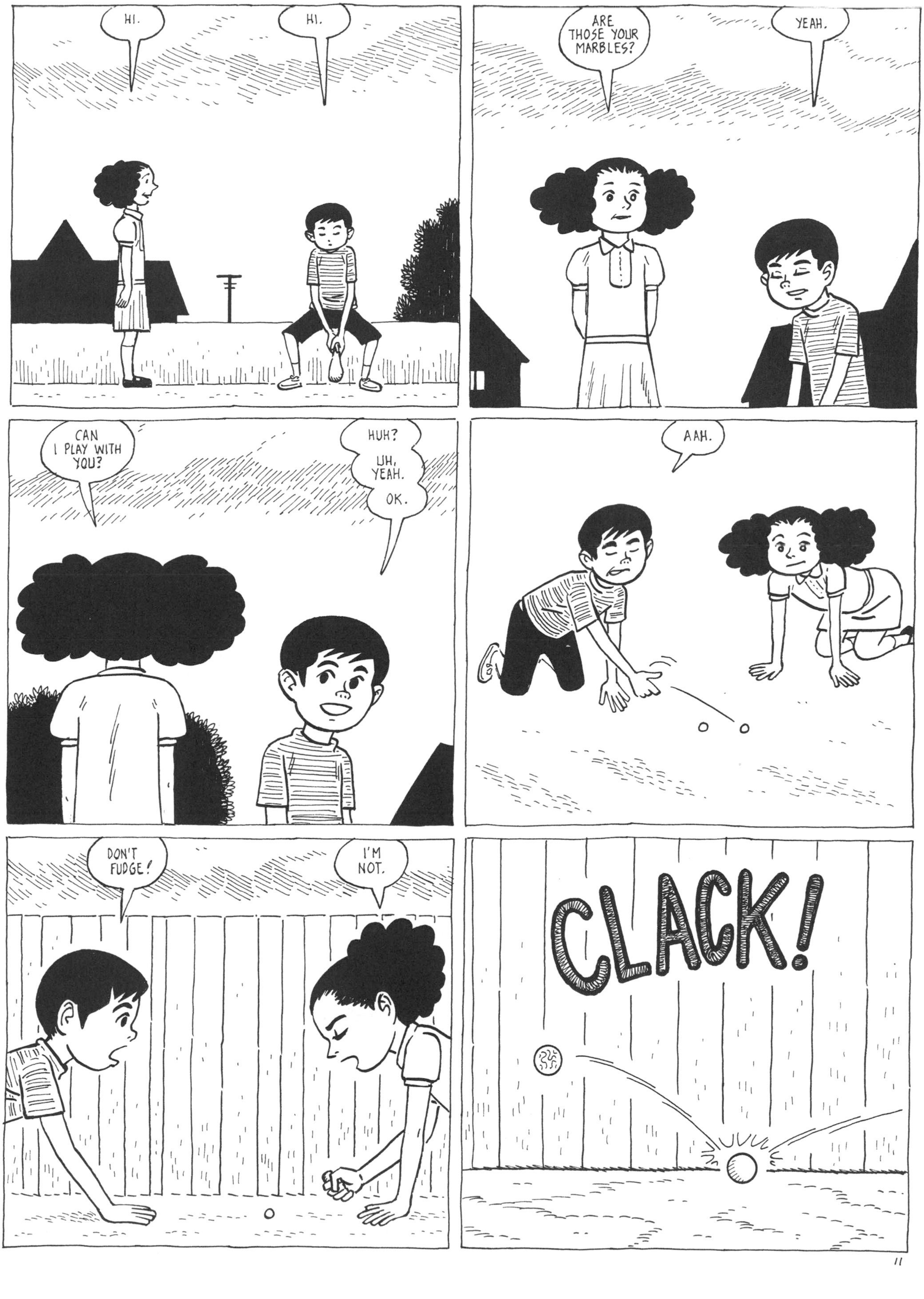
HI.
HI.
ARE THOSE YOUR MARBLES?
YEAH.
CAN I PLAY WITH YOU?
HUH?
UH, YEAH.
OK.
AAH.
DON'T FUDGE!
I'M NOT.
CLACK!

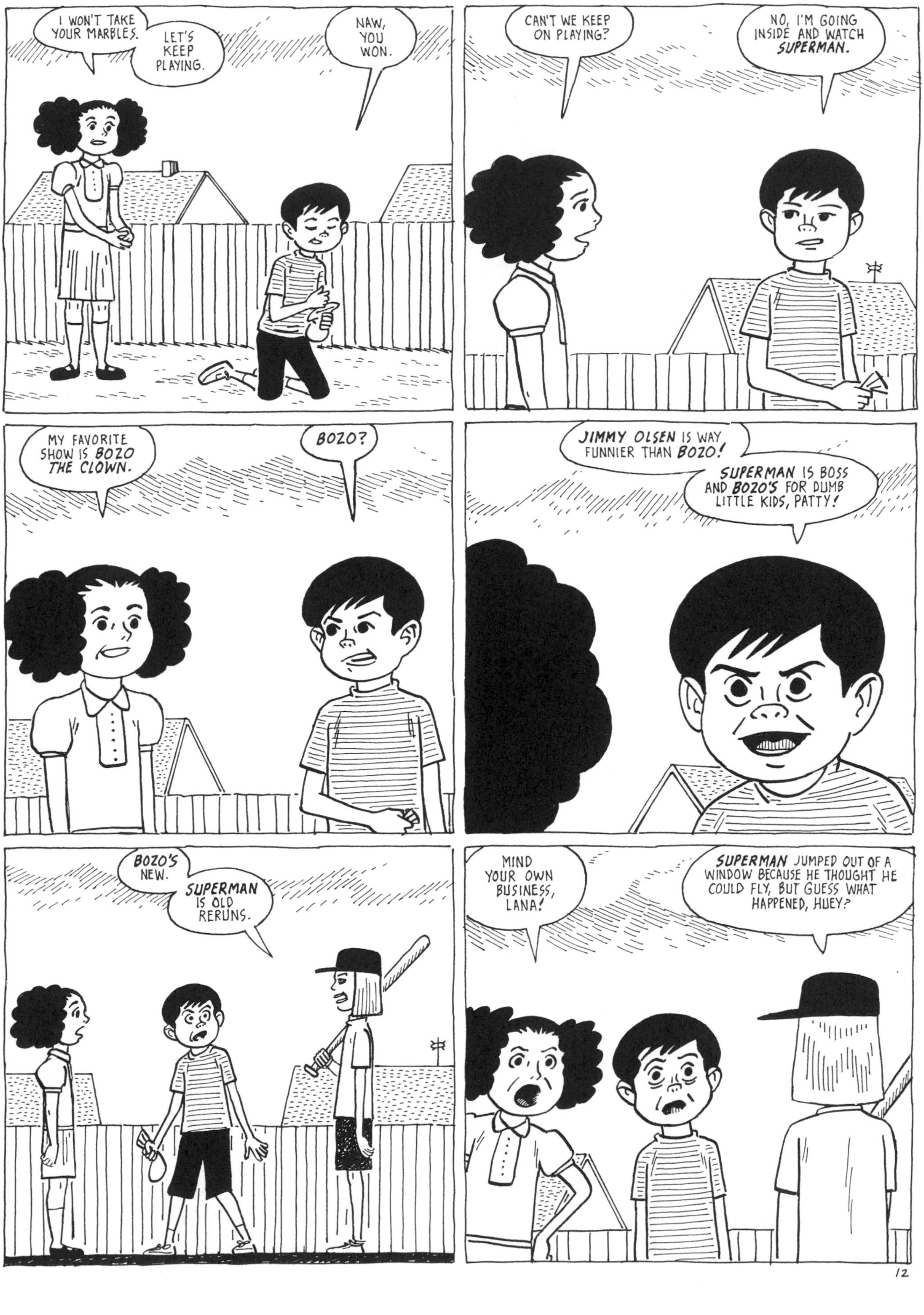
I WON'T TAKE YOUR MARBLES.
LET'S KEEP PLAYING.
NAW, YOU WON.
CAN'T WE KEEP ON PLAYING?
NO, I'M GOING INSIDE AND WATCH SUPERMAN.
MY FAVORITE SHOW IS BOZO THE CLOWN.
BOZO?
JIMMY OLSEN IS WAY FUNNIER THAN BOZO!
SUPERMAN IS BOSS AND BOZO'S FOR DUMB LITTLE KIDS, PATTY!
BOZO'S NEW.
SUPERMAN IS OLD RERUNS.
MIND YOUR OWN BUSINESS, LANA!
SUPERMAN JUMPED OUT OF A WINDOW BECAUSE HE THOUGHT HE COULD FLY, BUT GUESS WHAT HAPPENED, HUEY?

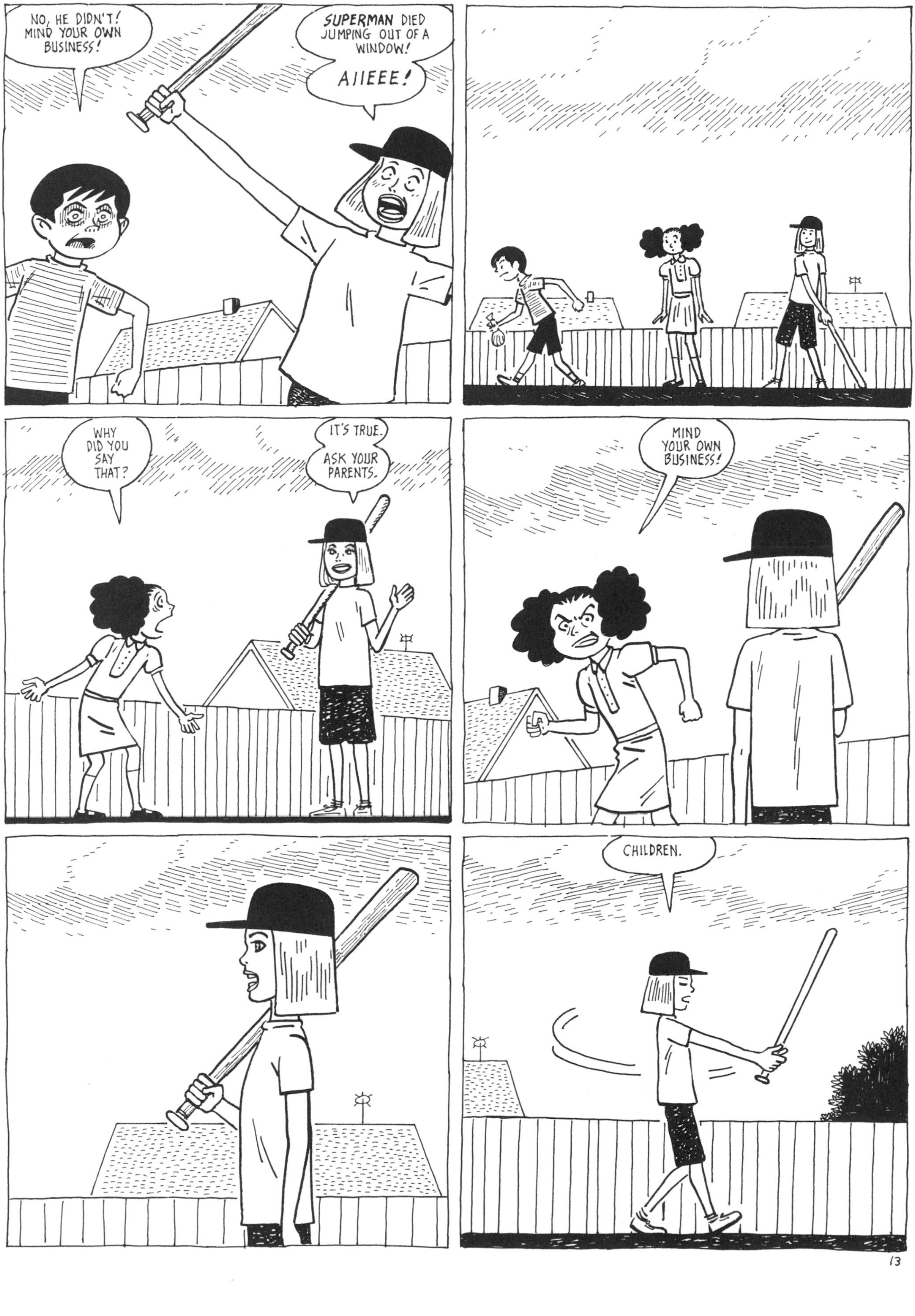
NO, HE DIDN'T! MIND YOUR OWN BUSINESS!
SUPERMAN DIED JUMPING OUT OF A WINDOW!
AIIEEE!
WHY DID YOU SAY THAT?
IT'S TRUE.
ASK YOUR PARENTS.
MIND YOUR OWN BUSINESS!
CHILDREN.

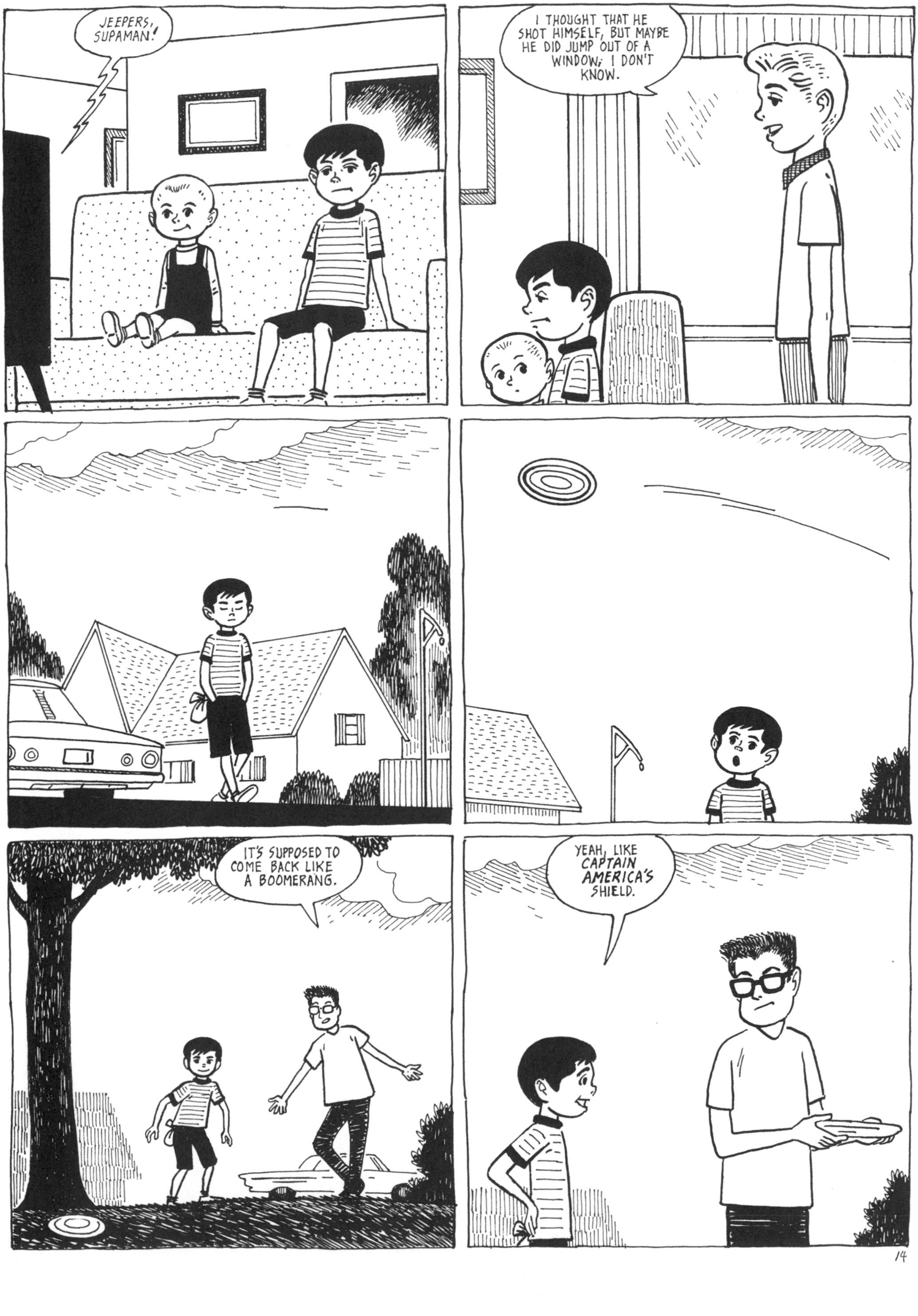
JEEPERS, SUPAMAN!
I THOUGHT THAT HE SHOT HIMSELF, BUT MAYBE HE DID JUMP OUT OF A WINDOW; I DON'T KNOW.
IT'S SUPPOSED TO COME BACK LIKE A BOOMERANG.
YEAH, LIKE CAPTAIN AMERICA'S SHIELD.

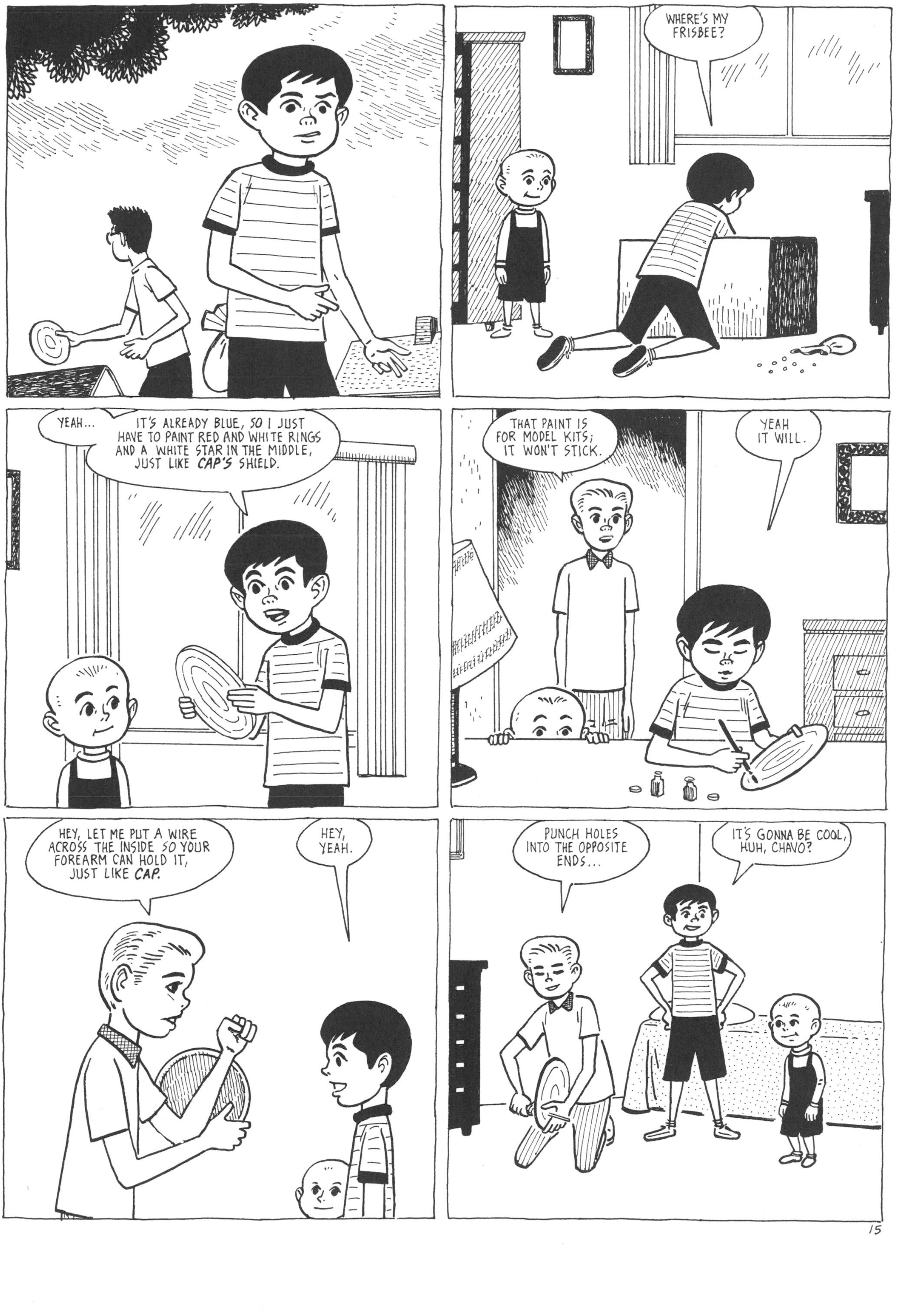
WHERE'S MY FRISBEE?
YEAH...
IT'S ALREADY BLUE, SO I JUST HAVE TO PAINT RED AND WHITE RINGS AND A WHITE STAR IN THE MIDDLE, JUST LIKE CAP'S SHIELD.
THAT PAINT IS FOR MODEL KITS; IT WON'T STICK.
YEAH IT WILL.
HEY, LET ME PUT A WIRE ACROSS THE INSIDE SO YOUR FOREARM CAN HOLD IT, JUST LIKE CAP.
HEY, YEAH.
PUNCH HOLES INTO THE OPPOSITE ENDS...
IT'S GONNA BE COOL, HUH, CHAVO?

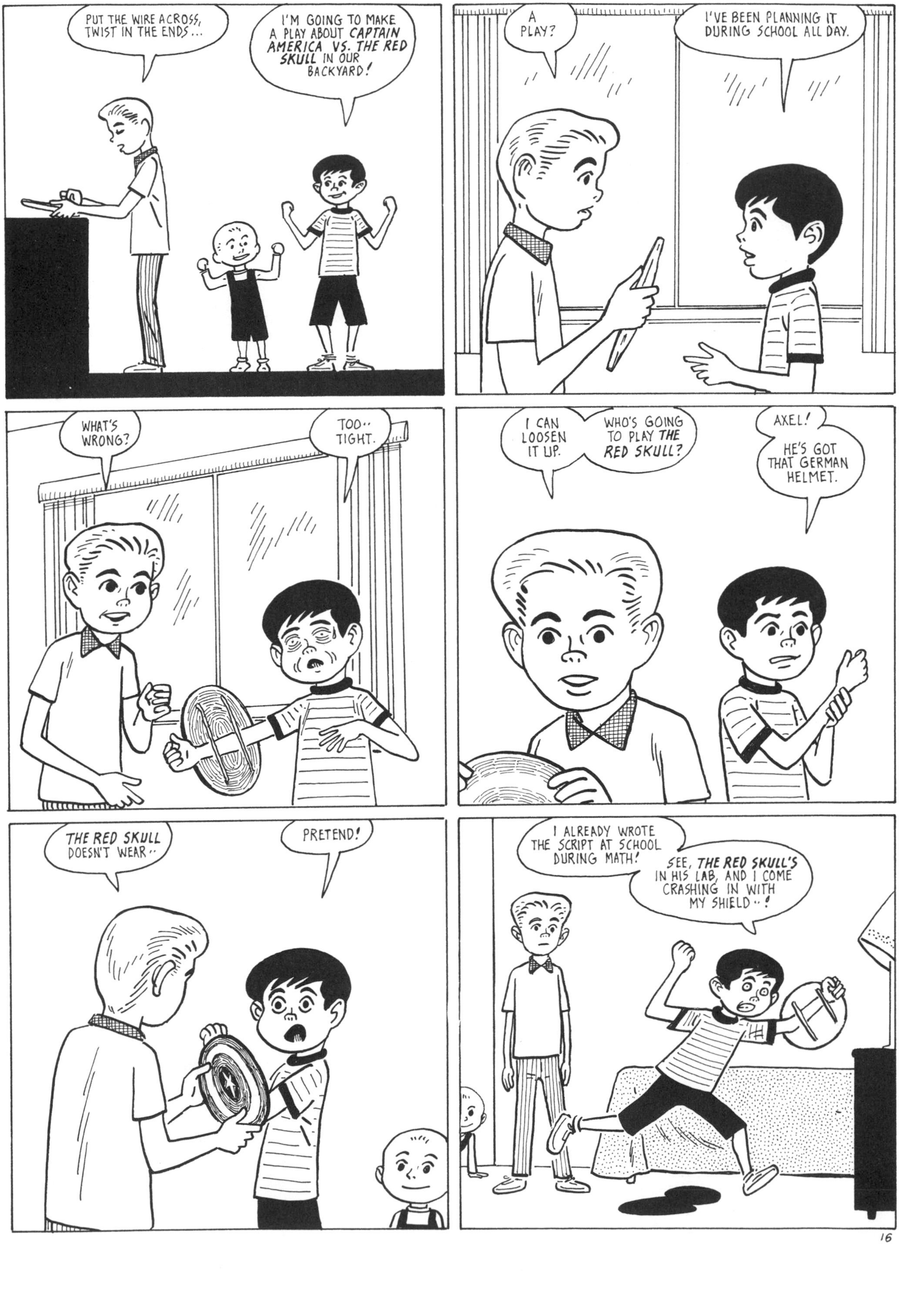
PUT THE WIRE ACROSS, TWIST IN THE ENDS...
I'M GOING TO MAKE A PLAY ABOUT **CAPTAIN AMERICA VS. THE RED SKULL** IN OUR BACKYARD!
A PLAY?
I'VE BEEN PLANNING IT DURING SCHOOL ALL DAY.
WHAT'S WRONG?
TOO.. TIGHT.
I CAN LOOSEN IT UP.
WHO'S GOING TO PLAY **THE RED SKULL?**
AXEL!
HE'S GOT THAT GERMAN HELMET.
THE RED SKULL DOESN'T WEAR..
PRETEND!
I ALREADY WROTE THE SCRIPT AT SCHOOL DURING MATH!
SEE, **THE RED SKULL'S** IN HIS LAB, AND I COME CRASHING IN WITH MY SHIELD..!

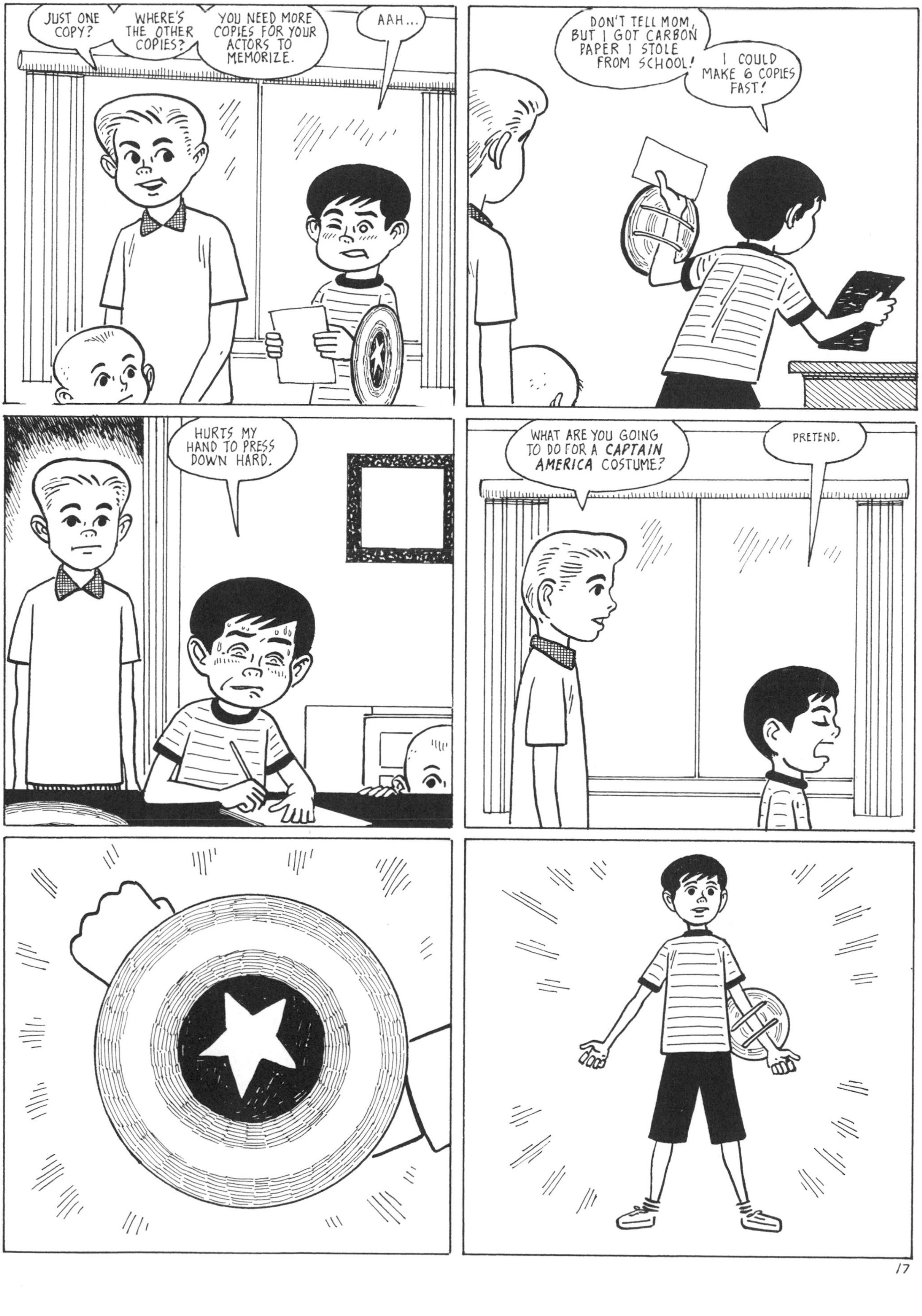
JUST ONE COPY?
WHERE'S THE OTHER COPIES?
YOU NEED MORE COPIES FOR YOUR ACTORS TO MEMORIZE.
AAH...
DON'T TELL MOM, BUT I GOT CARBON PAPER I STOLE FROM SCHOOL!
I COULD MAKE 6 COPIES FAST!
HURTS MY HAND TO PRESS DOWN HARD.
WHAT ARE YOU GOING TO DO FOR A CAPTAIN AMERICA COSTUME?
PRETEND.

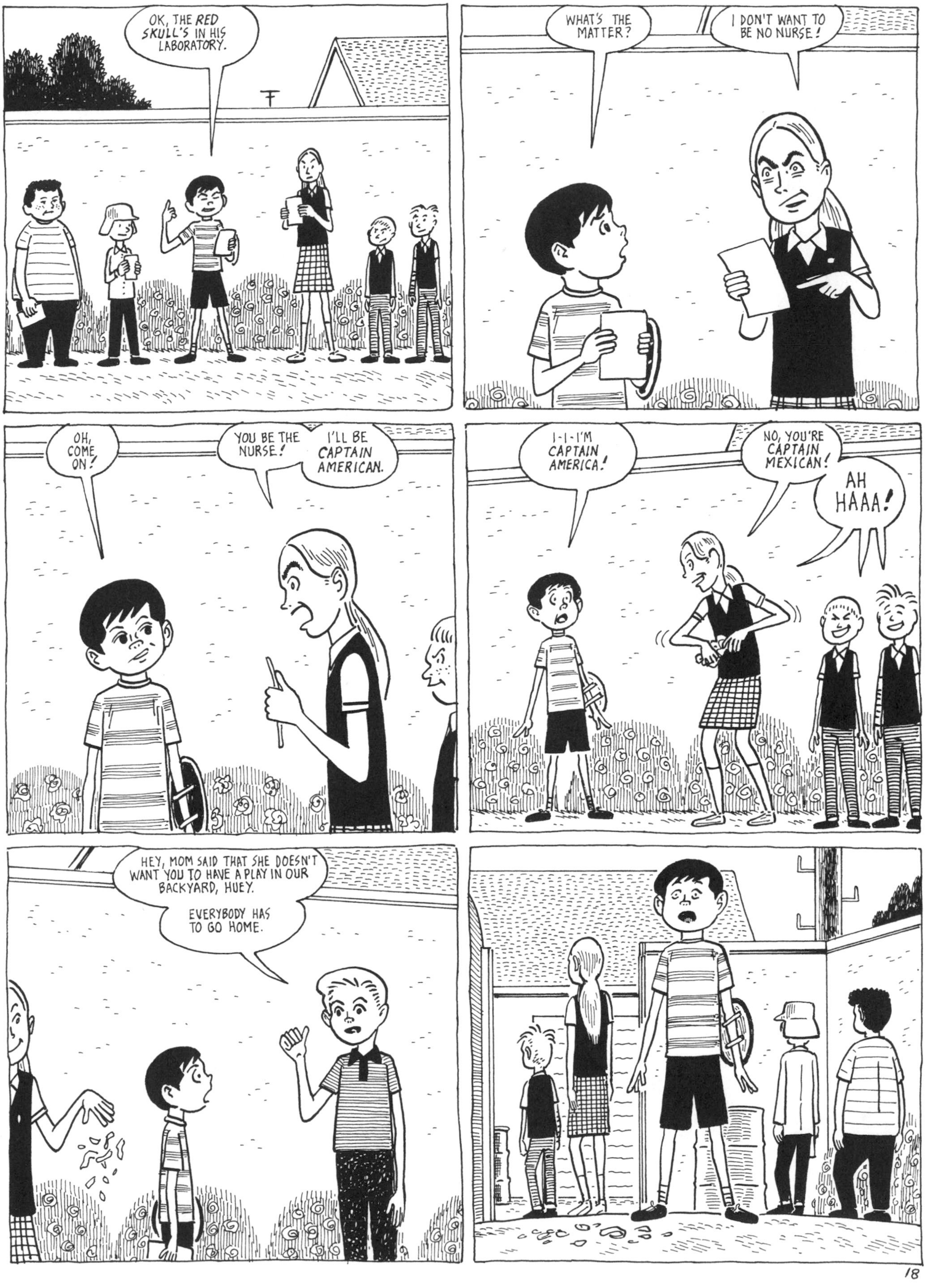
OK, THE RED SKULL'S IN HIS LABORATORY.
WHAT'S THE MATTER?
I DON'T WANT TO BE NO NURSE!
OH, COME ON!
YOU BE THE NURSE!
I'LL BE CAPTAIN AMERICAN.
I-I-I'M CAPTAIN AMERICA!
NO, YOU'RE CAPTAIN MEXICAN!
AH HAAA!
HEY, MOM SAID THAT SHE DOESN'T WANT YOU TO HAVE A PLAY IN OUR BACKYARD, HUEY.
EVERYBODY HAS TO GO HOME.

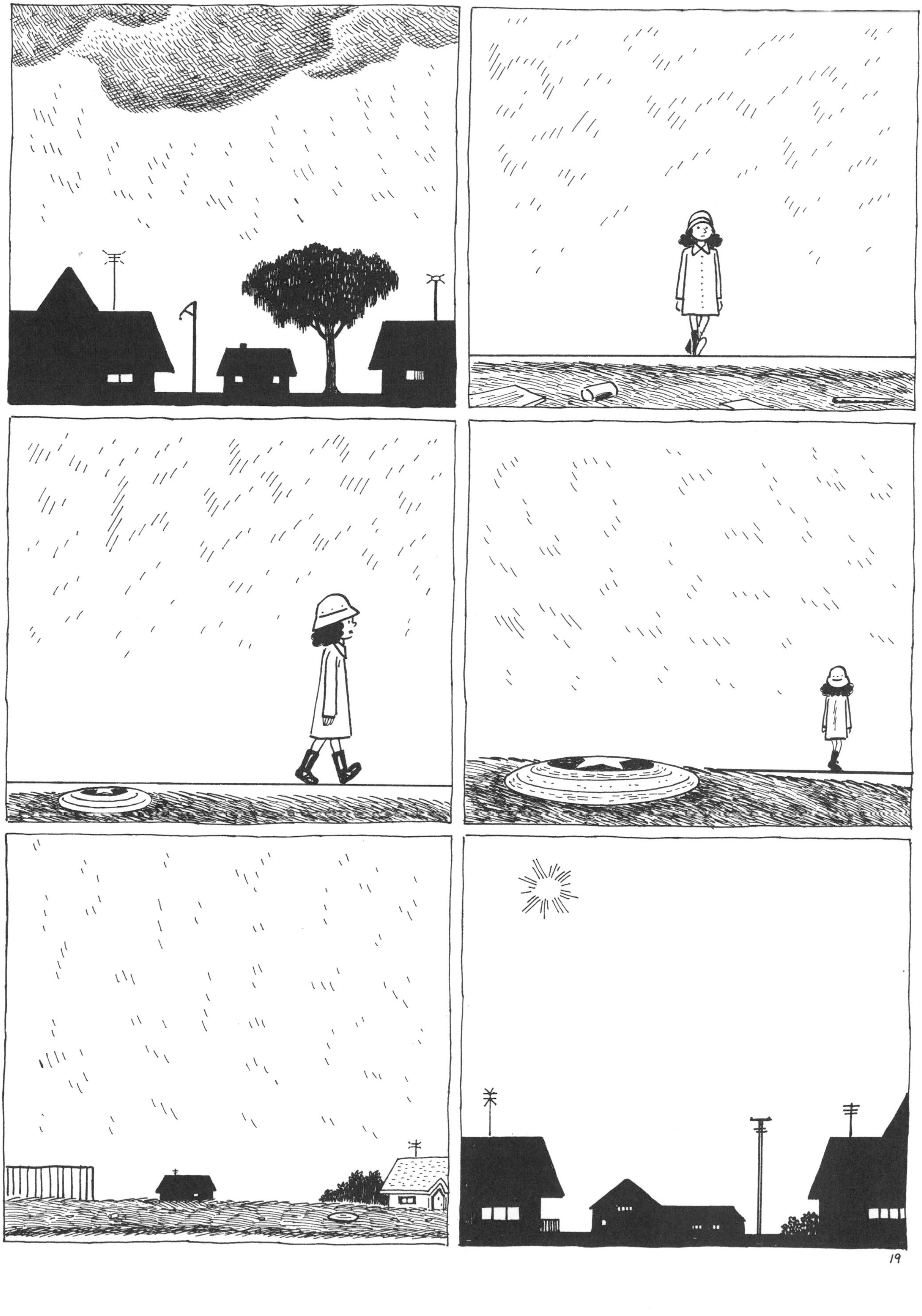

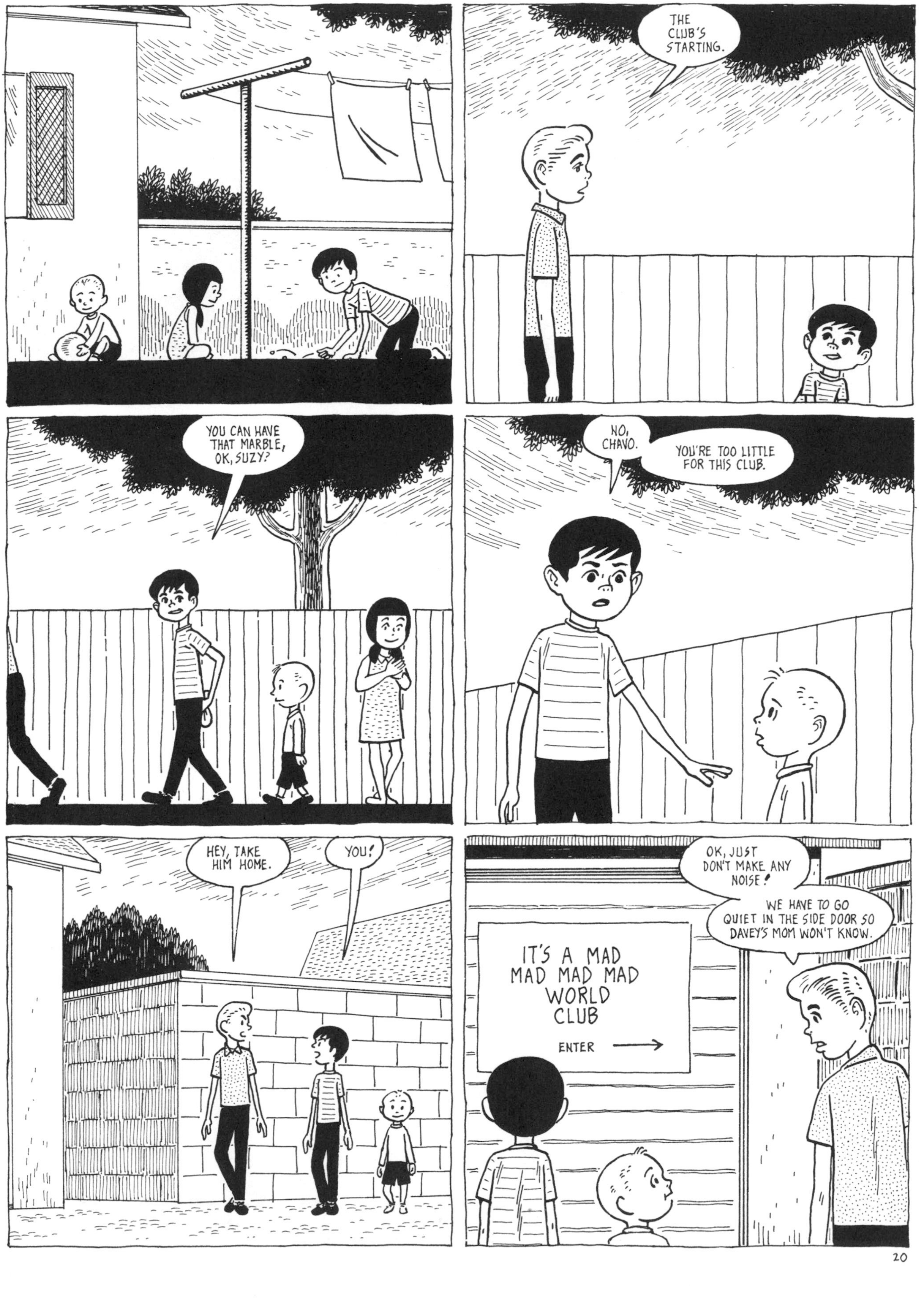
THE CLUB'S STARTING.
YOU CAN HAVE THAT MARBLE, OK, SUZY?
NO, CHAVO.
YOU'RE TOO LITTLE FOR THIS CLUB.
HEY, TAKE HIM HOME.
YOU!
OK, JUST DON'T MAKE ANY NOISE!
WE HAVE TO GO QUIET IN THE SIDE DOOR SO DAVEY'S MOM WON'T KNOW.
IT'S A MAD MAD MAD MAD WORLD CLUB
ENTER

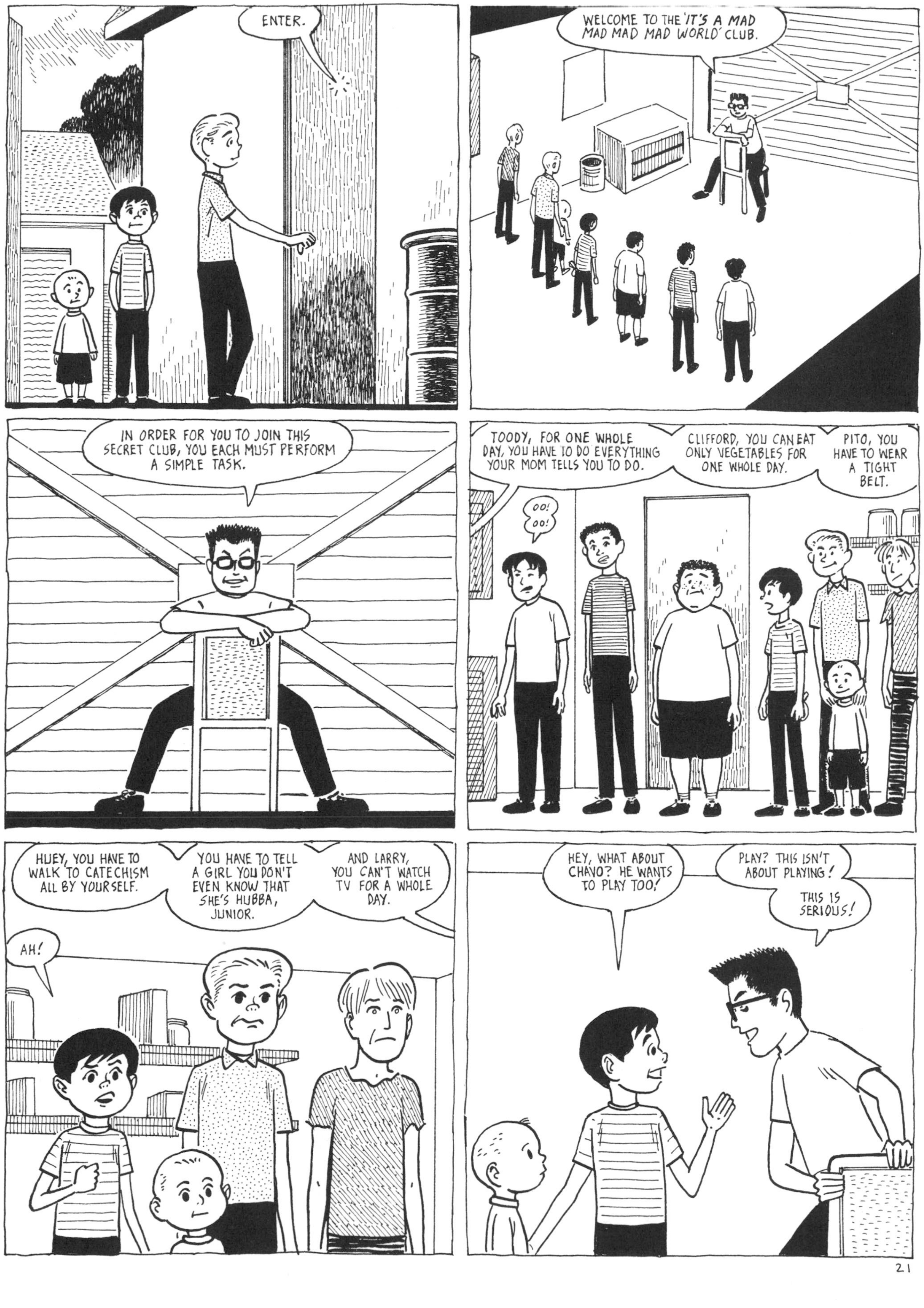
ENTER.
WELCOME TO THE 'IT'S A MAD MAD MAD MAD WORLD' CLUB.
IN ORDER FOR YOU TO JOIN THIS SECRET CLUB, YOU EACH MUST PERFORM A SIMPLE TASK.
TOODY, FOR ONE WHOLE DAY, YOU HAVE TO DO EVERYTHING YOUR MOM TELLS YOU TO DO.
OO! OO!
CLIFFORD, YOU CAN EAT ONLY VEGETABLES FOR ONE WHOLE DAY.
PITO, YOU HAVE TO WEAR A TIGHT BELT.
HUEY, YOU HAVE TO WALK TO CATECHISM ALL BY YOURSELF.
AH!
YOU HAVE TO TELL A GIRL YOU DON'T EVEN KNOW THAT SHE'S HUBBA, JUNIOR.
AND LARRY, YOU CAN'T WATCH TV FOR A WHOLE DAY.
HEY, WHAT ABOUT CHAVO? HE WANTS TO PLAY TOO!
PLAY? THIS ISN'T ABOUT PLAYING!
THIS IS SERIOUS!

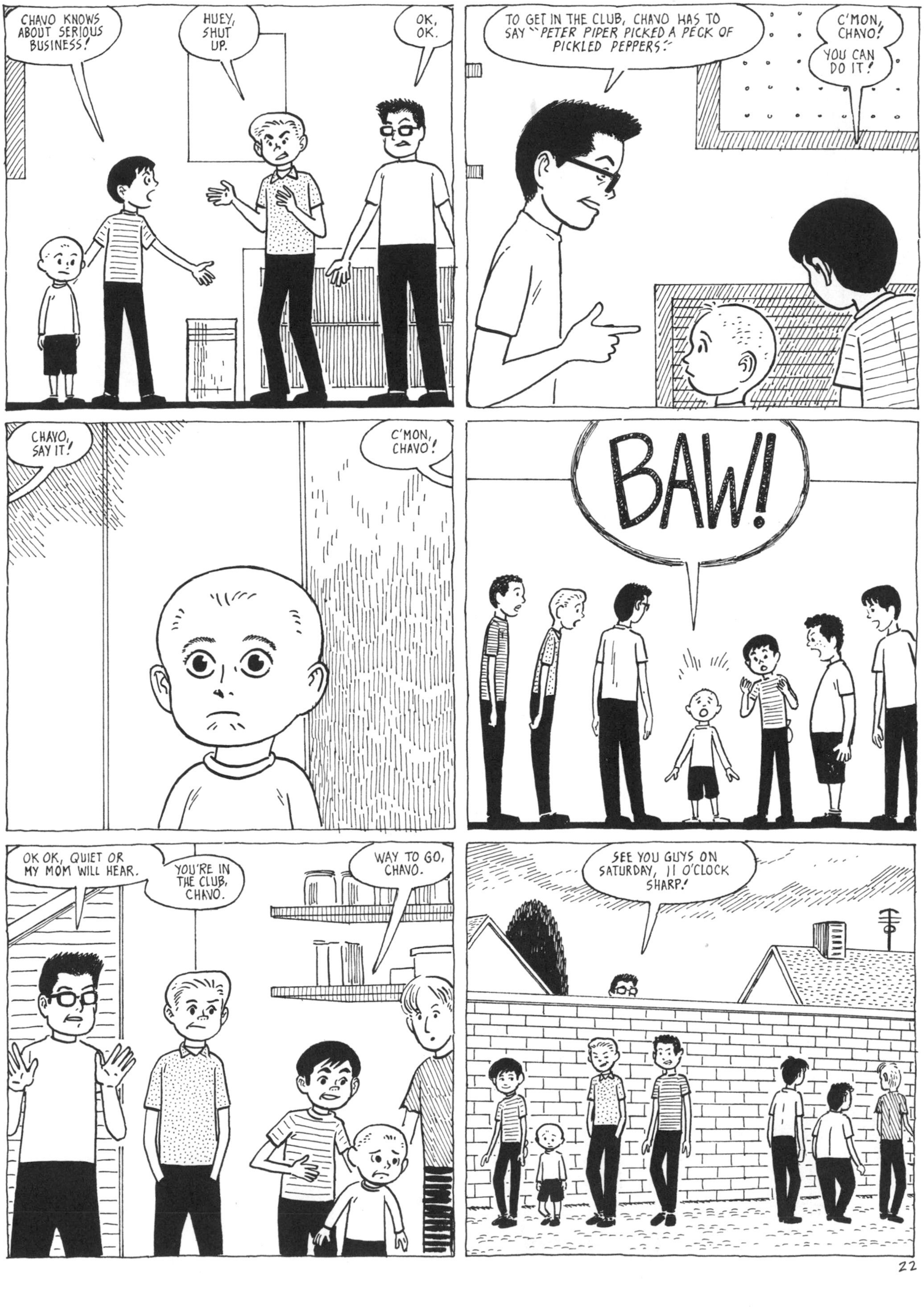

CHAVO KNOWS ABOUT SERIOUS BUSINESS!
HUEY, SHUT UP.
OK, OK.
TO GET IN THE CLUB, CHAVO HAS TO SAY "PETER PIPER PICKED A PECK OF PICKLED PEPPERS."
C'MON, CHAVO!
YOU CAN DO IT!
CHAVO, SAY IT!
C'MON, CHAVO!
BAW!
OK OK, QUIET OR MY MOM WILL HEAR.
YOU'RE IN THE CLUB, CHAVO.
WAY TO GO, CHAVO.
SEE YOU GUYS ON SATURDAY, 11 O'CLOCK SHARP!

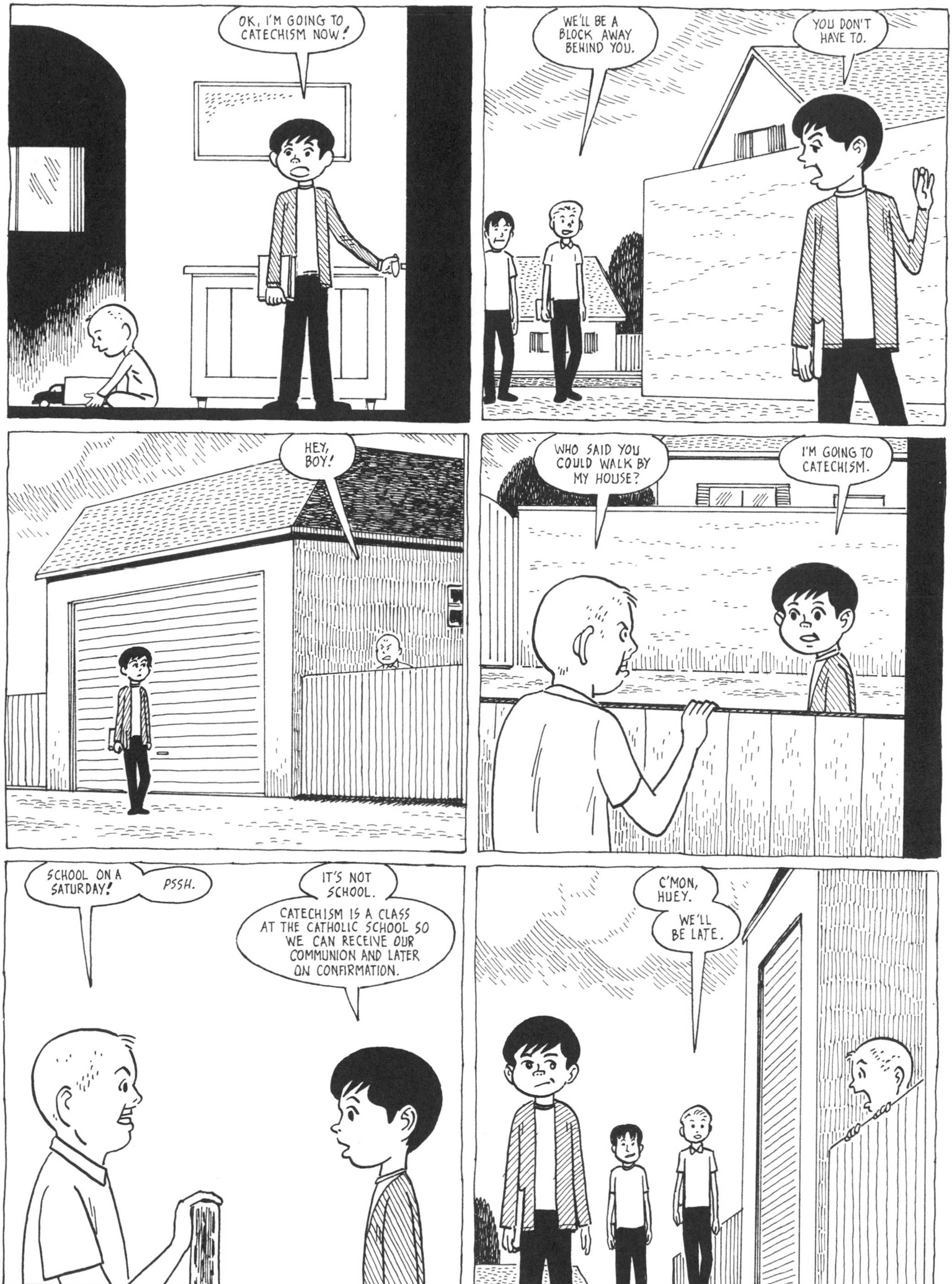
OK, I'M GOING TO CATECHISM NOW!
WE'LL BE A BLOCK AWAY BEHIND YOU.
YOU DON'T HAVE TO.
HEY, BOY!
WHO SAID YOU COULD WALK BY MY HOUSE?
I'M GOING TO CATECHISM.
SCHOOL ON A SATURDAY!
PSSH.
IT'S NOT SCHOOL.
CATECHISM IS A CLASS AT THE CATHOLIC SCHOOL SO WE CAN RECEIVE OUR COMMUNION AND LATER ON CONFIRMATION.
C'MON, HUEY.
WE'LL BE LATE.

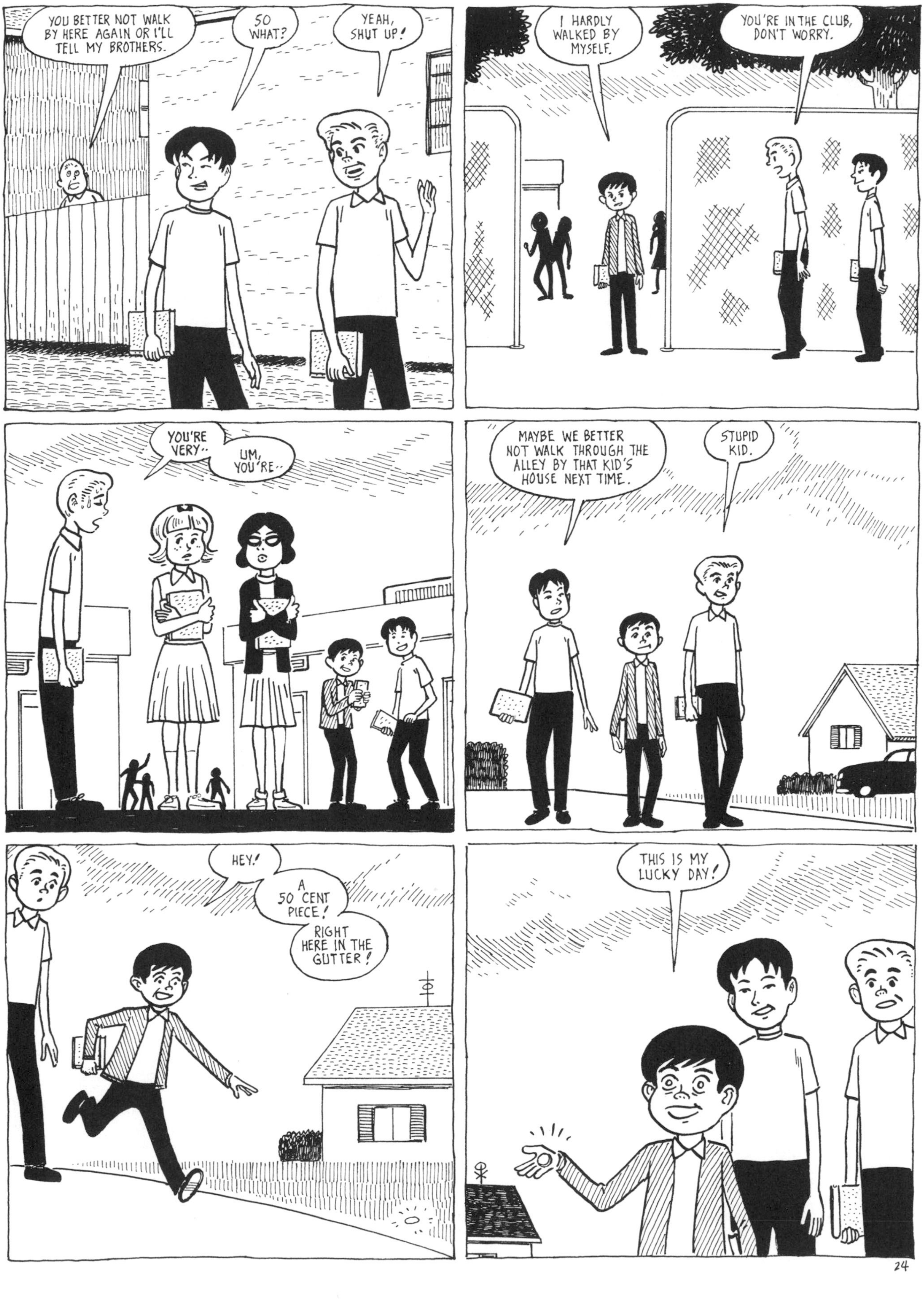
YOU BETTER NOT WALK BY HERE AGAIN OR I'LL TELL MY BROTHERS.
SO WHAT?
YEAH, SHUT UP!
I HARDLY WALKED BY MYSELF.
YOU'RE IN THE CLUB, DON'T WORRY.
YOU'RE VERY..
UM, YOU'RE..
MAYBE WE BETTER NOT WALK THROUGH THE ALLEY BY THAT KID'S HOUSE NEXT TIME.
STUPID KID.
HEY!
A 50 CENT PIECE!
RIGHT HERE IN THE GUTTER!
THIS IS MY LUCKY DAY!

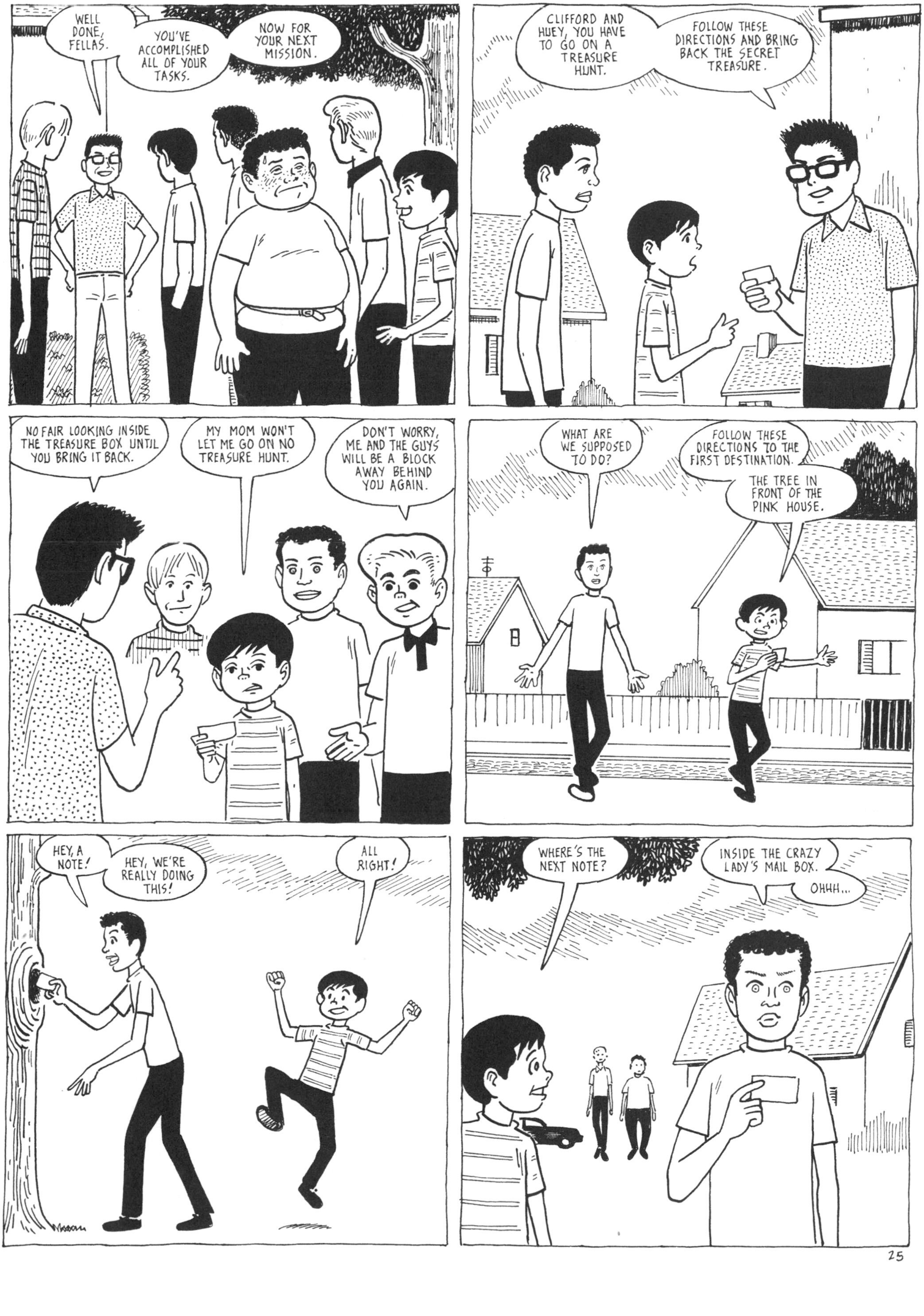

WELL DONE, FELLAS.
YOU'VE ACCOMPLISHED ALL OF YOUR TASKS.
NOW FOR YOUR NEXT MISSION.
CLIFFORD AND HUEY, YOU HAVE TO GO ON A TREASURE HUNT.
FOLLOW THESE DIRECTIONS AND BRING BACK THE SECRET TREASURE.
NO FAIR LOOKING INSIDE THE TREASURE BOX UNTIL YOU BRING IT BACK.
MY MOM WON'T LET ME GO ON NO TREASURE HUNT.
DON'T WORRY, ME AND THE GUYS WILL BE A BLOCK AWAY BEHIND YOU AGAIN.
WHAT ARE WE SUPPOSED TO DO?
FOLLOW THESE DIRECTIONS TO THE FIRST DESTINATION.
THE TREE IN FRONT OF THE PINK HOUSE.
HEY, A NOTE!
HEY, WE'RE REALLY DOING THIS!
ALL RIGHT!
WHERE'S THE NEXT NOTE?
INSIDE THE CRAZY LADY'S MAIL BOX.
OHHH...

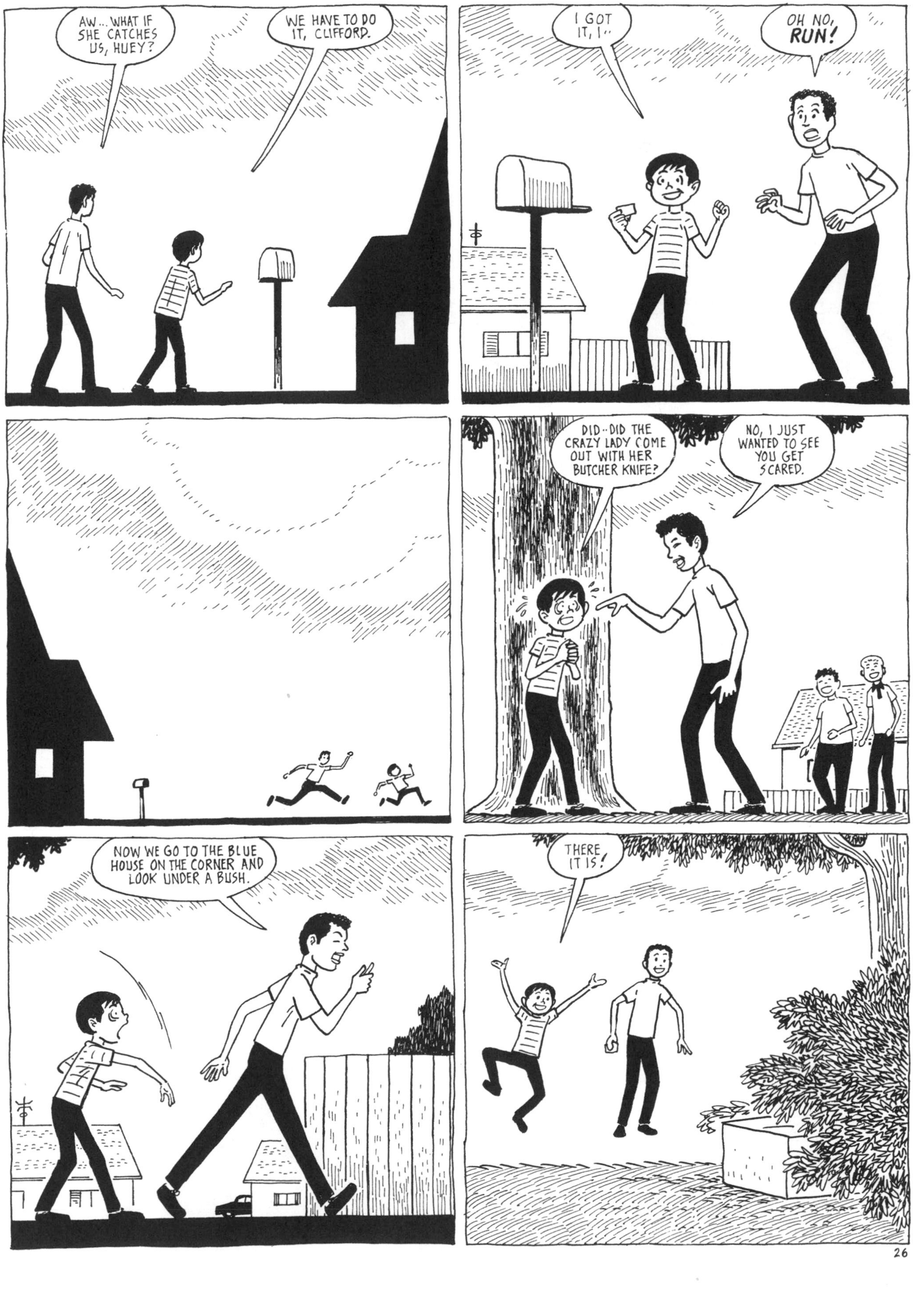
AW... WHAT IF SHE CATCHES US, HUEY?
WE HAVE TO DO IT, CLIFFORD.
I GOT IT, I..
OH NO, RUN!
DID.. DID THE CRAZY LADY COME OUT WITH HER BUTCHER KNIFE?
NO, I JUST WANTED TO SEE YOU GET SCARED.
NOW WE GO TO THE BLUE HOUSE ON THE CORNER AND LOOK UNDER A BUSH.
THERE IT IS!

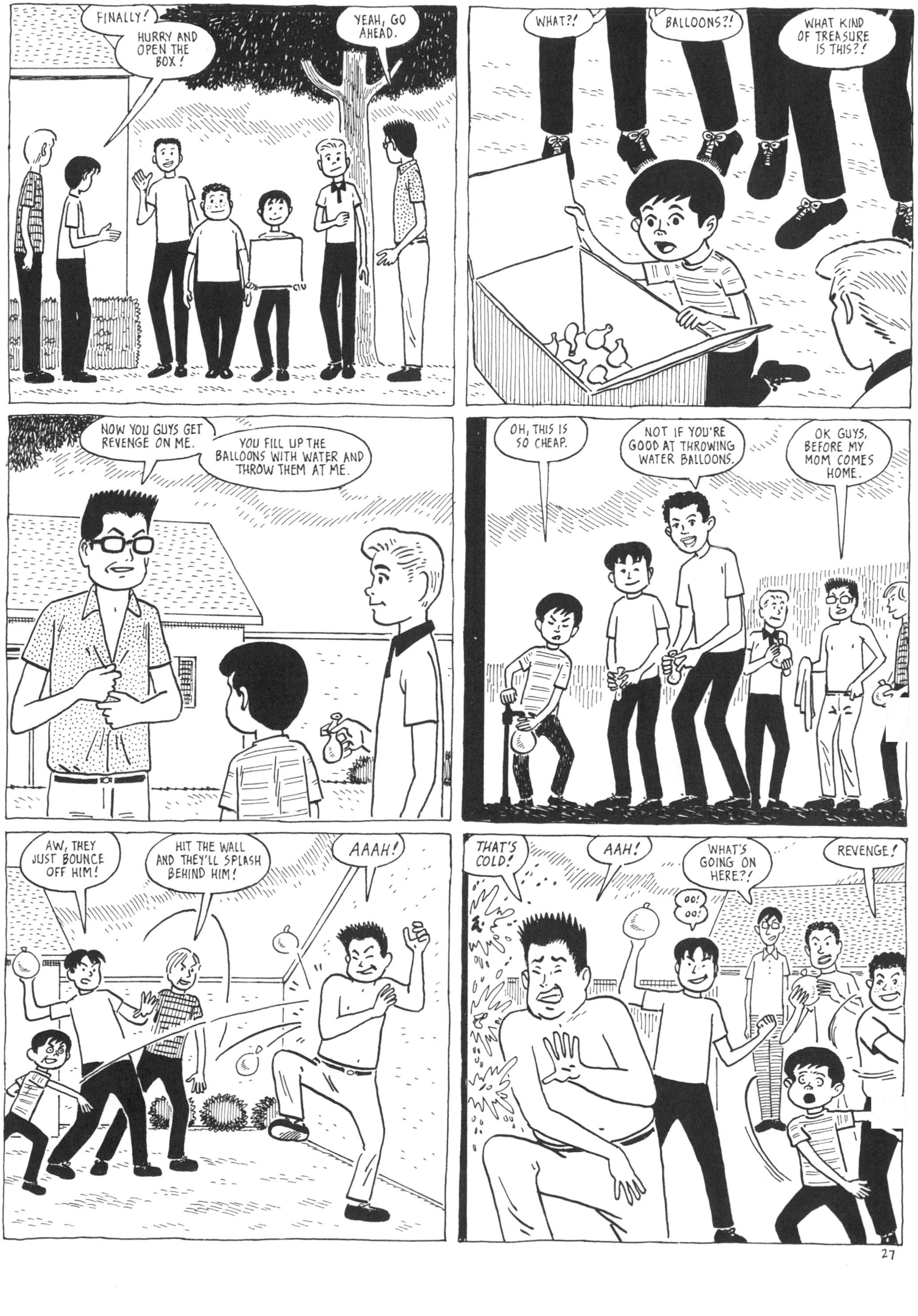
FINALLY!
HURRY AND OPEN THE BOX!
YEAH, GO AHEAD.
WHAT?!
BALLOONS?!
WHAT KIND OF TREASURE IS THIS?!
NOW YOU GUYS GET REVENGE ON ME.
YOU FILL UP THE BALLOONS WITH WATER AND THROW THEM AT ME.
OH, THIS IS SO CHEAP.
NOT IF YOU'RE GOOD AT THROWING WATER BALLOONS.
OK GUYS, BEFORE MY MOM COMES HOME.
AW, THEY JUST BOUNCE OFF HIM!
HIT THE WALL AND THEY'LL SPLASH BEHIND HIM!
AAAH!
THAT'S COLD!
AAH!
WHAT'S GOING ON HERE?!
OO! OO!
REVENGE!

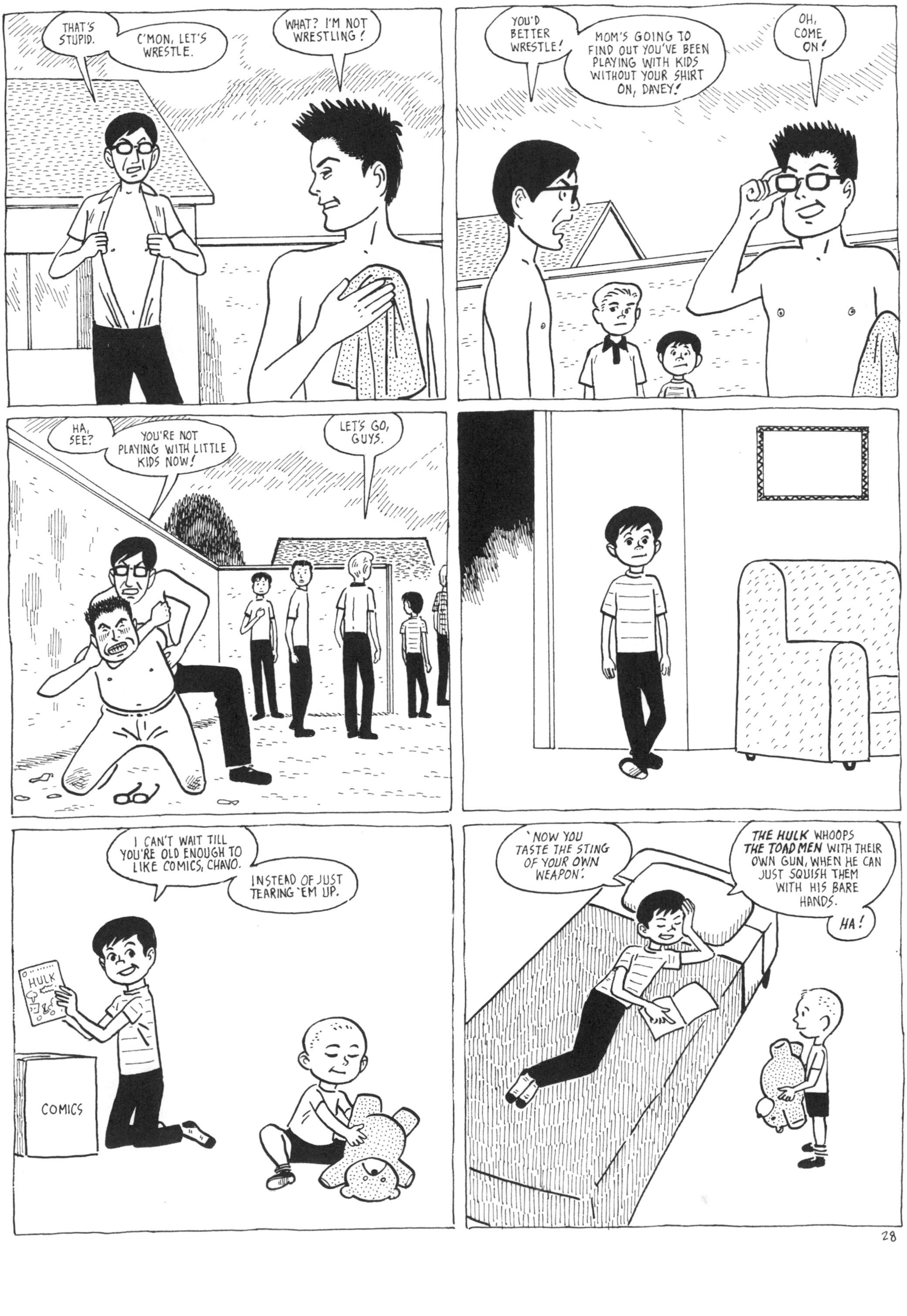
THAT'S STUPID.
C'MON, LET'S WRESTLE.
WHAT? I'M NOT WRESTLING!
YOU'D BETTER WRESTLE!
MOM'S GOING TO FIND OUT YOU'VE BEEN PLAYING WITH KIDS WITHOUT YOUR SHIRT ON, DAVEY!
OH, COME ON!
HA, SEE?
YOU'RE NOT PLAYING WITH LITTLE KIDS NOW!
LET'S GO, GUYS.
I CAN'T WAIT TILL YOU'RE OLD ENOUGH TO LIKE COMICS, CHAVO.
INSTEAD OF JUST TEARING 'EM UP.
HULK
COMICS
'NOW YOU TASTE THE STING OF YOUR OWN WEAPON.'
THE HULK WHOOPS THE TOAD MEN WITH THEIR OWN GUN, WHEN HE CAN JUST SQUISH THEM WITH HIS BARE HANDS.
HA!

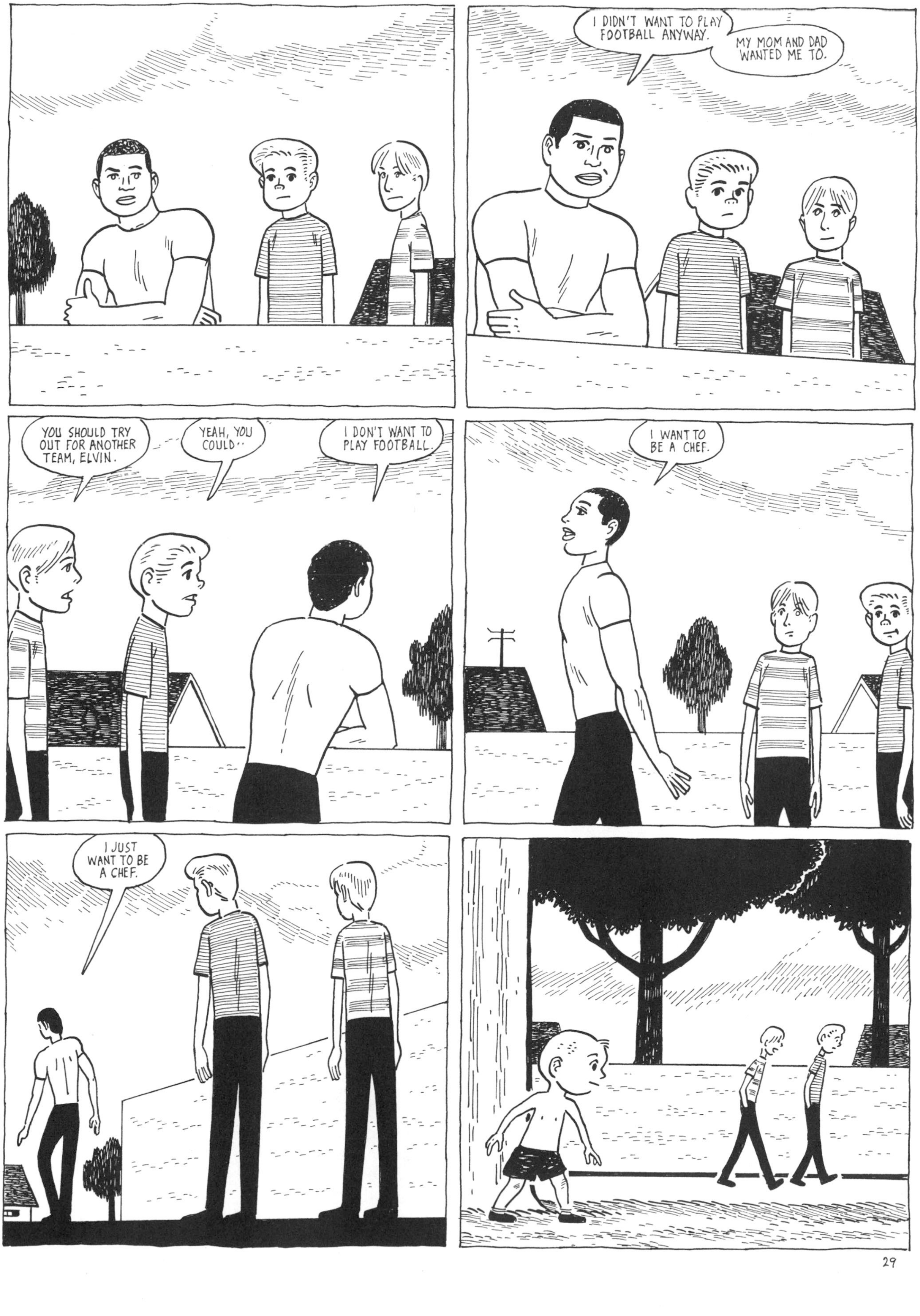
I DIDN'T WANT TO PLAY FOOTBALL ANYWAY.
MY MOM AND DAD WANTED ME TO.
YOU SHOULD TRY OUT FOR ANOTHER TEAM, ELVIN.
YEAH, YOU COULD..
I DON'T WANT TO PLAY FOOTBALL.
I WANT TO BE A CHEF.
I JUST WANT TO BE A CHEF.

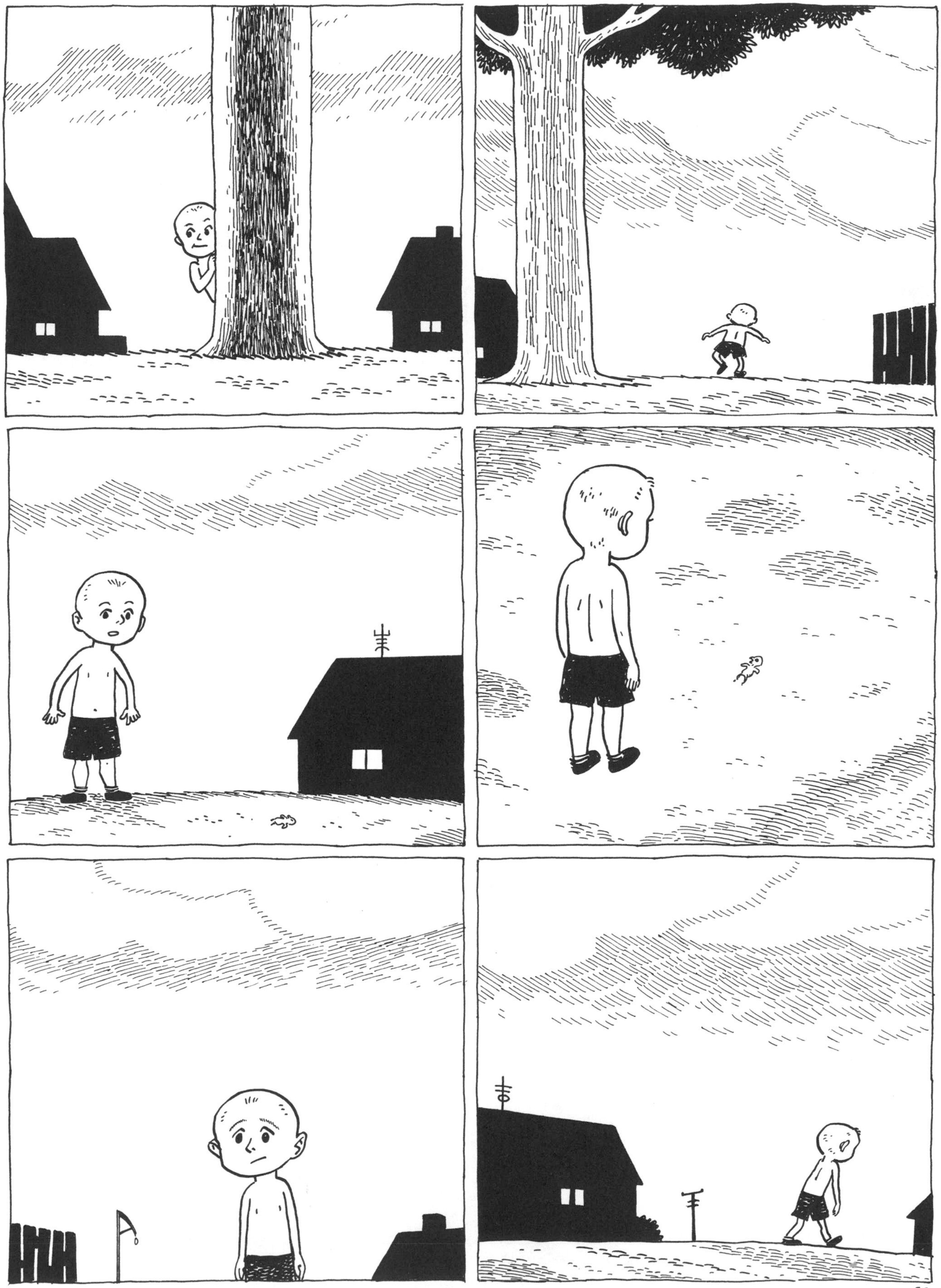

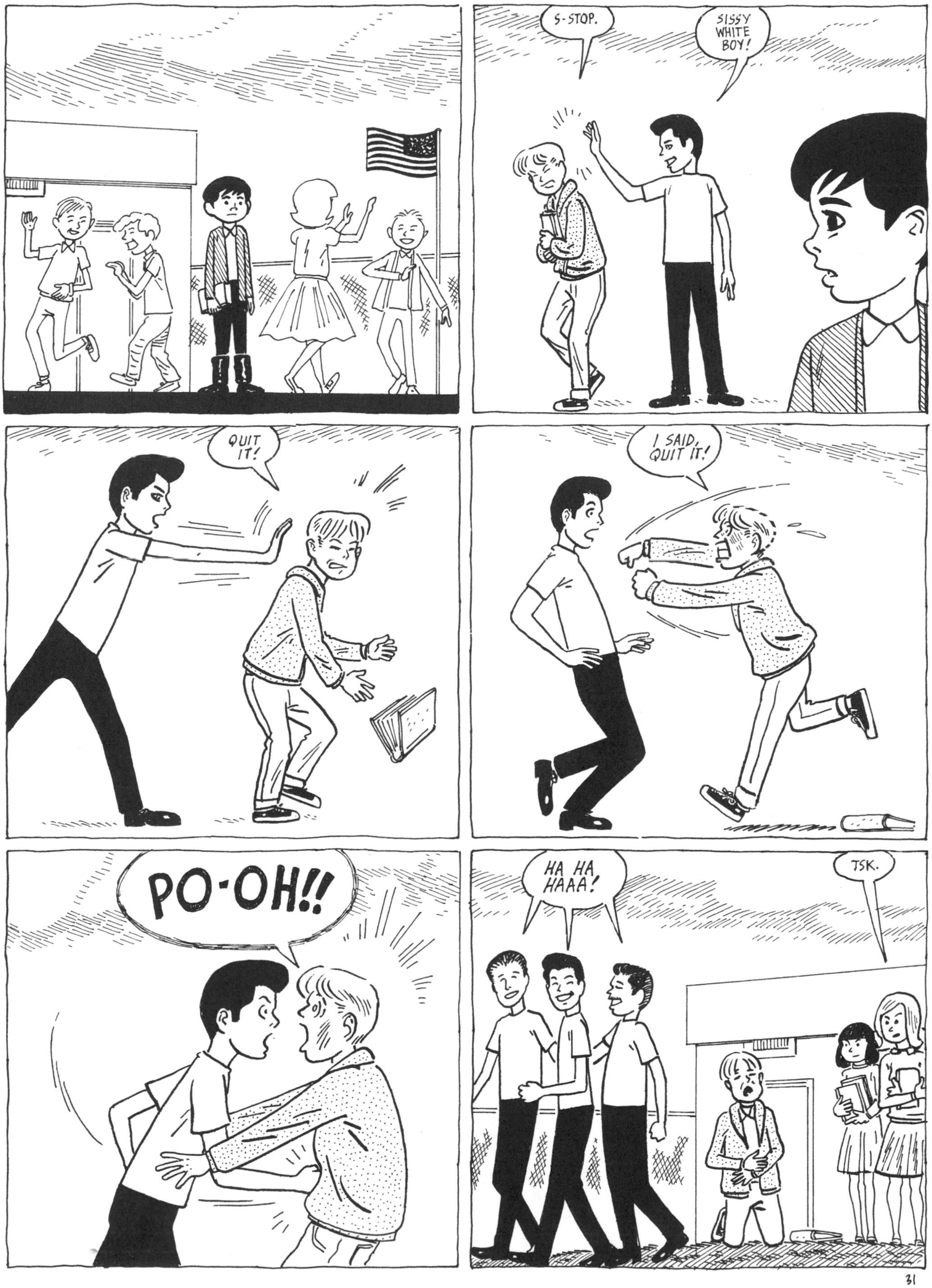
S-STOP.
SISSY WHITE BOY!
QUIT IT!
I SAID, QUIT IT!
PO-OH!!
HA HA HAAA!
TSK.

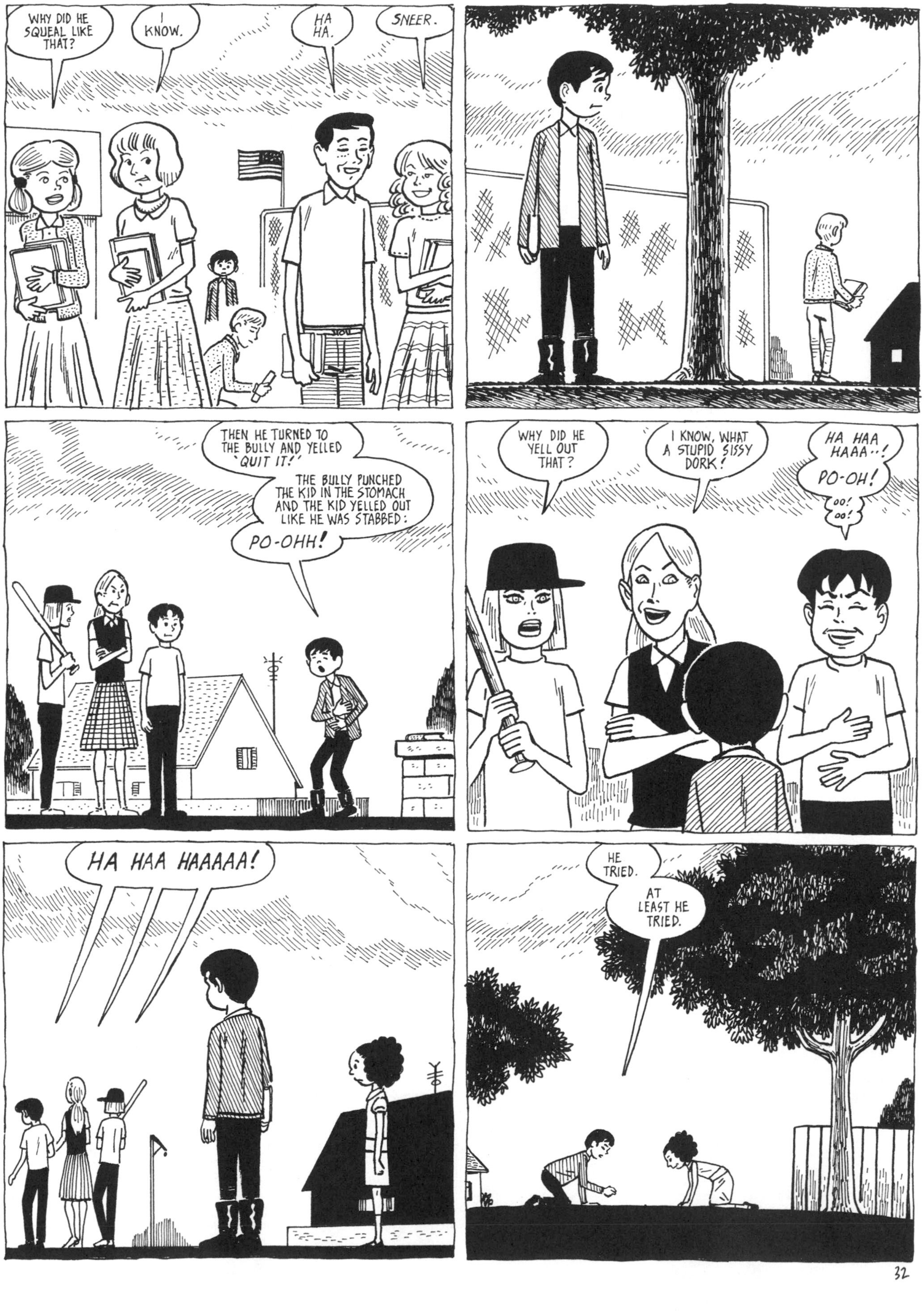

WHY DID HE SQUEAL LIKE THAT?
I KNOW.
HA HA.
SNEER.
THEN HE TURNED TO THE BULLY AND YELLED 'QUIT IT!'
THE BULLY PUNCHED THE KID IN THE STOMACH AND THE KID YELLED OUT LIKE HE WAS STABBED:
PO-OHH!
WHY DID HE YELL OUT THAT?
I KNOW, WHAT A STUPID SISSY DORK!
HA HAA HAAA..!
PO-OH!
OO! OO!
HA HAA HAAAAA!
HE TRIED.
AT LEAST HE TRIED.

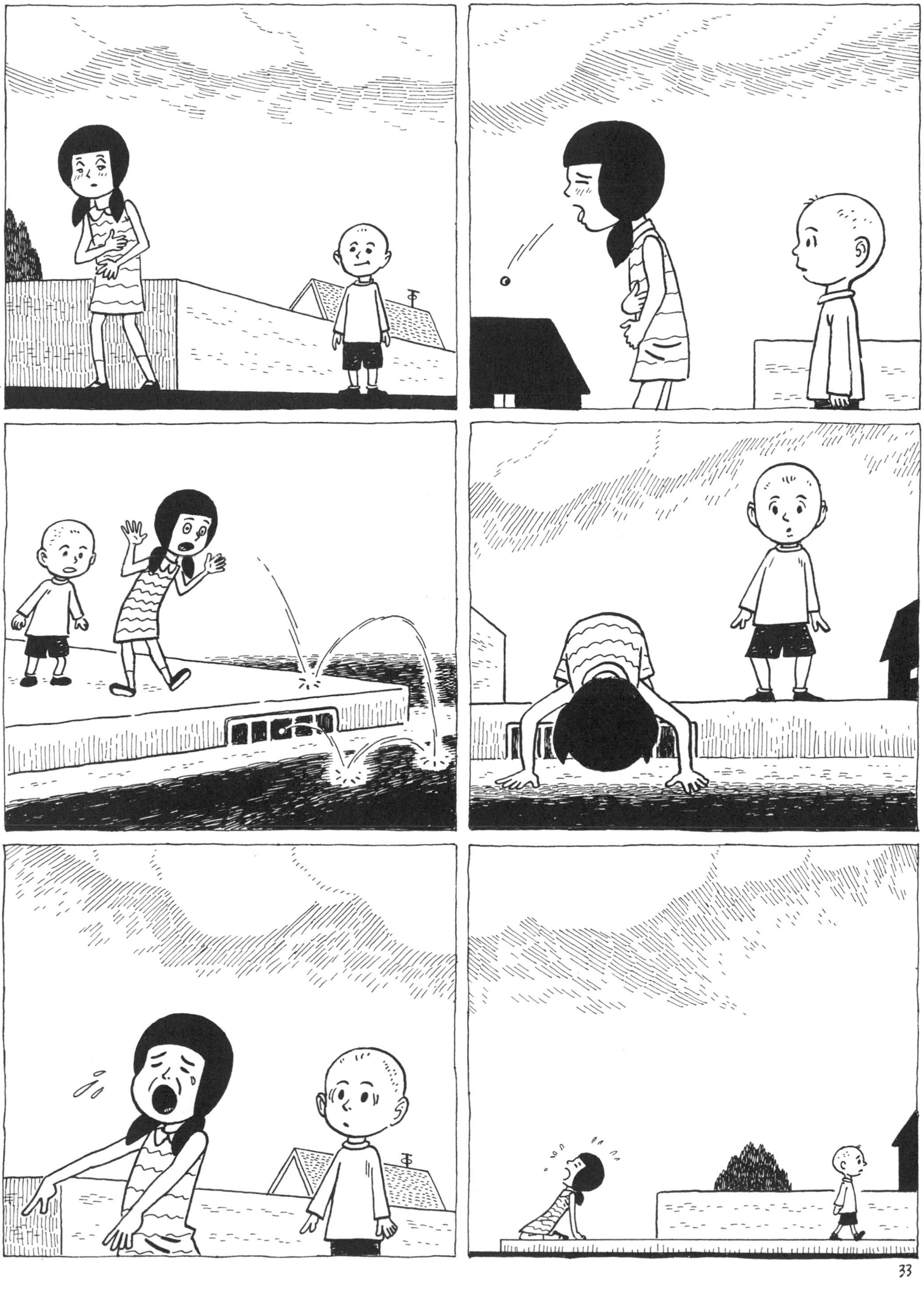

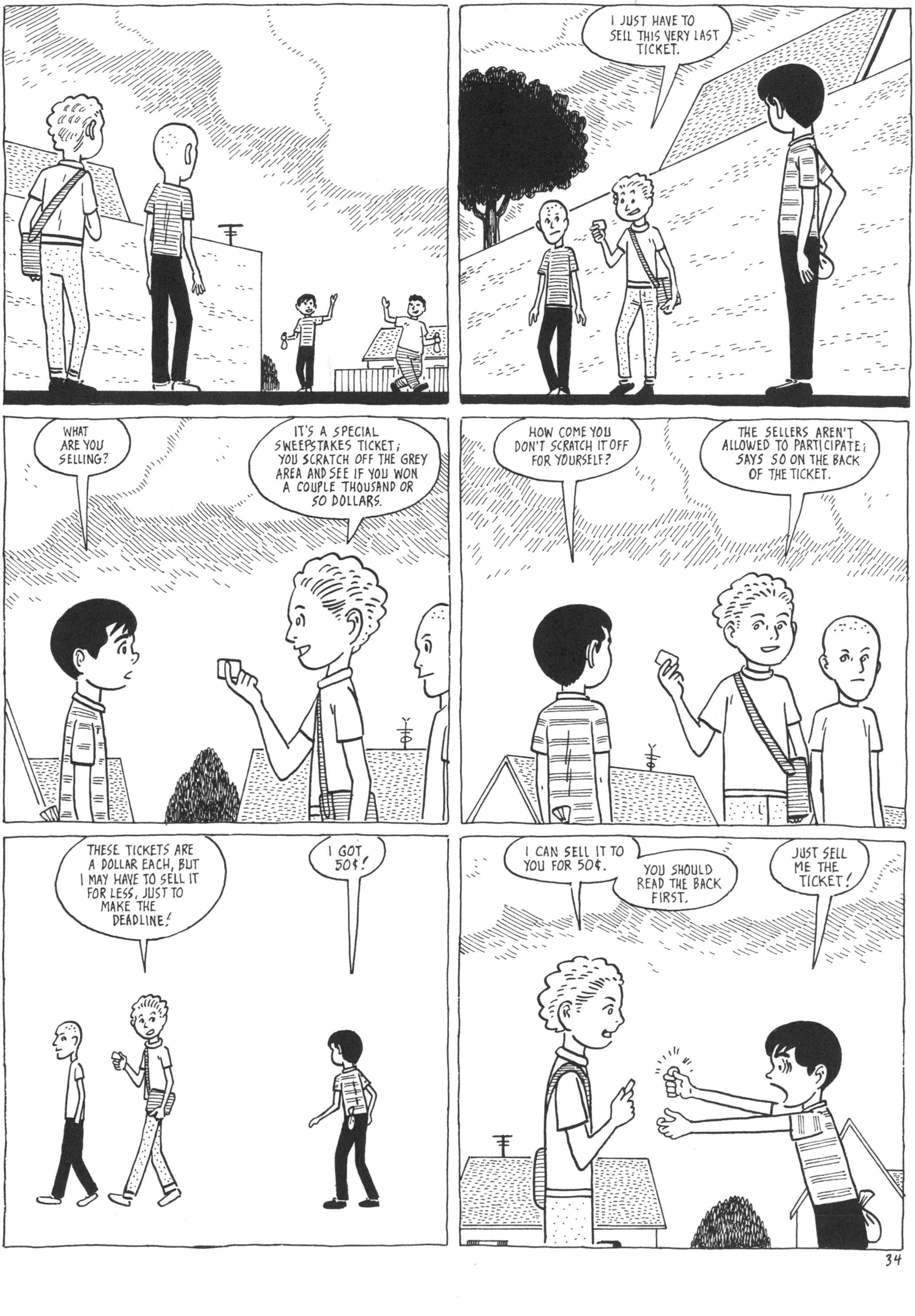

I JUST HAVE TO SELL THIS VERY LAST TICKET.
WHAT ARE YOU SELLING?
IT'S A SPECIAL SWEEPSTAKES TICKET; YOU SCRATCH OFF THE GREY AREA AND SEE IF YOU WON A COUPLE THOUSAND OR 50 DOLLARS.
HOW COME YOU DON'T SCRATCH IT OFF FOR YOURSELF?
THE SELLERS AREN'T ALLOWED TO PARTICIPATE; SAYS SO ON THE BACK OF THE TICKET.
THESE TICKETS ARE A DOLLAR EACH, BUT I MAY HAVE TO SELL IT FOR LESS, JUST TO MAKE THE DEADLINE!
I GOT 50¢!
I CAN SELL IT TO YOU FOR 50¢.
YOU SHOULD READ THE BACK FIRST.
JUST SELL ME THE TICKET!

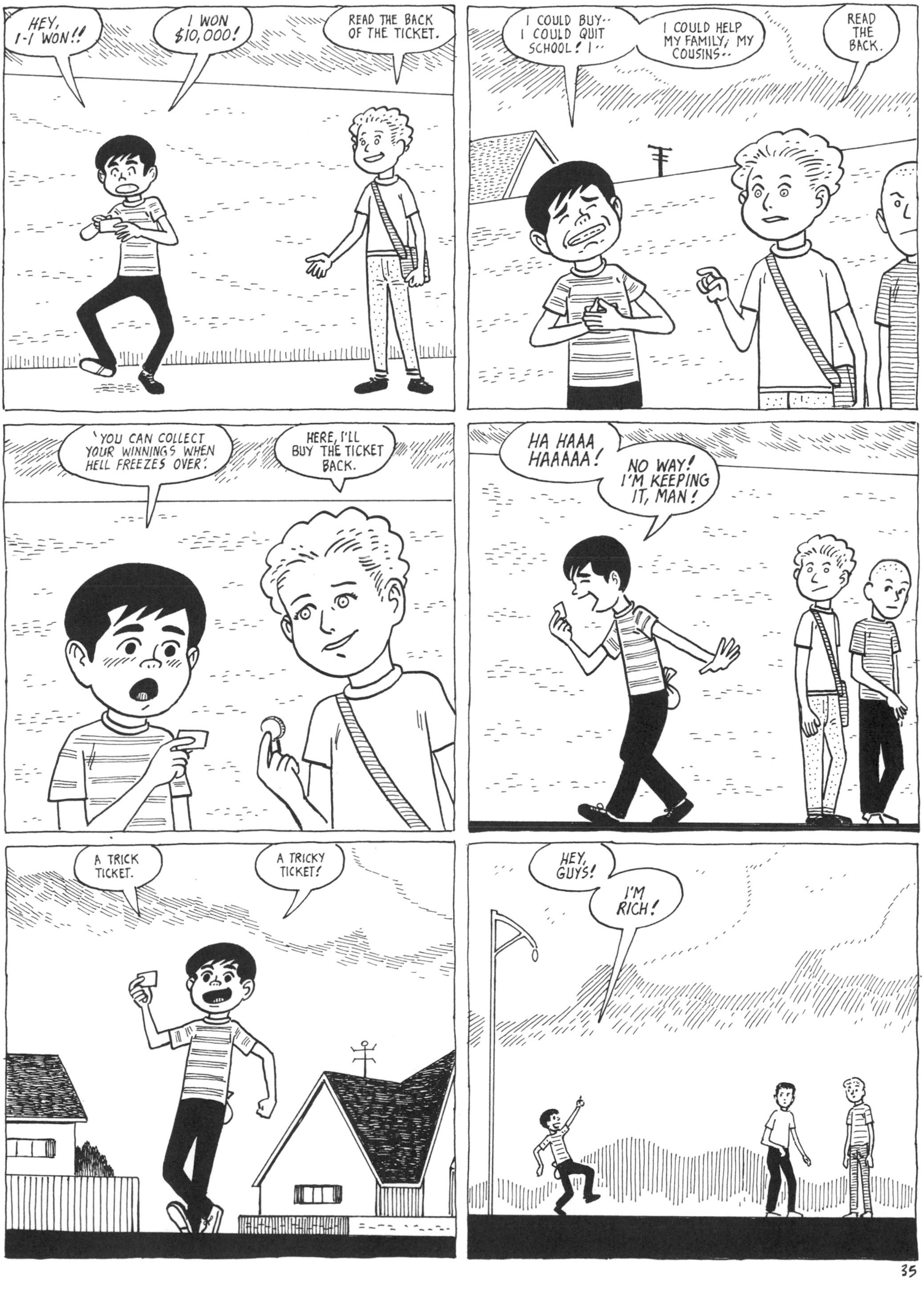
HEY, I-I WON!!
I WON $10,000!
READ THE BACK OF THE TICKET.
I COULD BUY.. I COULD QUIT SCHOOL! I..
I COULD HELP MY FAMILY, MY COUSINS..
READ THE BACK.
'YOU CAN COLLECT YOUR WINNINGS WHEN HELL FREEZES OVER.'
HERE, I'LL BUY THE TICKET BACK.
HA HAAA HAAAAA!
NO WAY! I'M KEEPING IT, MAN!
A TRICK TICKET.
A TRICKY TICKET!
HEY, GUYS!
I'M RICH!

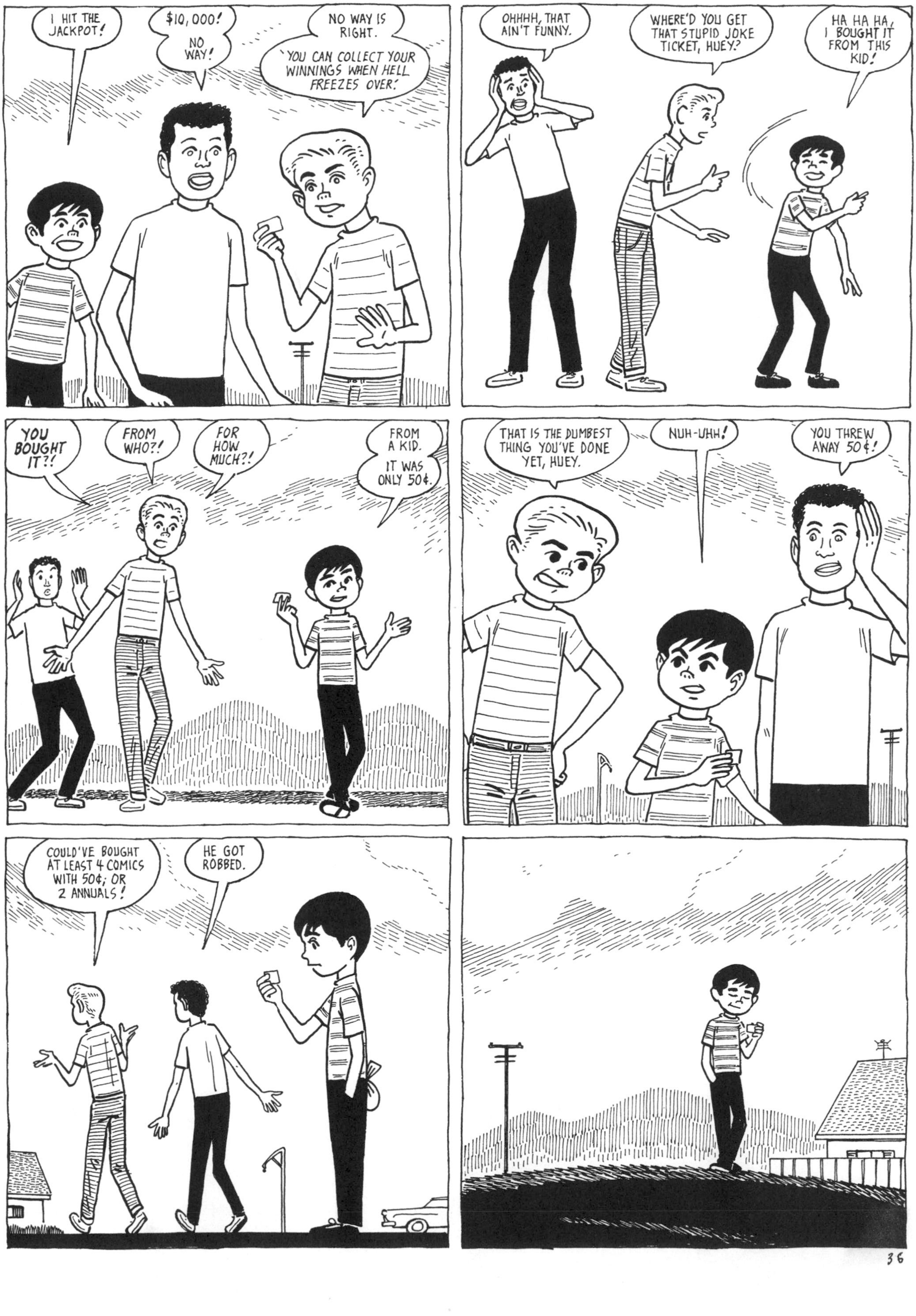
I HIT THE JACKPOT!
$10,000! NO WAY!
NO WAY IS RIGHT. 'YOU CAN COLLECT YOUR WINNINGS WHEN HELL FREEZES OVER.'
OHHHH, THAT AIN'T FUNNY.
WHERE'D YOU GET THAT STUPID JOKE TICKET, HUEY?
HA HA HA, I BOUGHT IT FROM THIS KID!
YOU BOUGHT IT?!
FROM WHO?!
FOR HOW MUCH?!
FROM A KID. IT WAS ONLY 50¢.
THAT IS THE DUMBEST THING YOU'VE DONE YET, HUEY.
NUH-UHH!
YOU THREW AWAY 50¢!
COULD'VE BOUGHT AT LEAST 4 COMICS WITH 50¢; OR 2 ANNUALS!
HE GOT ROBBED.

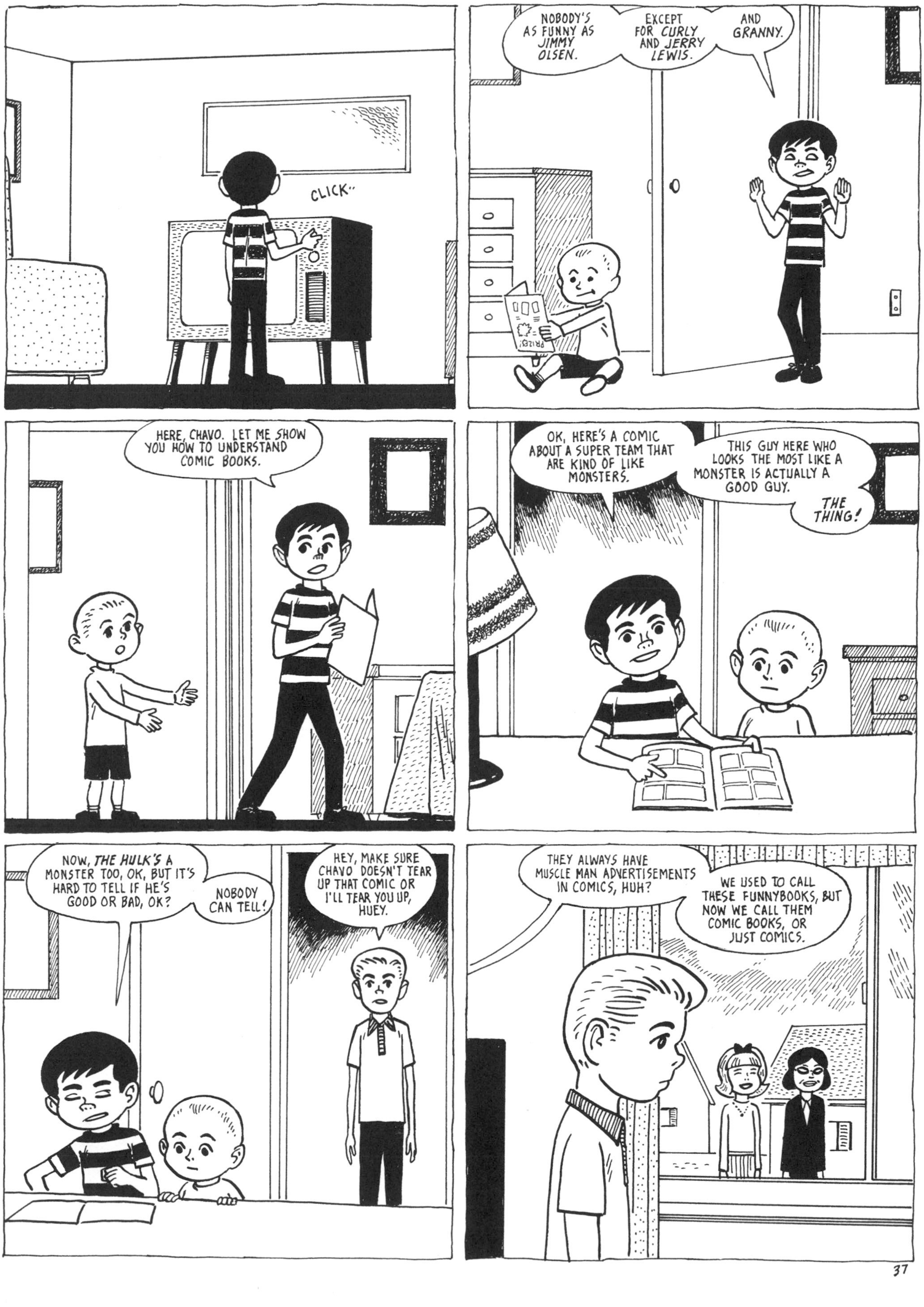

CLICK..
NOBODY'S AS FUNNY AS JIMMY OLSEN.
EXCEPT FOR CURLY AND JERRY LEWIS.
AND GRANNY.
PRIZES!
HERE, CHAVO. LET ME SHOW YOU HOW TO UNDERSTAND COMIC BOOKS.
OK, HERE'S A COMIC ABOUT A SUPER TEAM THAT ARE KIND OF LIKE MONSTERS.
THIS GUY HERE WHO LOOKS THE MOST LIKE A MONSTER IS ACTUALLY A GOOD GUY.
THE THING!
NOW, THE HULK'S A MONSTER TOO, OK, BUT IT'S HARD TO TELL IF HE'S GOOD OR BAD, OK?
NOBODY CAN TELL!
HEY, MAKE SURE CHAVO DOESN'T TEAR UP THAT COMIC OR I'LL TEAR YOU UP, HUEY.
THEY ALWAYS HAVE MUSCLE MAN ADVERTISEMENTS IN COMICS, HUH?
WE USED TO CALL THESE FUNNYBOOKS, BUT NOW WE CALL THEM COMIC BOOKS, OR JUST COMICS.

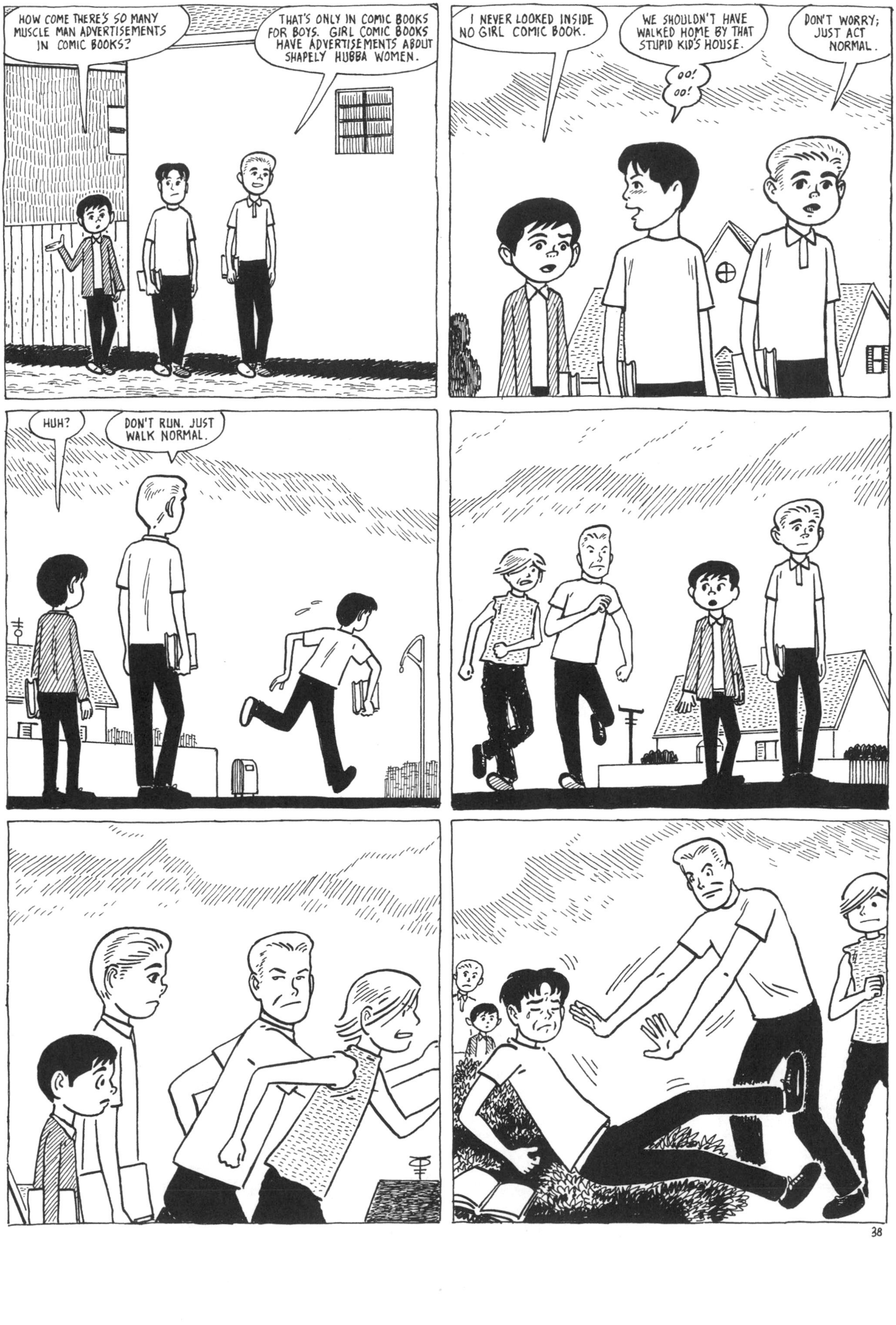
HOW COME THERE'S SO MANY MUSCLE MAN ADVERTISEMENTS IN COMIC BOOKS?
THAT'S ONLY IN COMIC BOOKS FOR BOYS. GIRL COMIC BOOKS HAVE ADVERTISEMENTS ABOUT SHAPELY HUBBA WOMEN.
I NEVER LOOKED INSIDE NO GIRL COMIC BOOK.
WE SHOULDN'T HAVE WALKED HOME BY THAT STUPID KID'S HOUSE.
OO! OO!
DON'T WORRY; JUST ACT NORMAL.
HUH?
DON'T RUN. JUST WALK NORMAL.

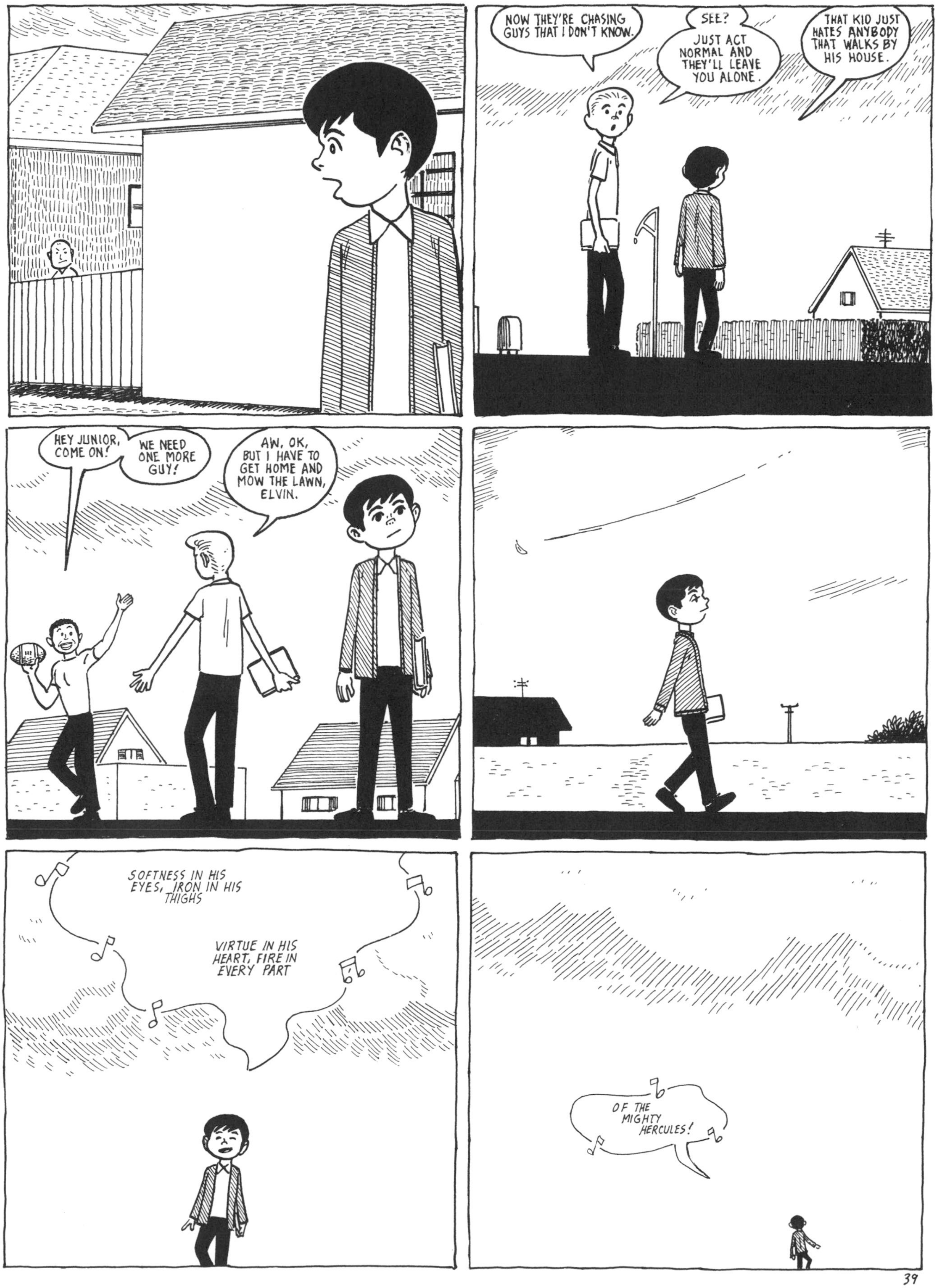
NOW THEY'RE CHASING GUYS THAT I DON'T KNOW.
SEE?
JUST ACT NORMAL AND THEY'LL LEAVE YOU ALONE.
THAT KID JUST HATES ANYBODY THAT WALKS BY HIS HOUSE.
HEY JUNIOR, COME ON!
WE NEED ONE MORE GUY!
AW, OK, BUT I HAVE TO GET HOME AND MOW THE LAWN, ELVIN.
SOFTNESS IN HIS EYES, IRON IN HIS THIGHS
VIRTUE IN HIS HEART, FIRE IN EVERY PART
OF THE MIGHTY HERCULES!

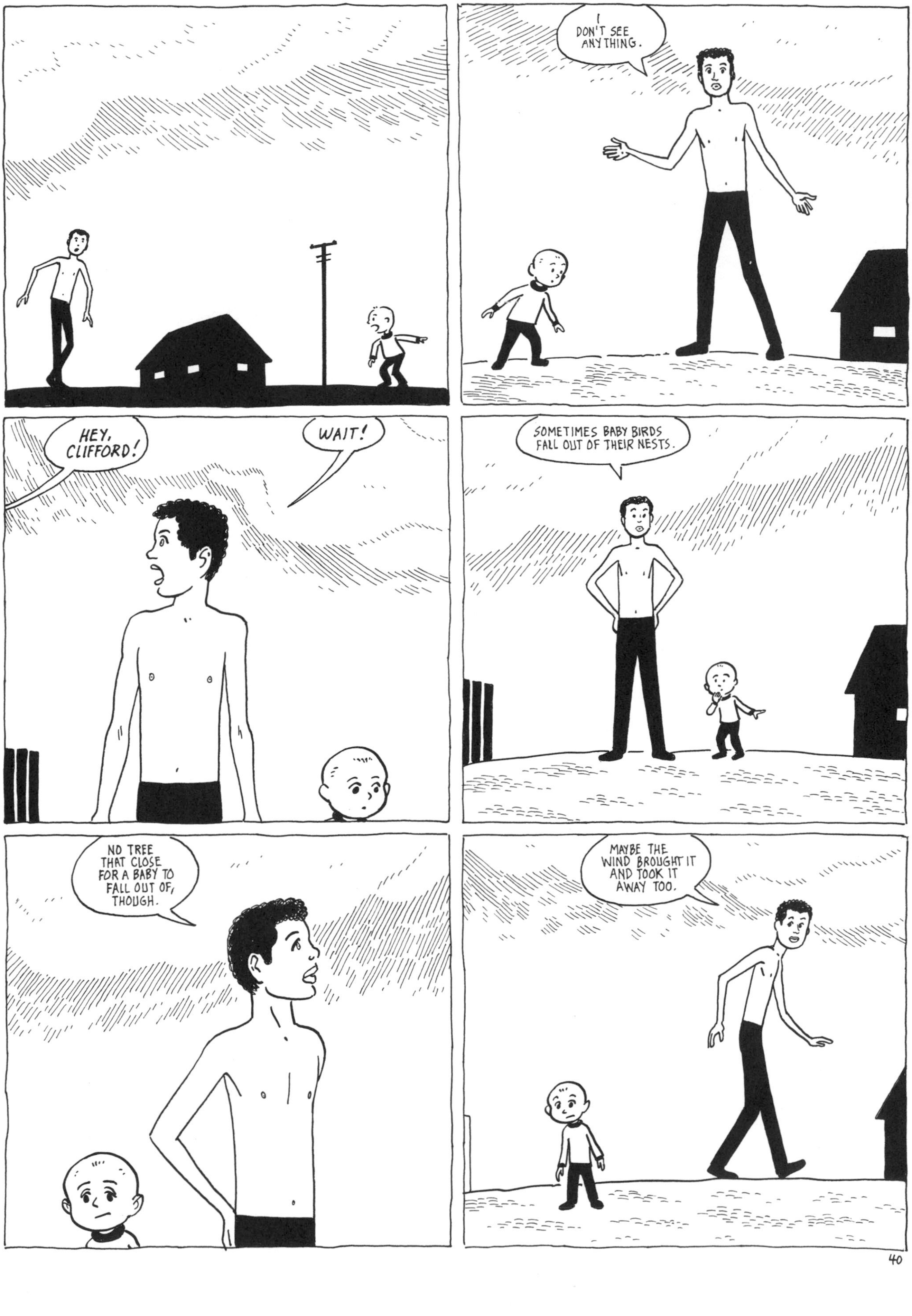
I DON'T SEE ANYTHING.
HEY, CLIFFORD!
WAIT!
SOMETIMES BABY BIRDS FALL OUT OF THEIR NESTS.
NO TREE THAT CLOSE FOR A BABY TO FALL OUT OF, THOUGH.
MAYBE THE WIND BROUGHT IT AND TOOK IT AWAY TOO.

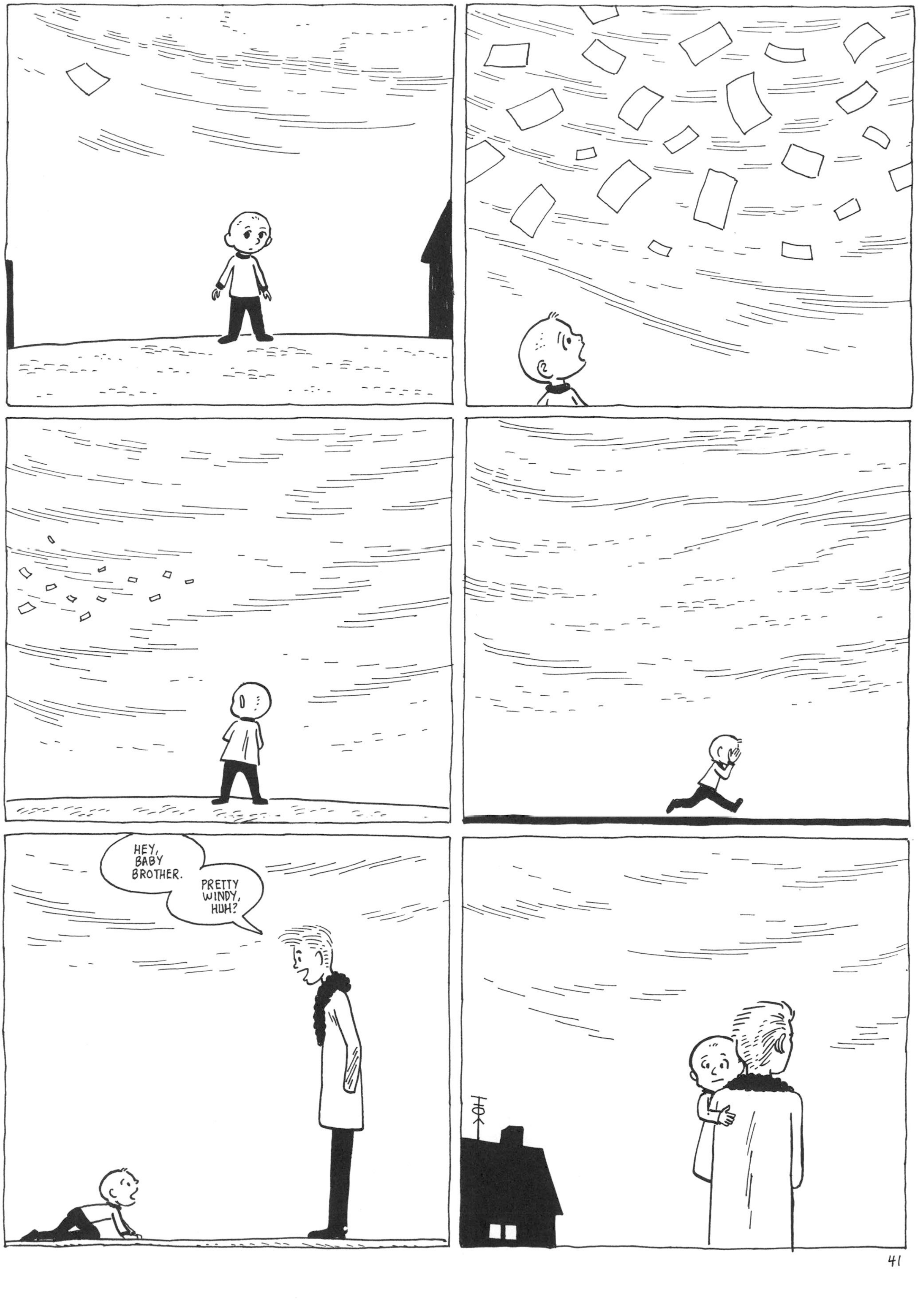
HEY, BABY BROTHER.
PRETTY WINDY, HUH?

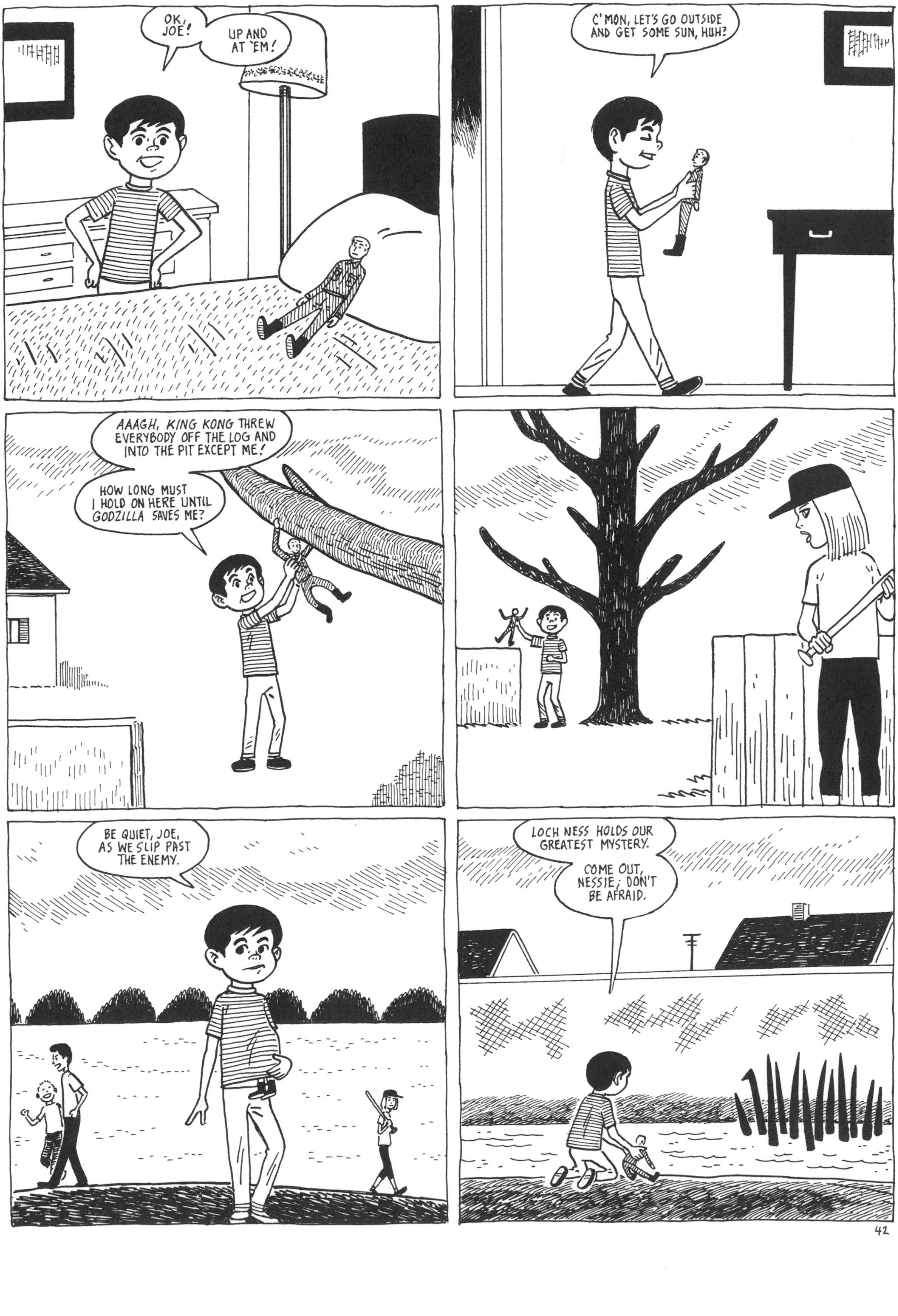
OK, JOE!
UP AND AT 'EM!
C'MON, LET'S GO OUTSIDE AND GET SOME SUN, HUH?
AAAGH, KING KONG THREW EVERYBODY OFF THE LOG AND INTO THE PIT EXCEPT ME!
HOW LONG MUST I HOLD ON HERE UNTIL GODZILLA SAVES ME?
BE QUIET, JOE, AS WE SLIP PAST THE ENEMY.
LOCH NESS HOLDS OUR GREATEST MYSTERY.
COME OUT, NESSIE; DON'T BE AFRAID.

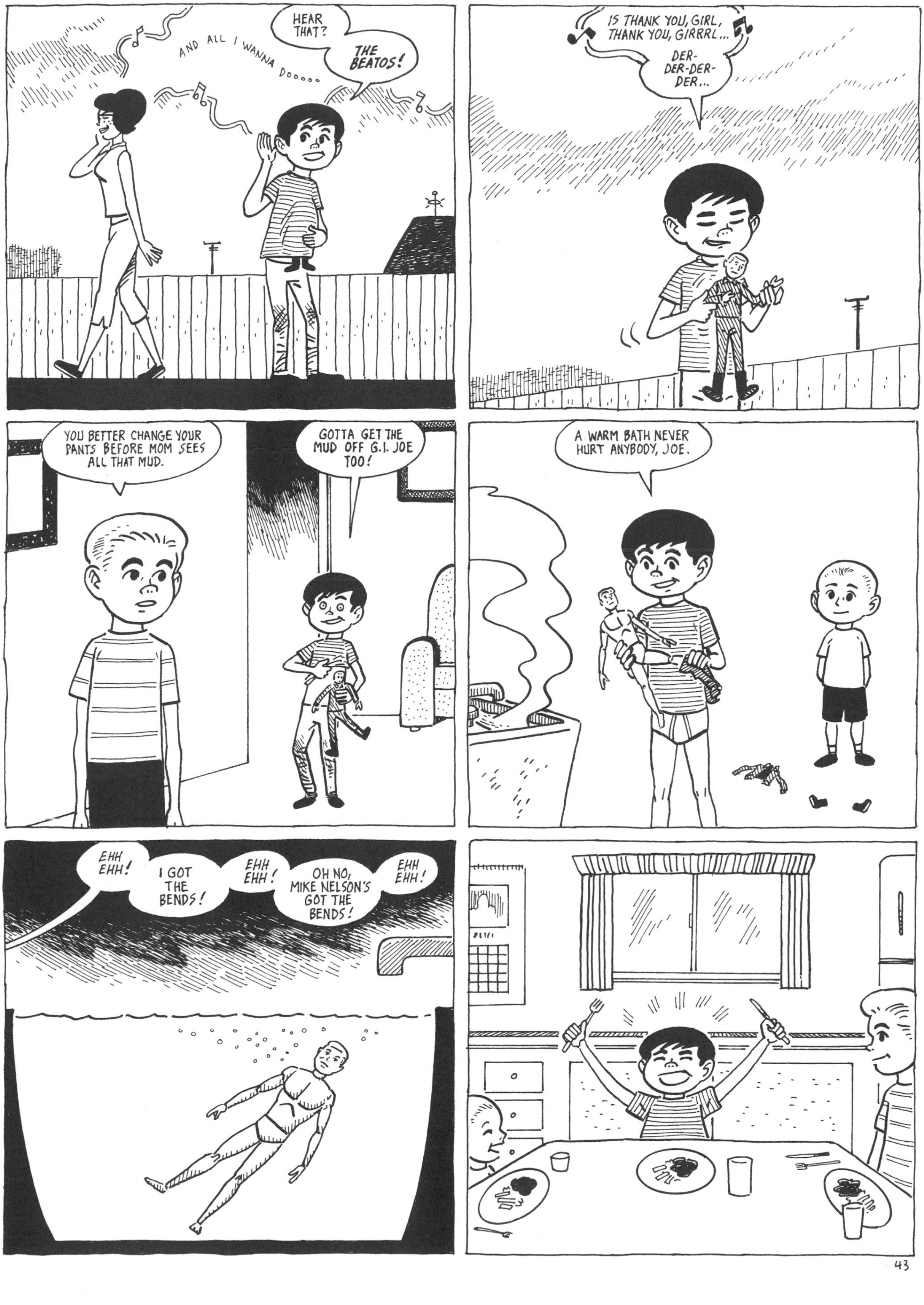
AND ALL I WANNA DOOOOO
HEAR THAT?
THE BEATOS!
IS THANK YOU, GIRL, THANK YOU, GIRRRL...
DER-DER-DER-DER...
YOU BETTER CHANGE YOUR PANTS BEFORE MOM SEES ALL THAT MUD.
GOTTA GET THE MUD OFF G.I. JOE TOO!
A WARM BATH NEVER HURT ANYBODY, JOE.
EHH EHH!
I GOT THE BENDS!
EHH EHH!
OH NO, MIKE NELSON'S GOT THE BENDS!
EHH EHH!

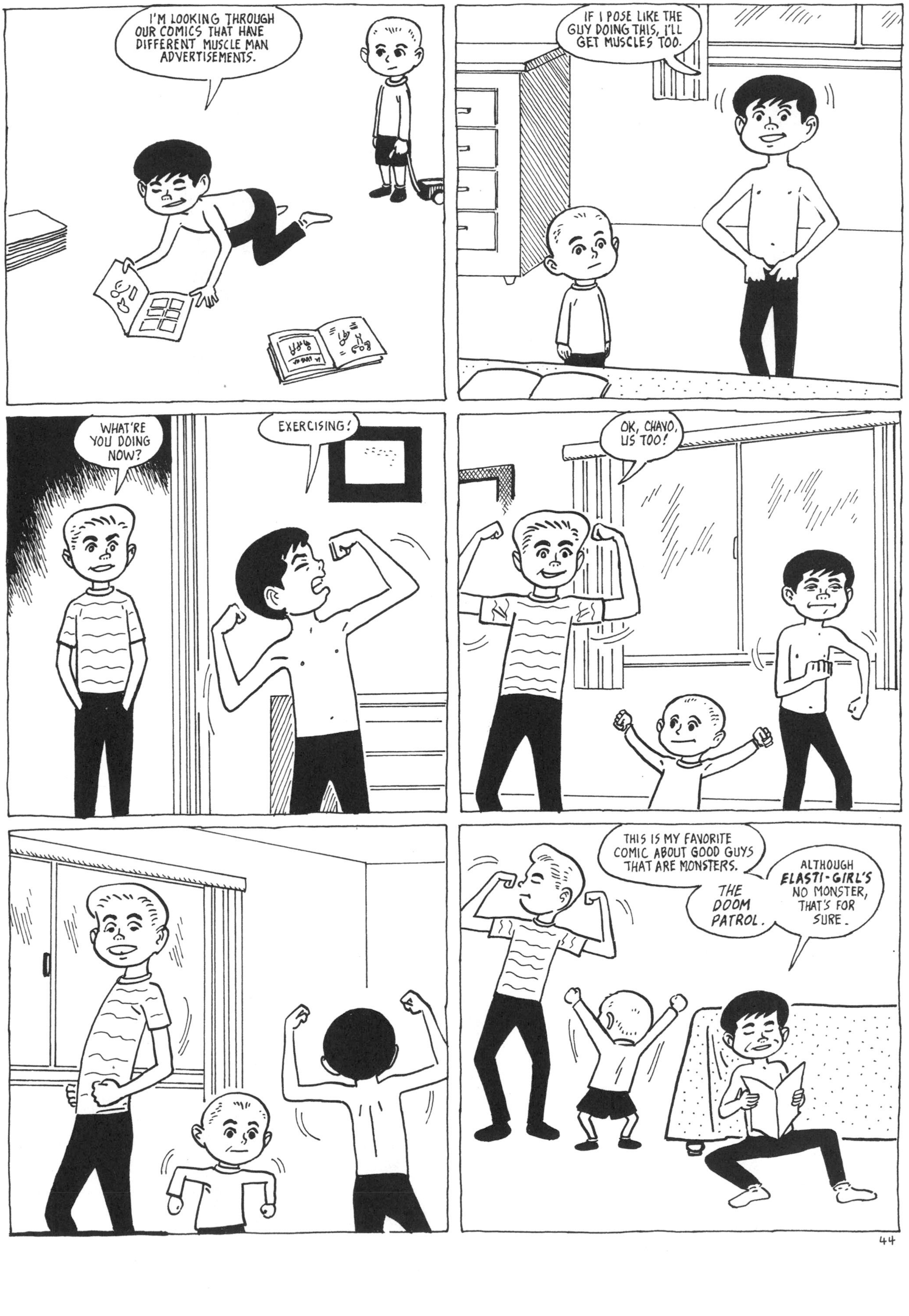
I'M LOOKING THROUGH OUR COMICS THAT HAVE DIFFERENT MUSCLE MAN ADVERTISEMENTS.
IF I POSE LIKE THE GUY DOING THIS, I'LL GET MUSCLES TOO.
WHAT'RE YOU DOING NOW?
EXERCISING!
OK, CHAVO, US TOO!
THIS IS MY FAVORITE COMIC ABOUT GOOD GUYS THAT ARE MONSTERS.
THE DOOM PATROL.
ALTHOUGH ELASTI-GIRL'S NO MONSTER, THAT'S FOR SURE.

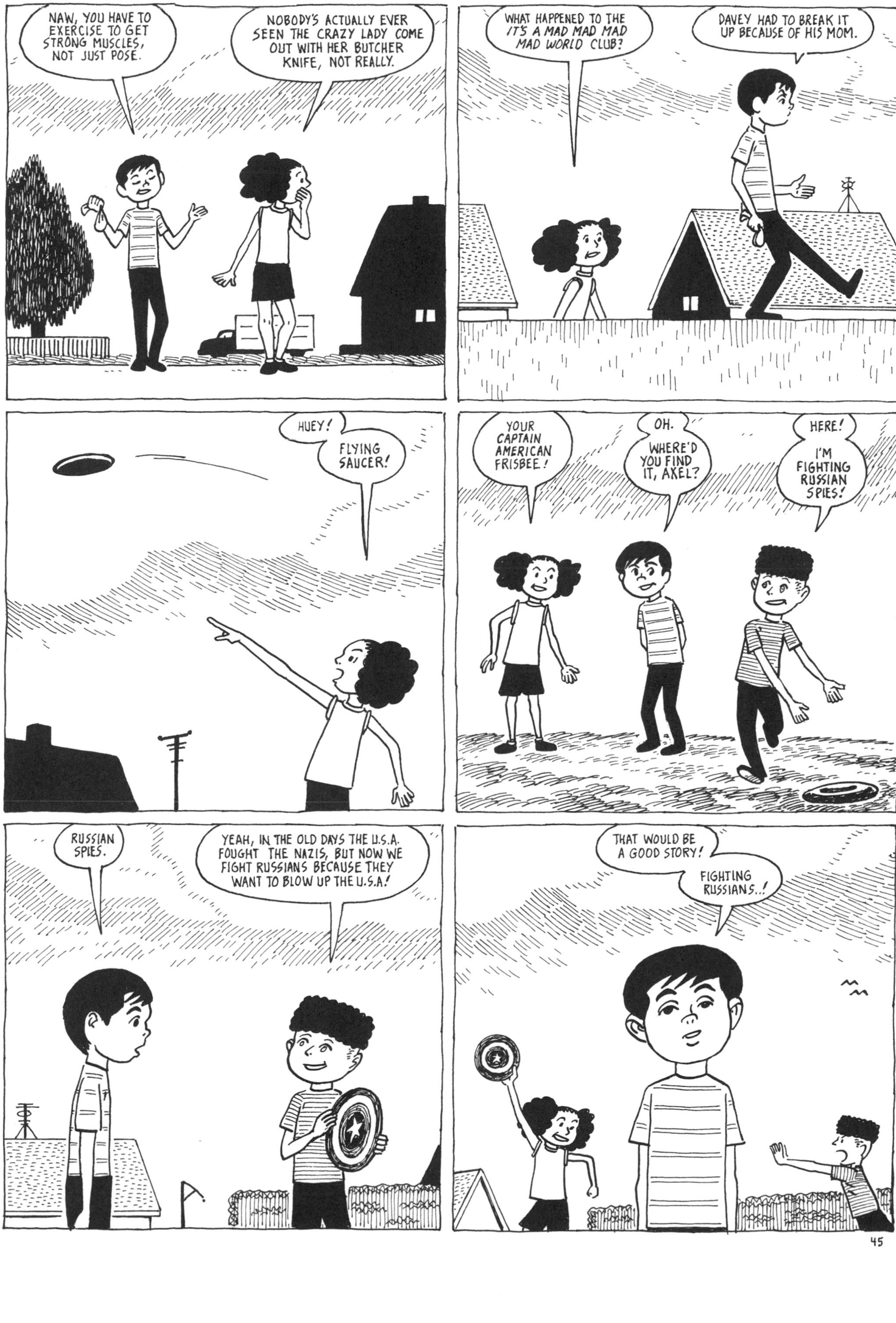
NAW, YOU HAVE TO EXERCISE TO GET STRONG MUSCLES, NOT JUST POSE.
NOBODY'S ACTUALLY EVER SEEN THE CRAZY LADY COME OUT WITH HER BUTCHER KNIFE, NOT REALLY.
WHAT HAPPENED TO THE *IT'S A MAD MAD MAD MAD WORLD* CLUB?
DAVEY HAD TO BREAK IT UP BECAUSE OF HIS MOM.
HUEY!
FLYING SAUCER!
YOUR CAPTAIN AMERICAN FRISBEE!
OH.
WHERE'D YOU FIND IT, AXEL?
HERE!
I'M FIGHTING RUSSIAN SPIES!
RUSSIAN SPIES.
YEAH, IN THE OLD DAYS THE U.S.A. FOUGHT THE NAZIS, BUT NOW WE FIGHT RUSSIANS BECAUSE THEY WANT TO BLOW UP THE U.S.A!
THAT WOULD BE A GOOD STORY!
FIGHTING RUSSIANS..!

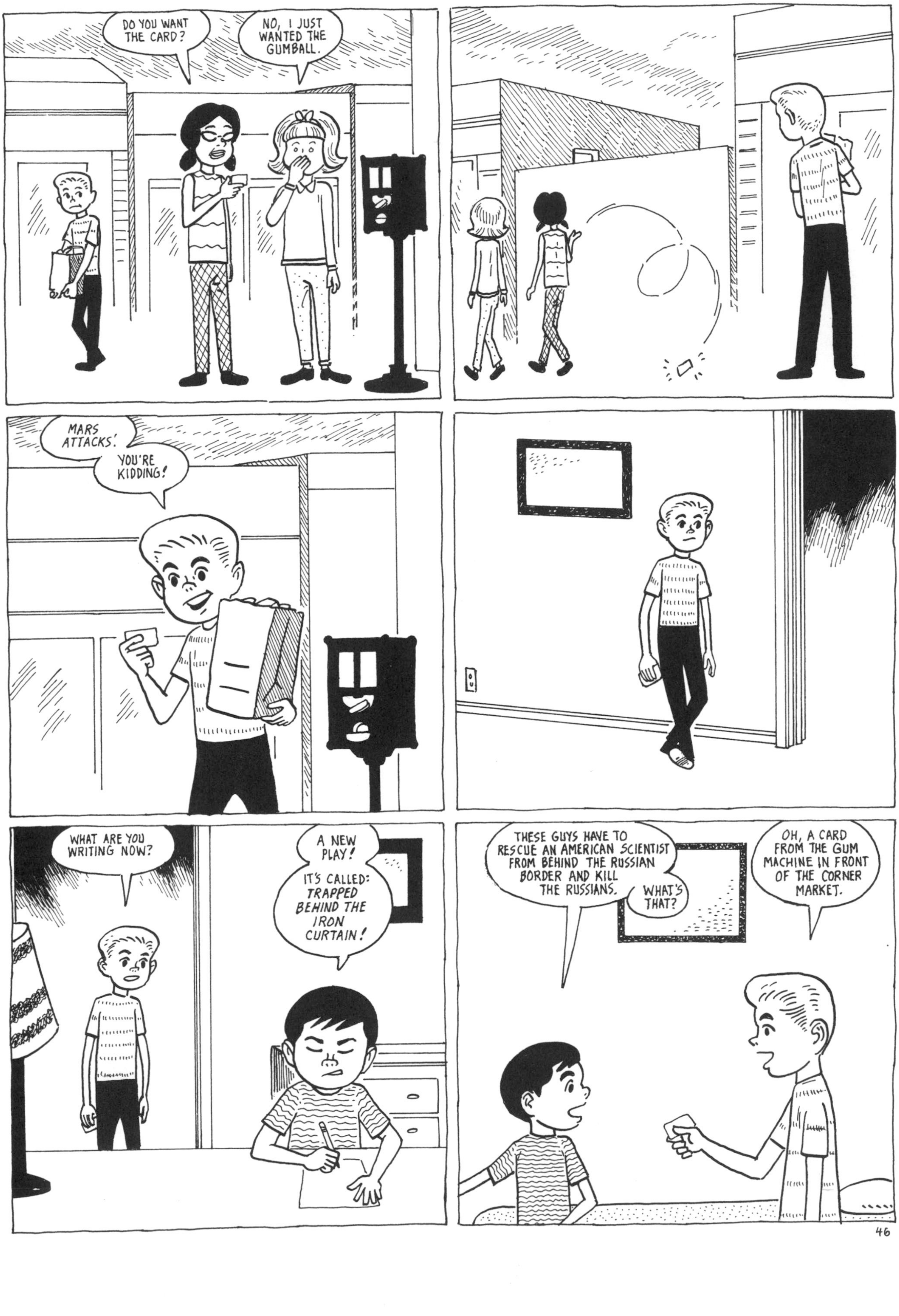
DO YOU WANT THE CARD?
NO, I JUST WANTED THE GUMBALL.
MARS ATTACKS!
YOU'RE KIDDING!
WHAT ARE YOU WRITING NOW?
A NEW PLAY!
IT'S CALLED: TRAPPED BEHIND THE IRON CURTAIN!
THESE GUYS HAVE TO RESCUE AN AMERICAN SCIENTIST FROM BEHIND THE RUSSIAN BORDER AND KILL THE RUSSIANS.
WHAT'S THAT?
OH, A CARD FROM THE GUM MACHINE IN FRONT OF THE CORNER MARKET.

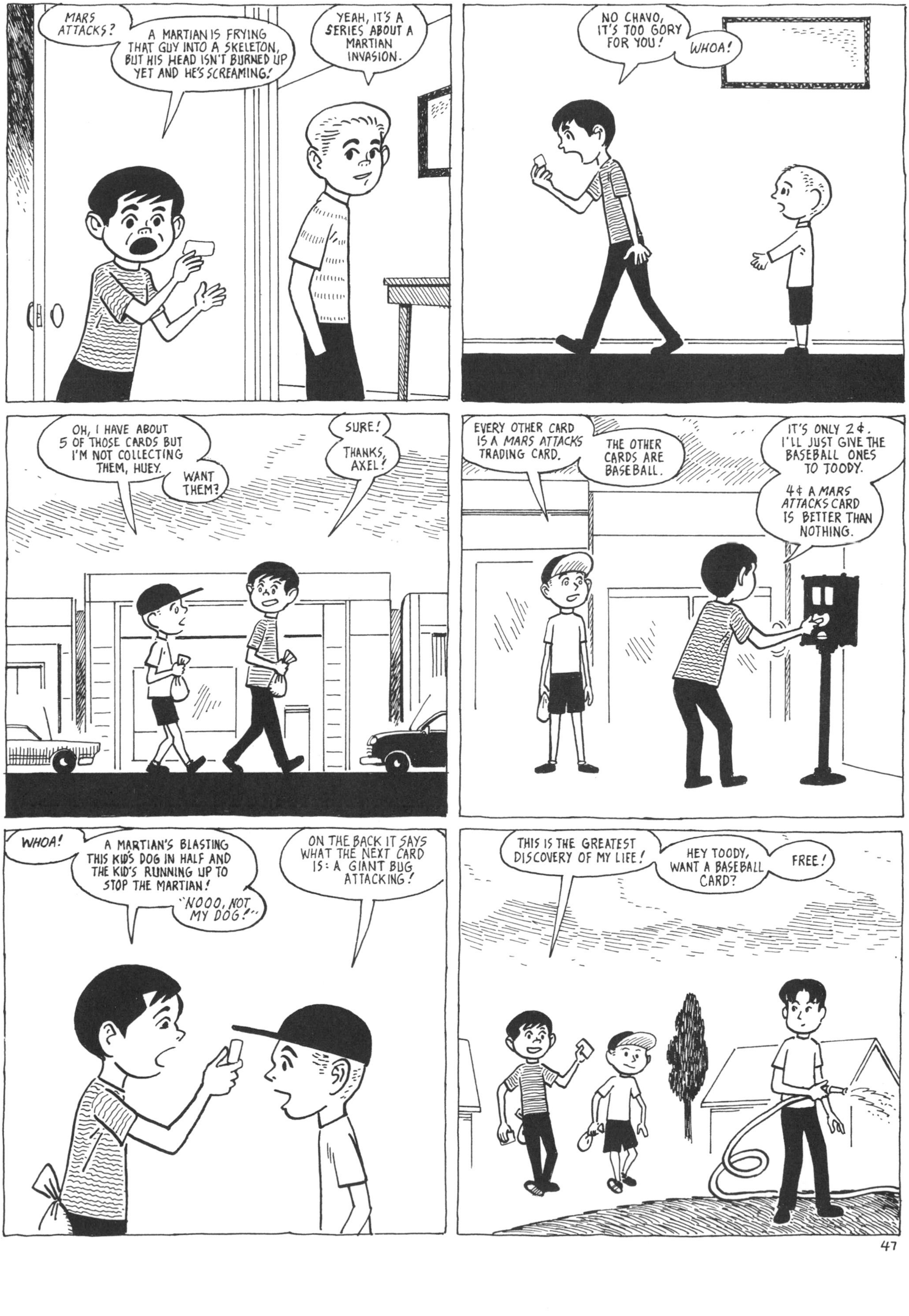
MARS ATTACKS?
A MARTIAN IS FRYING THAT GUY INTO A SKELETON, BUT HIS HEAD ISN'T BURNED UP YET AND HE'S SCREAMING!
YEAH, IT'S A SERIES ABOUT A MARTIAN INVASION.
NO CHAVO, IT'S TOO GORY FOR YOU!
WHOA!
OH, I HAVE ABOUT 5 OF THOSE CARDS BUT I'M NOT COLLECTING THEM, HUEY.
WANT THEM?
SURE!
THANKS, AXEL!
EVERY OTHER CARD IS A MARS ATTACKS TRADING CARD.
THE OTHER CARDS ARE BASEBALL.
IT'S ONLY 2¢. I'LL JUST GIVE THE BASEBALL ONES TO TOODY.
4¢ A MARS ATTACKS CARD IS BETTER THAN NOTHING.
WHOA!
A MARTIAN'S BLASTING THIS KID'S DOG IN HALF AND THE KID'S RUNNING UP TO STOP THE MARTIAN!
"NOOO, NOT MY DOG!"
ON THE BACK IT SAYS WHAT THE NEXT CARD IS: A GIANT BUG ATTACKING!
THIS IS THE GREATEST DISCOVERY OF MY LIFE!
HEY TOODY, WANT A BASEBALL CARD?
FREE!

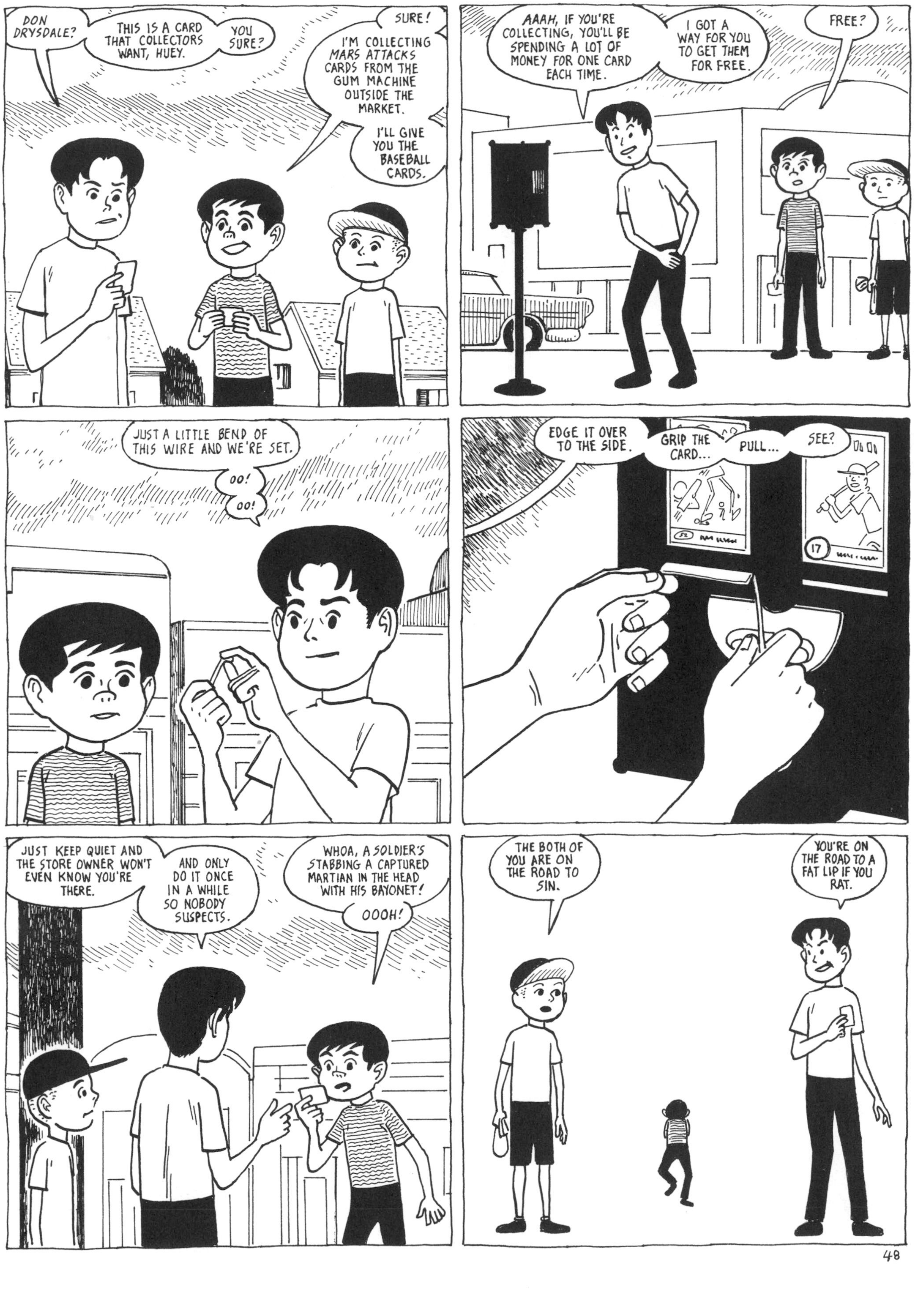
DON DRYSDALE?
THIS IS A CARD THAT COLLECTORS WANT, HUEY.
YOU SURE?
SURE!
I'M COLLECTING MARS ATTACKS CARDS FROM THE GUM MACHINE OUTSIDE THE MARKET.
I'LL GIVE YOU THE BASEBALL CARDS.
AAAH, IF YOU'RE COLLECTING, YOU'LL BE SPENDING A LOT OF MONEY FOR ONE CARD EACH TIME.
I GOT A WAY FOR YOU TO GET THEM FOR FREE.
FREE?
JUST A LITTLE BEND OF THIS WIRE AND WE'RE SET.
OO!
OO!
EDGE IT OVER TO THE SIDE.
GRIP THE CARD...
PULL...
SEE?
JUST KEEP QUIET AND THE STORE OWNER WON'T EVEN KNOW YOU'RE THERE.
AND ONLY DO IT ONCE IN A WHILE SO NOBODY SUSPECTS.
WHOA, A SOLDIER'S STABBING A CAPTURED MARTIAN IN THE HEAD WITH HIS BAYONET!
OOOH!
THE BOTH OF YOU ARE ON THE ROAD TO SIN.
YOU'RE ON THE ROAD TO A FAT LIP IF YOU RAT.

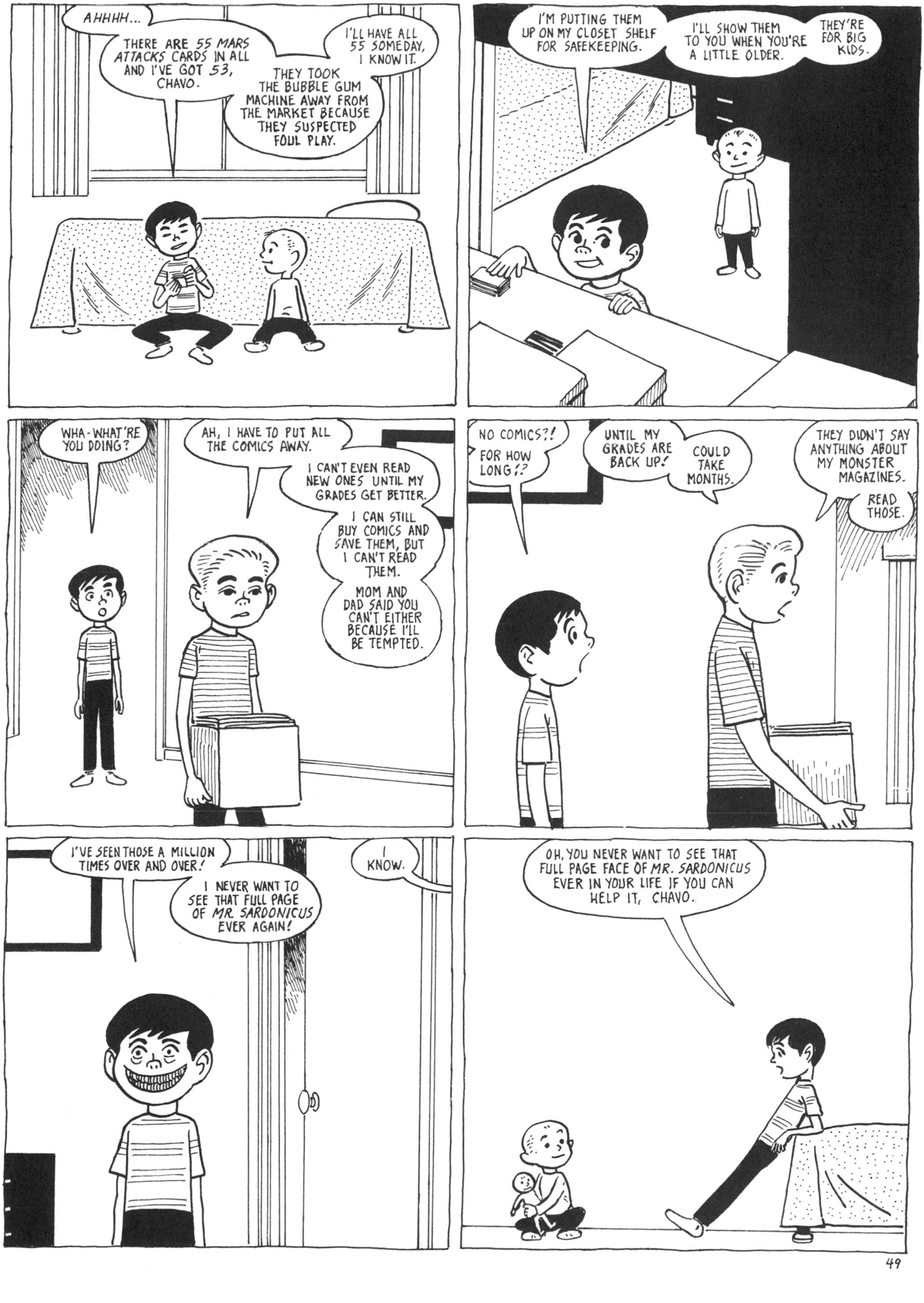
AHHHH...
THERE ARE 55 *MARS ATTACKS* CARDS IN ALL AND I'VE GOT 53, CHAVO.
I'LL HAVE ALL 55 SOMEDAY, I KNOW IT.
THEY TOOK THE BUBBLE GUM MACHINE AWAY FROM THE MARKET BECAUSE THEY SUSPECTED FOUL PLAY.
I'M PUTTING THEM UP ON MY CLOSET SHELF FOR SAFEKEEPING.
I'LL SHOW THEM TO YOU WHEN YOU'RE A LITTLE OLDER.
THEY'RE FOR BIG KIDS.
WHA-WHAT'RE YOU DOING?
AH, I HAVE TO PUT ALL THE COMICS AWAY.
I CAN'T EVEN READ NEW ONES UNTIL MY GRADES GET BETTER.
I CAN STILL BUY COMICS AND SAVE THEM, BUT I CAN'T READ THEM.
MOM AND DAD SAID YOU CAN'T EITHER BECAUSE I'LL BE TEMPTED.
NO COMICS?!
FOR HOW LONG!?
UNTIL MY GRADES ARE BACK UP!
COULD TAKE MONTHS.
THEY DIDN'T SAY ANYTHING ABOUT MY MONSTER MAGAZINES.
READ THOSE.
I'VE SEEN THOSE A MILLION TIMES OVER AND OVER!
I NEVER WANT TO SEE THAT FULL PAGE OF *MR. SARDONICUS* EVER AGAIN!
I KNOW.
OH, YOU NEVER WANT TO SEE THAT FULL PAGE FACE OF *MR. SARDONICUS* EVER IN YOUR LIFE IF YOU CAN HELP IT, CHAVO.

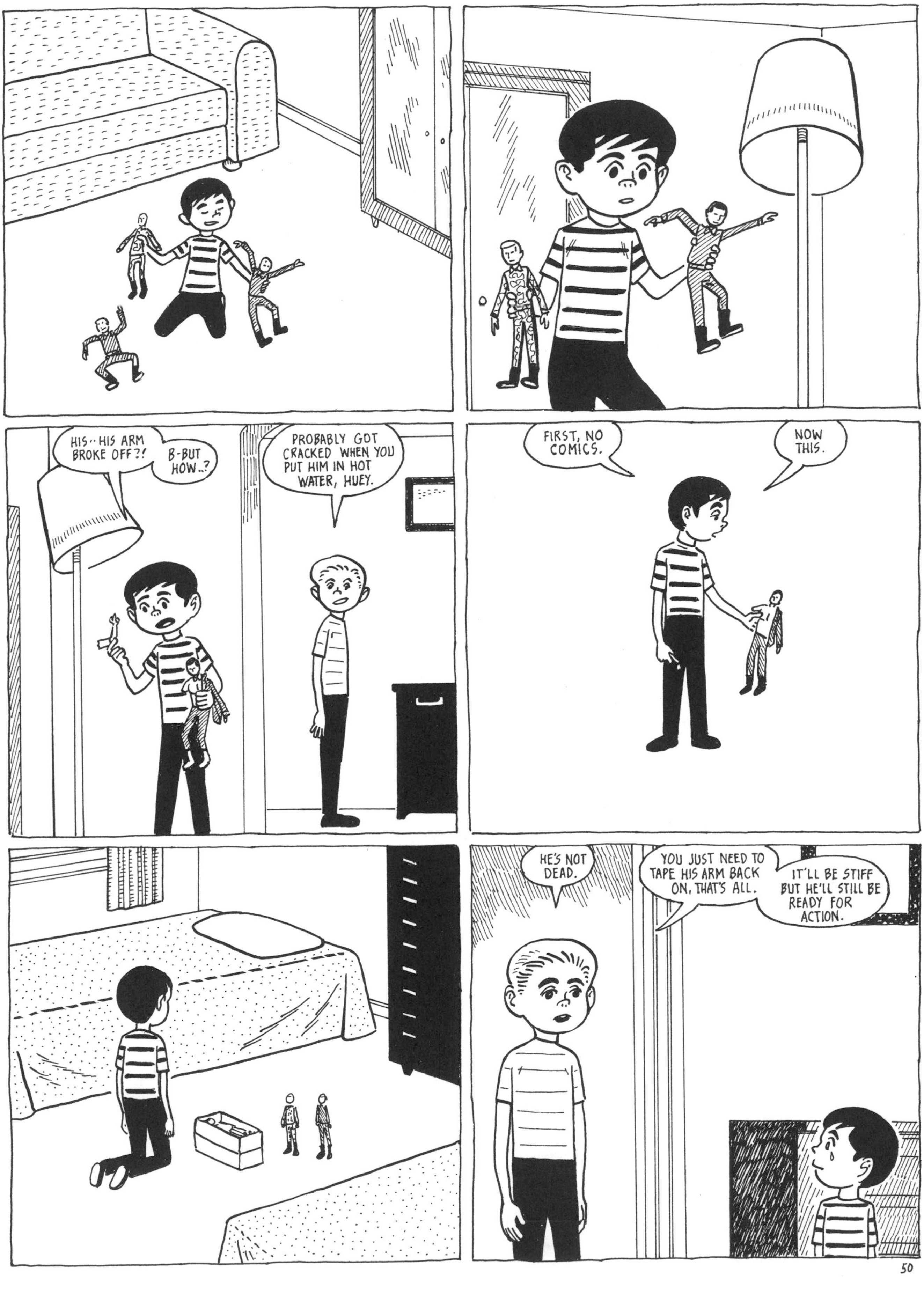

HIS.. HIS ARM BROKE OFF?!
B-BUT HOW..?
PROBABLY GOT CRACKED WHEN YOU PUT HIM IN HOT WATER, HUEY.
FIRST, NO COMICS.
NOW THIS.
HE'S NOT DEAD.
YOU JUST NEED TO TAPE HIS ARM BACK ON, THAT'S ALL.
IT'LL BE STIFF BUT HE'LL STILL BE READY FOR ACTION.

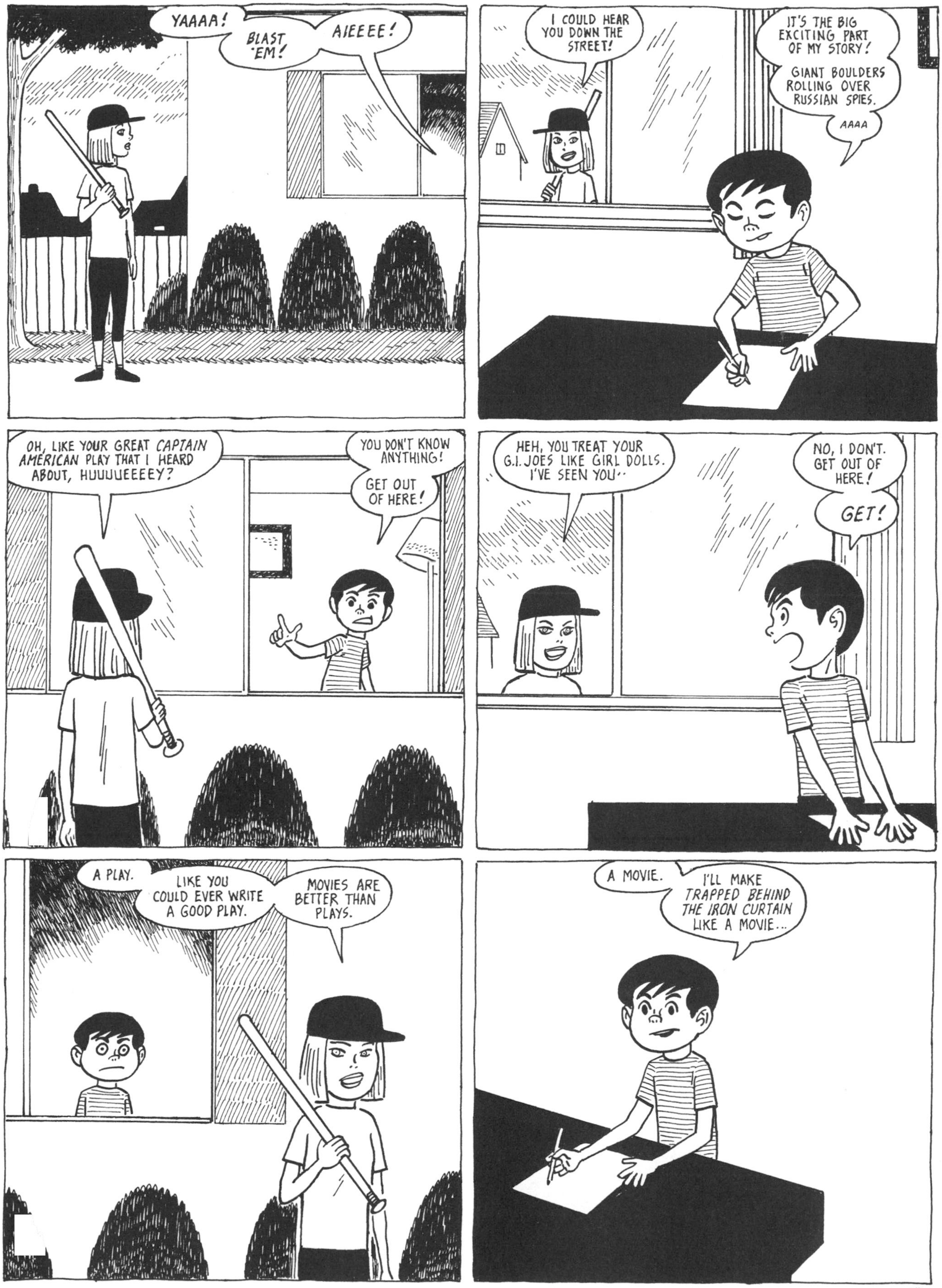
YAAAA!
BLAST 'EM!
AIEEEE!
I COULD HEAR YOU DOWN THE STREET!
IT'S THE BIG EXCITING PART OF MY STORY!
GIANT BOULDERS ROLLING OVER RUSSIAN SPIES.
AAAA
OH, LIKE YOUR GREAT *CAPTAIN AMERICAN* PLAY THAT I HEARD ABOUT, HUUUUEEEEY?
YOU DON'T KNOW ANYTHING!
GET OUT OF HERE!
HEH, YOU TREAT YOUR G.I. JOES LIKE GIRL DOLLS. I'VE SEEN YOU..
NO, I DON'T. GET OUT OF HERE!
GET!
A PLAY.
LIKE YOU COULD EVER WRITE A GOOD PLAY.
MOVIES ARE BETTER THAN PLAYS.
A MOVIE.
I'LL MAKE *TRAPPED BEHIND THE IRON CURTAIN* LIKE A MOVIE...

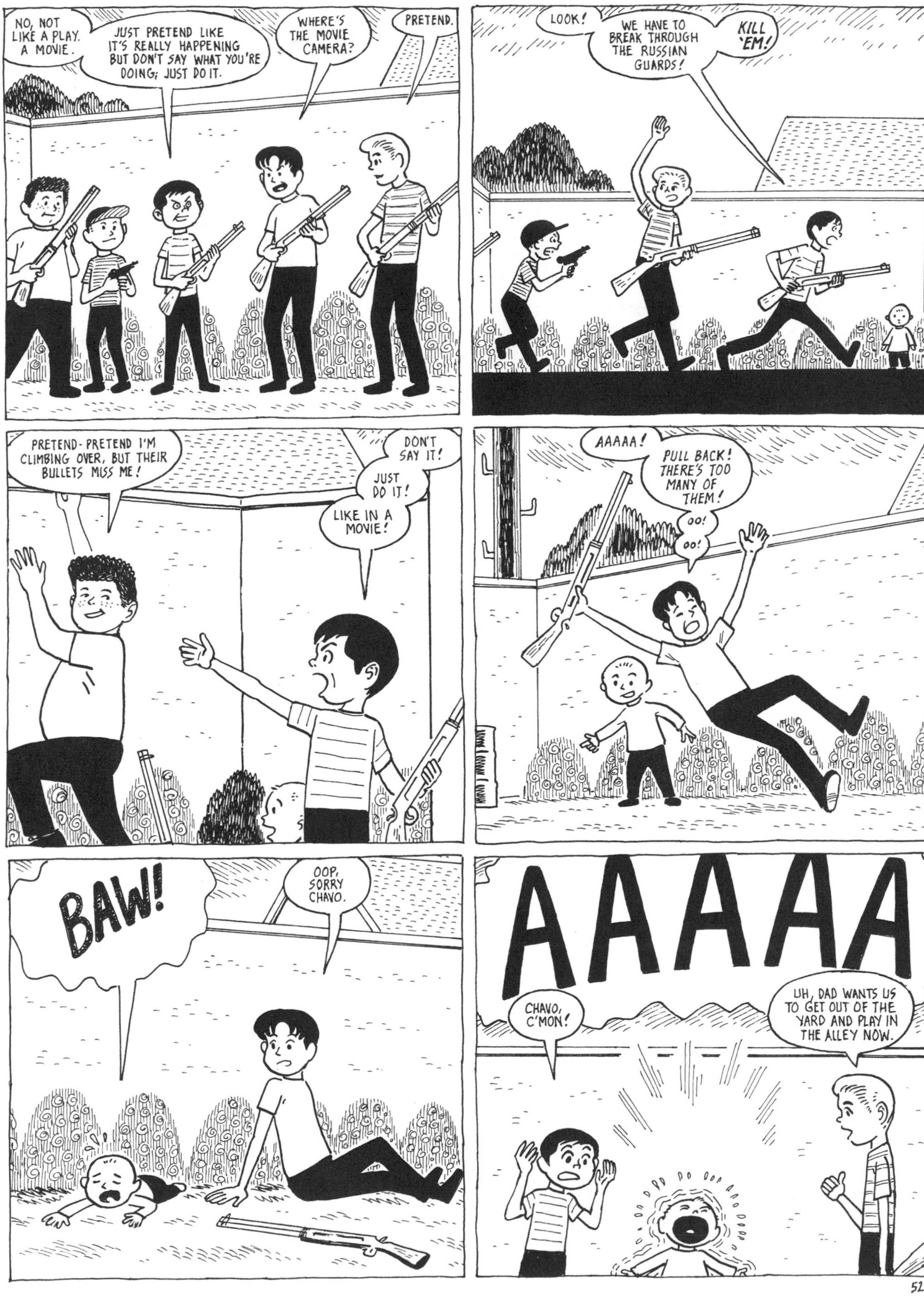
NO, NOT LIKE A PLAY. A MOVIE.
JUST PRETEND LIKE IT'S REALLY HAPPENING BUT DON'T SAY WHAT YOU'RE DOING; JUST DO IT.
WHERE'S THE MOVIE CAMERA?
PRETEND.
LOOK!
WE HAVE TO BREAK THROUGH THE RUSSIAN GUARDS!
KILL 'EM!
PRETEND- PRETEND I'M CLIMBING OVER, BUT THEIR BULLETS MISS ME!
DON'T SAY IT!
JUST DO IT!
LIKE IN A MOVIE!
AAAAA!
PULL BACK! THERE'S TOO MANY OF THEM!
OO!
OO!
BAW!
OOP, SORRY CHAVO.
AAAAA
CHAVO, C'MON!
UH, DAD WANTS US TO GET OUT OF THE YARD AND PLAY IN THE ALLEY NOW.

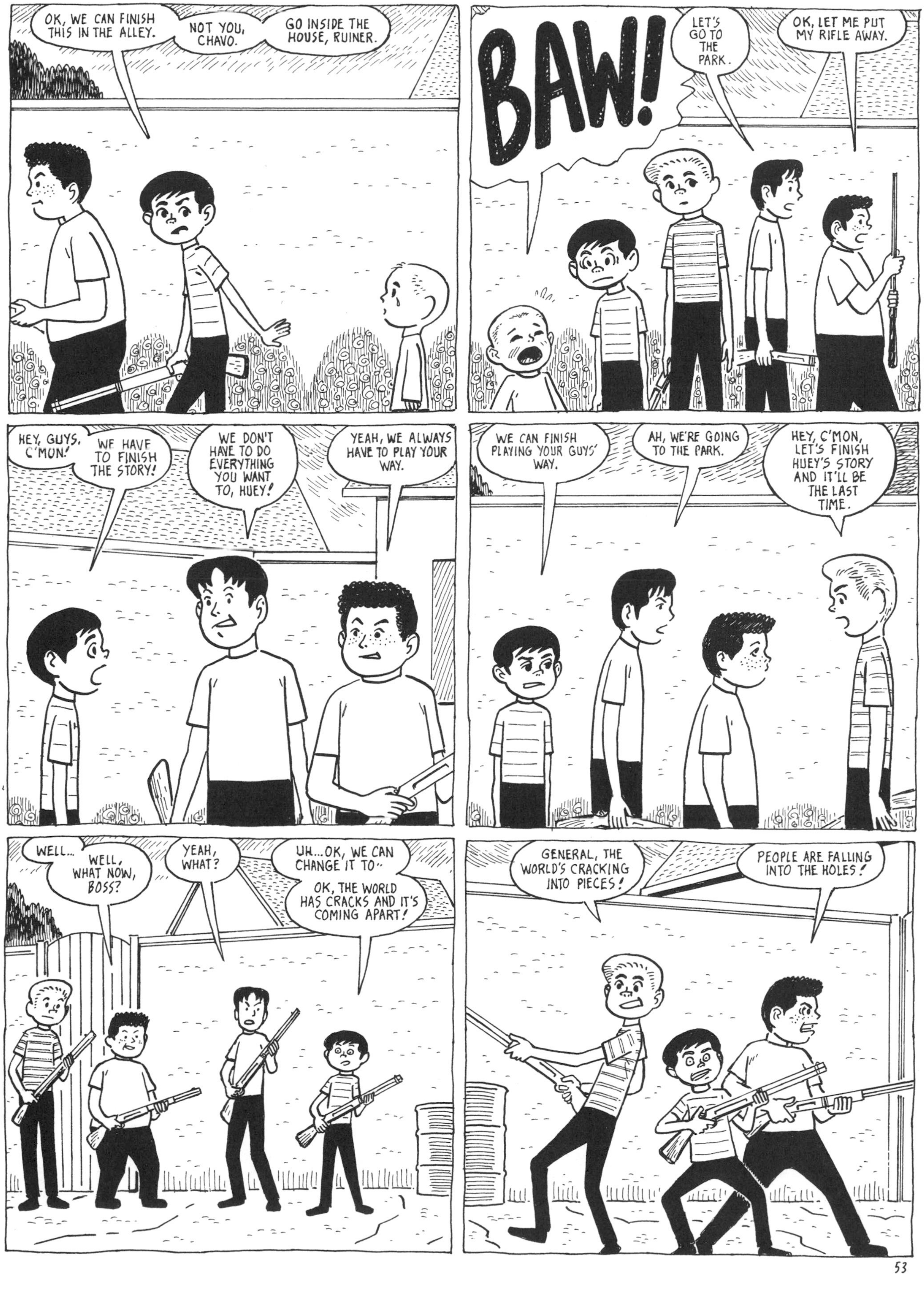
OK, WE CAN FINISH THIS IN THE ALLEY.
NOT YOU, CHAVO.
GO INSIDE THE HOUSE, RUINER.
BAW!
LET'S GO TO THE PARK.
OK, LET ME PUT MY RIFLE AWAY.
HEY, GUYS. C'MON!
WE HAVE TO FINISH THE STORY!
WE DON'T HAVE TO DO EVERYTHING YOU WANT TO, HUEY!
YEAH, WE ALWAYS HAVE TO PLAY YOUR WAY.
WE CAN FINISH PLAYING YOUR GUYS' WAY.
AH, WE'RE GOING TO THE PARK.
HEY, C'MON, LET'S FINISH HUEY'S STORY AND IT'LL BE THE LAST TIME.
WELL...
WELL, WHAT NOW, BOSS?
YEAH, WHAT?
UH...OK, WE CAN CHANGE IT TO--
OK, THE WORLD HAS CRACKS AND IT'S COMING APART!
GENERAL, THE WORLD'S CRACKING INTO PIECES!
PEOPLE ARE FALLING INTO THE HOLES!

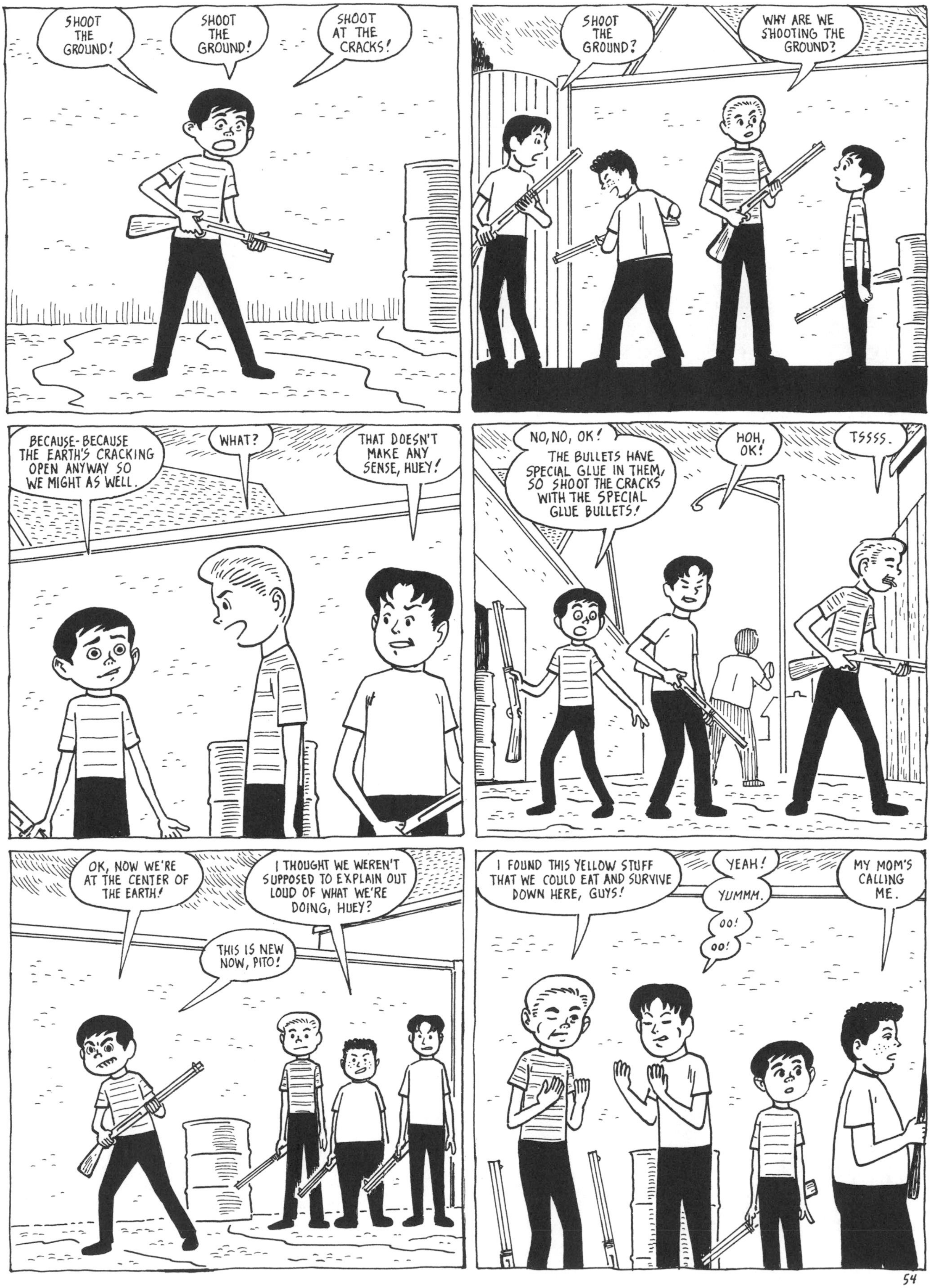
SHOOT THE GROUND!
SHOOT THE GROUND!
SHOOT AT THE CRACKS!
SHOOT THE GROUND?
WHY ARE WE SHOOTING THE GROUND?
BECAUSE-BECAUSE THE EARTH'S CRACKING OPEN ANYWAY SO WE MIGHT AS WELL.
WHAT?
THAT DOESN'T MAKE ANY SENSE, HUEY!
NO, NO, OK! THE BULLETS HAVE SPECIAL GLUE IN THEM, SO SHOOT THE CRACKS WITH THE SPECIAL GLUE BULLETS!
HOH, OK!
TSSSS.
OK, NOW WE'RE AT THE CENTER OF THE EARTH!
I THOUGHT WE WEREN'T SUPPOSED TO EXPLAIN OUT LOUD OF WHAT WE'RE DOING, HUEY?
THIS IS NEW NOW, PITO!
I FOUND THIS YELLOW STUFF THAT WE COULD EAT AND SURVIVE DOWN HERE, GUYS!
YEAH!
YUMMM.
OO!
OO!
MY MOM'S CALLING ME.

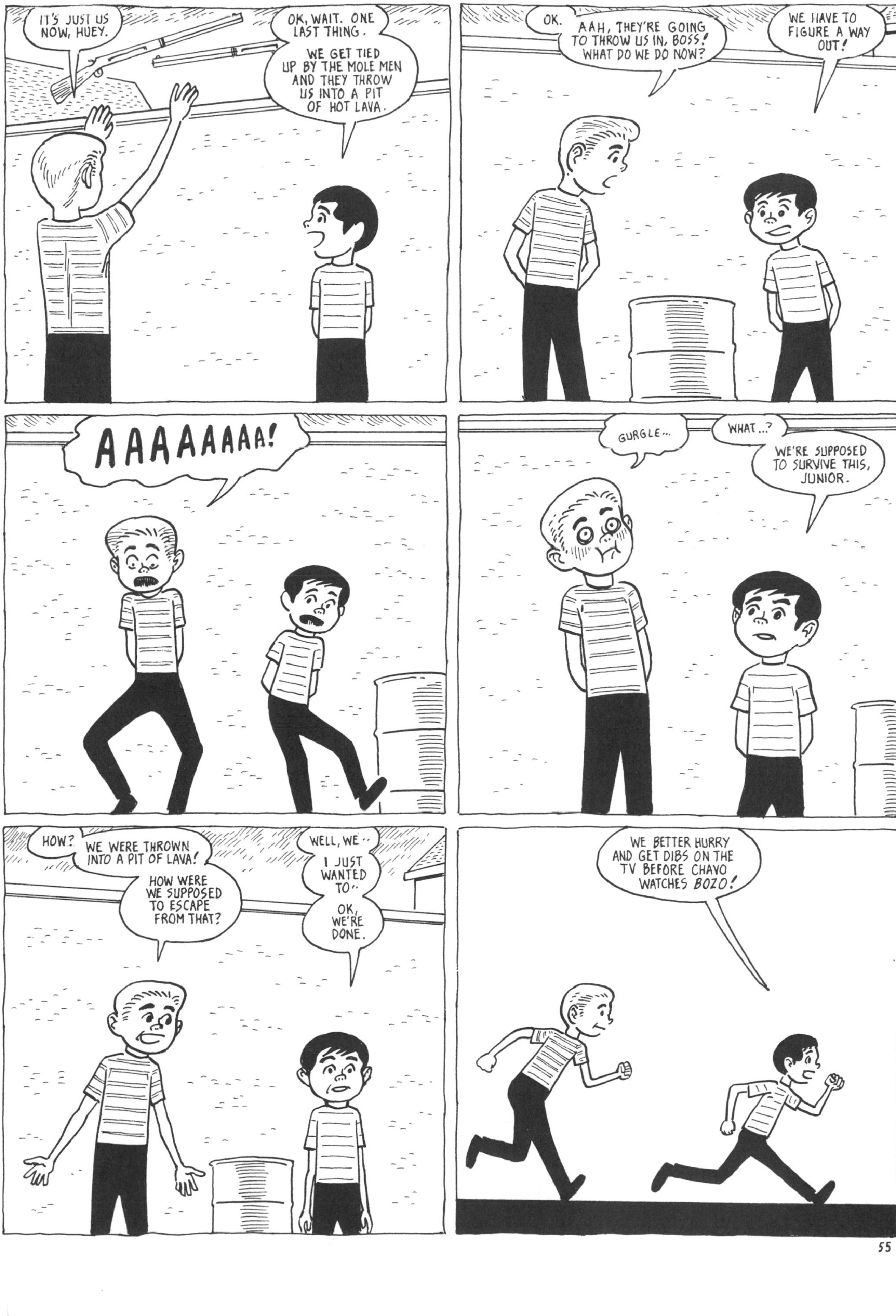
IT'S JUST US NOW, HUEY.
OK, WAIT. ONE LAST THING.
WE GET TIED UP BY THE MOLE MEN AND THEY THROW US INTO A PIT OF HOT LAVA.
OK.
AAH, THEY'RE GOING TO THROW US IN, BOSS! WHAT DO WE DO NOW?
WE HAVE TO FIGURE A WAY OUT!
AAAAAAAA!
GURGLE...
WHAT...?
WE'RE SUPPOSED TO SURVIVE THIS, JUNIOR.
HOW?
WE WERE THROWN INTO A PIT OF LAVA!
HOW WERE WE SUPPOSED TO ESCAPE FROM THAT?
WELL, WE..
I JUST WANTED TO..
OK, WE'RE DONE.
WE BETTER HURRY AND GET DIBS ON THE TV BEFORE CHAVO WATCHES BOZO!

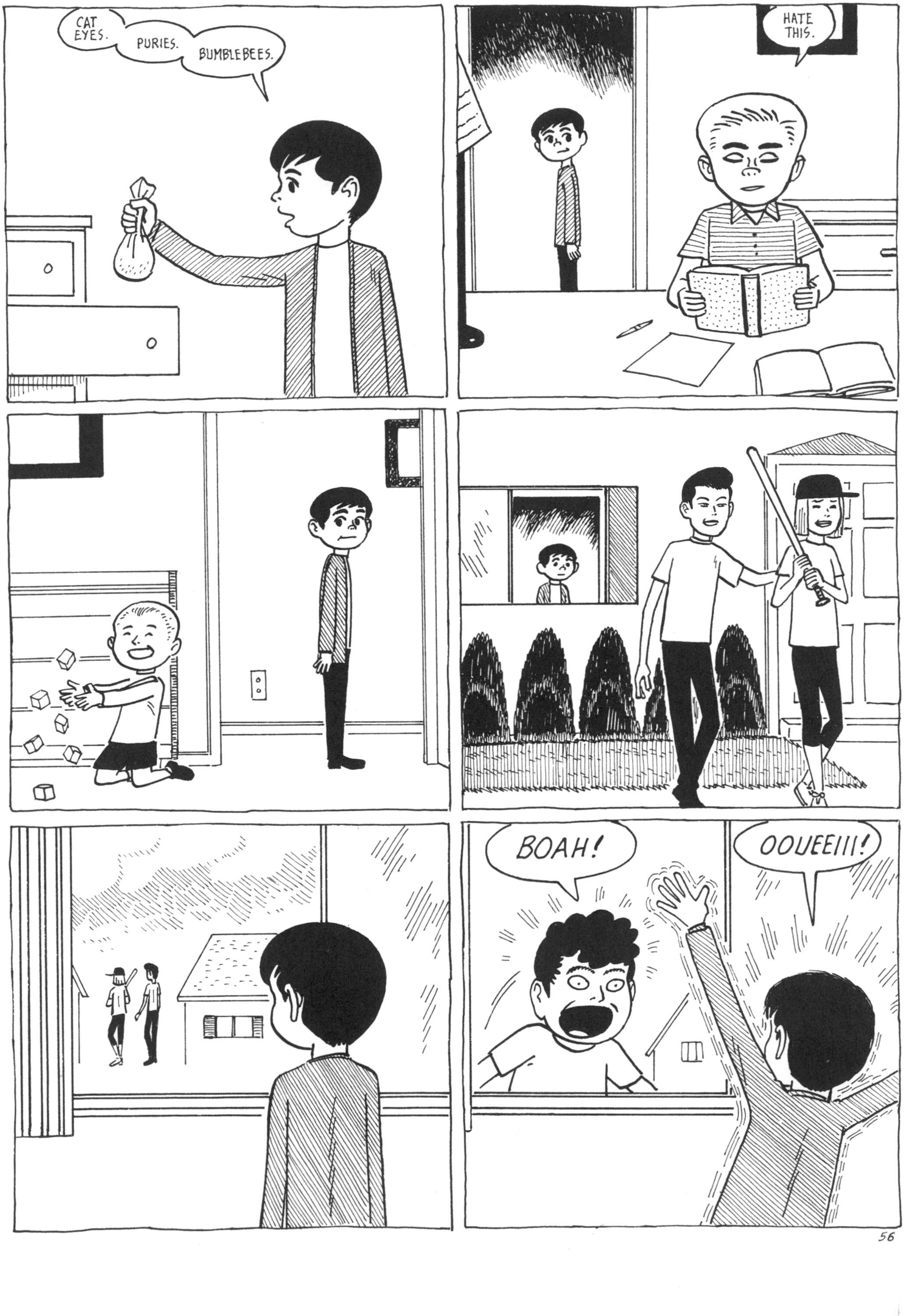
CAT EYES.
PURIES.
BUMBLEBEES.
HATE THIS.
BOAH!
OOUEEIII!

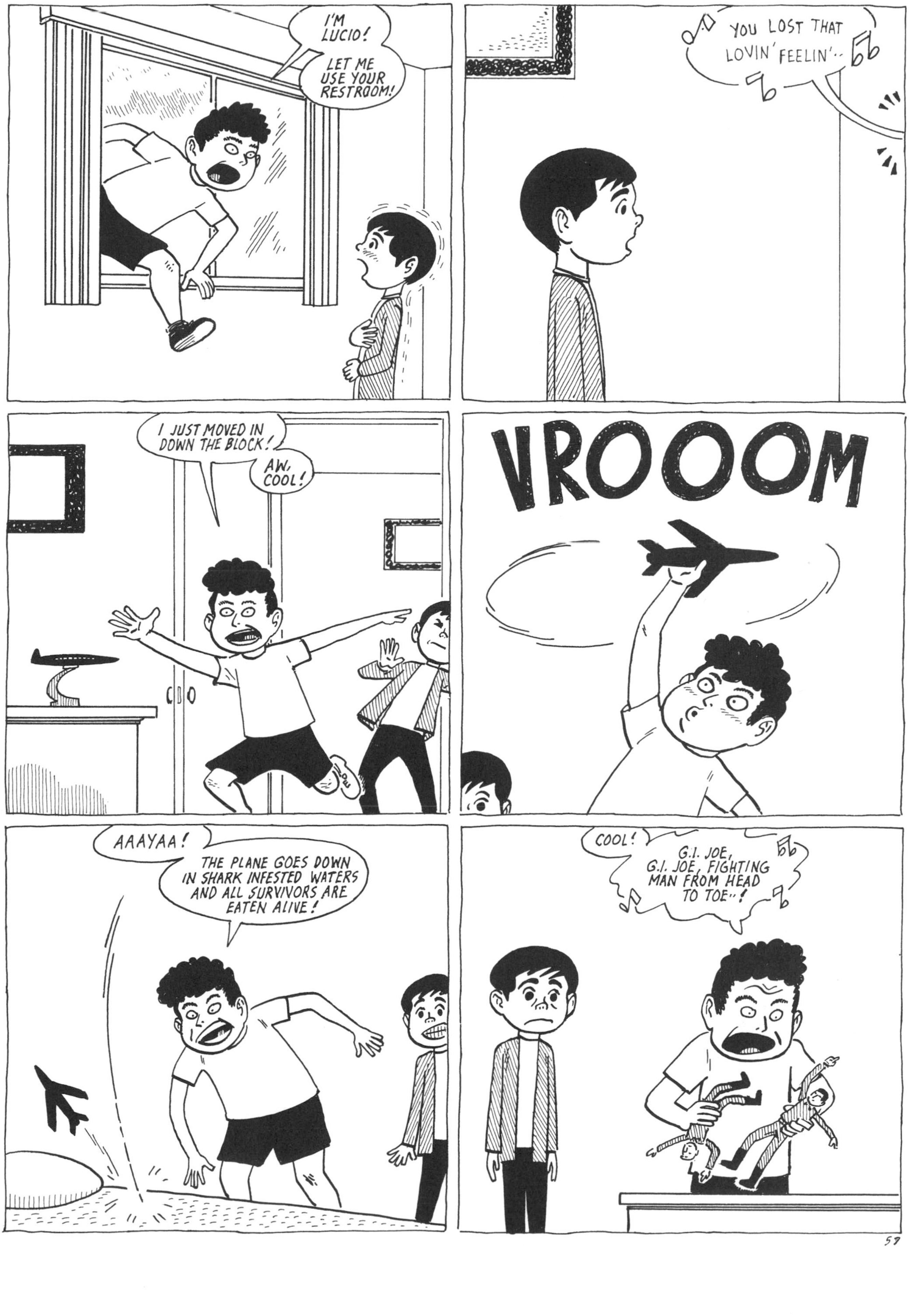
I'M LUCIO!
LET ME USE YOUR RESTROOM!
YOU LOST THAT LOVIN' FEELIN'..
I JUST MOVED IN DOWN THE BLOCK!
AW, COOL!
VROOOM
AAAYAA!
THE PLANE GOES DOWN IN SHARK INFESTED WATERS AND ALL SURVIVORS ARE EATEN ALIVE!
COOL!
G.I. JOE, G.I. JOE, FIGHTING MAN FROM HEAD TO TOE..!

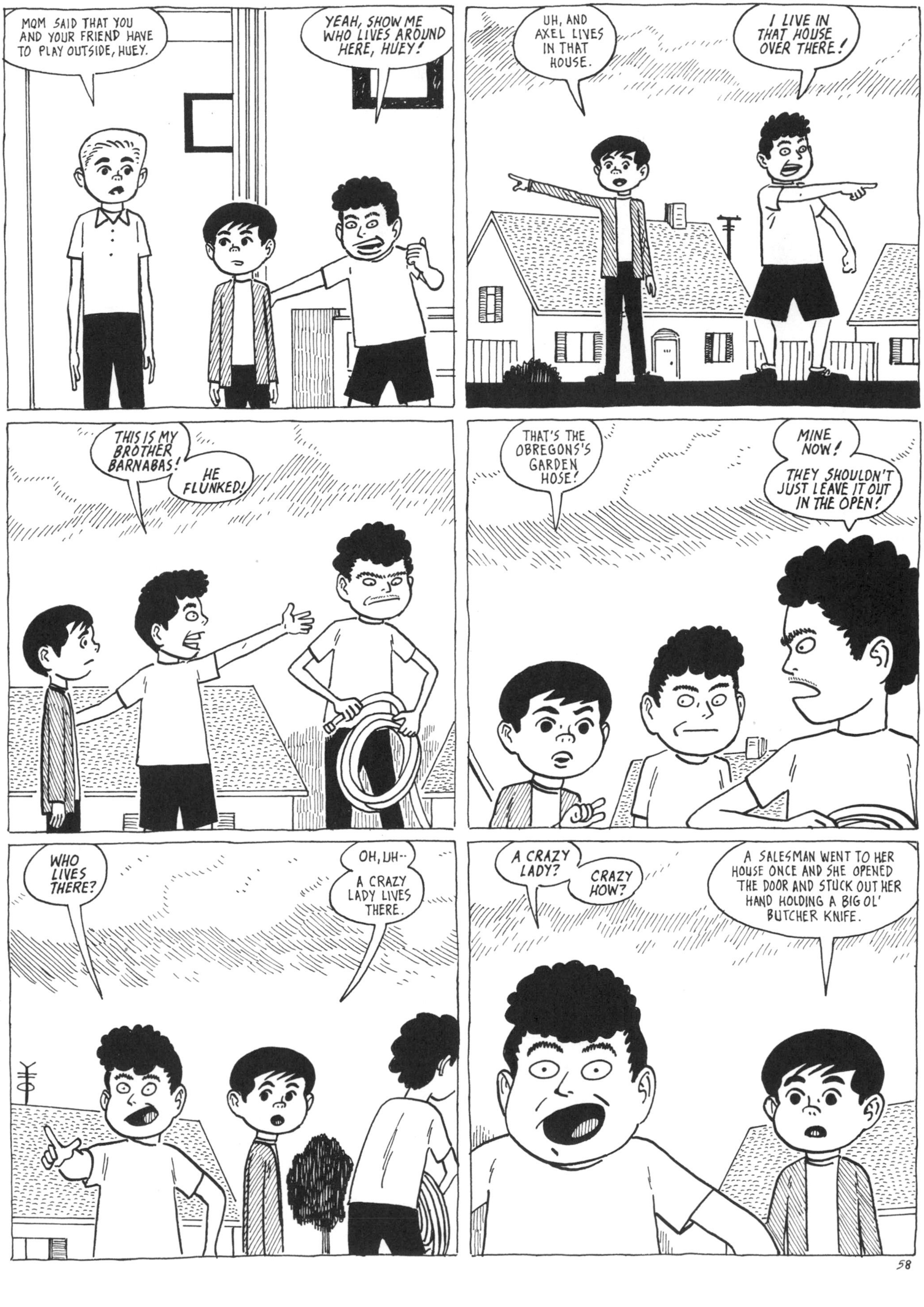
MOM SAID THAT YOU AND YOUR FRIEND HAVE TO PLAY OUTSIDE, HUEY.
YEAH, SHOW ME WHO LIVES AROUND HERE, HUEY!
UH, AND AXEL LIVES IN THAT HOUSE.
I LIVE IN THAT HOUSE OVER THERE!
THIS IS MY BROTHER BARNABAS!
HE FLUNKED!
THAT'S THE OBREGONS'S GARDEN HOSE!
MINE NOW!
THEY SHOULDN'T JUST LEAVE IT OUT IN THE OPEN!
WHO LIVES THERE?
OH, UH--
A CRAZY LADY LIVES THERE.
A CRAZY LADY?
CRAZY HOW?
A SALESMAN WENT TO HER HOUSE ONCE AND SHE OPENED THE DOOR AND STUCK OUT HER HAND HOLDING A BIG OL' BUTCHER KNIFE.

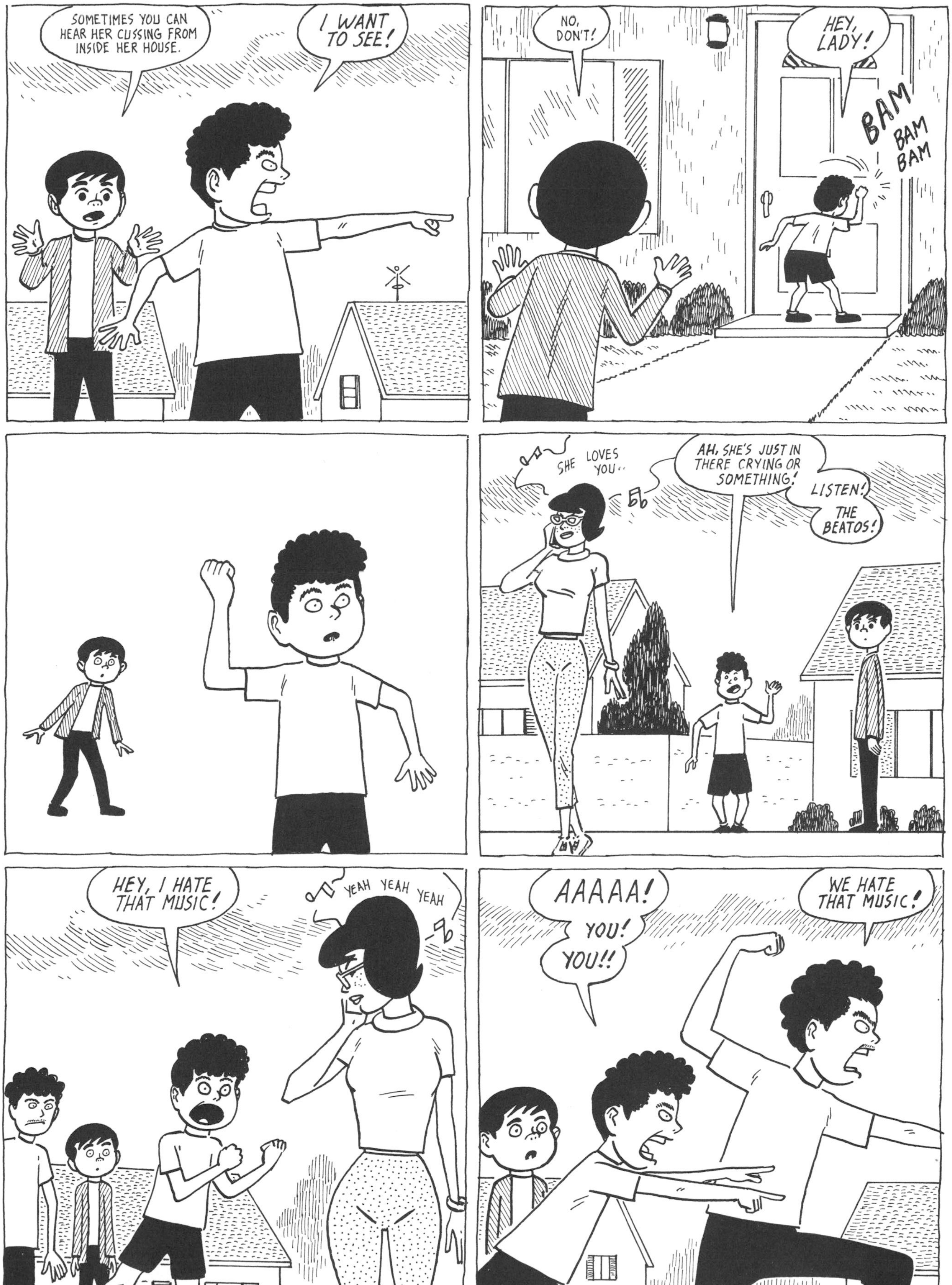
SOMETIMES YOU CAN HEAR HER CUSSING FROM INSIDE HER HOUSE.
I WANT TO SEE!
NO, DON'T!
HEY, LADY!
BAM BAM BAM
SHE LOVES YOU..
AH, SHE'S JUST IN THERE CRYING OR SOMETHING!
LISTEN! THE BEATOS!
HEY, I HATE THAT MUSIC!
YEAH YEAH YEAH
AAAAA! YOU! YOU!!
WE HATE THAT MUSIC!

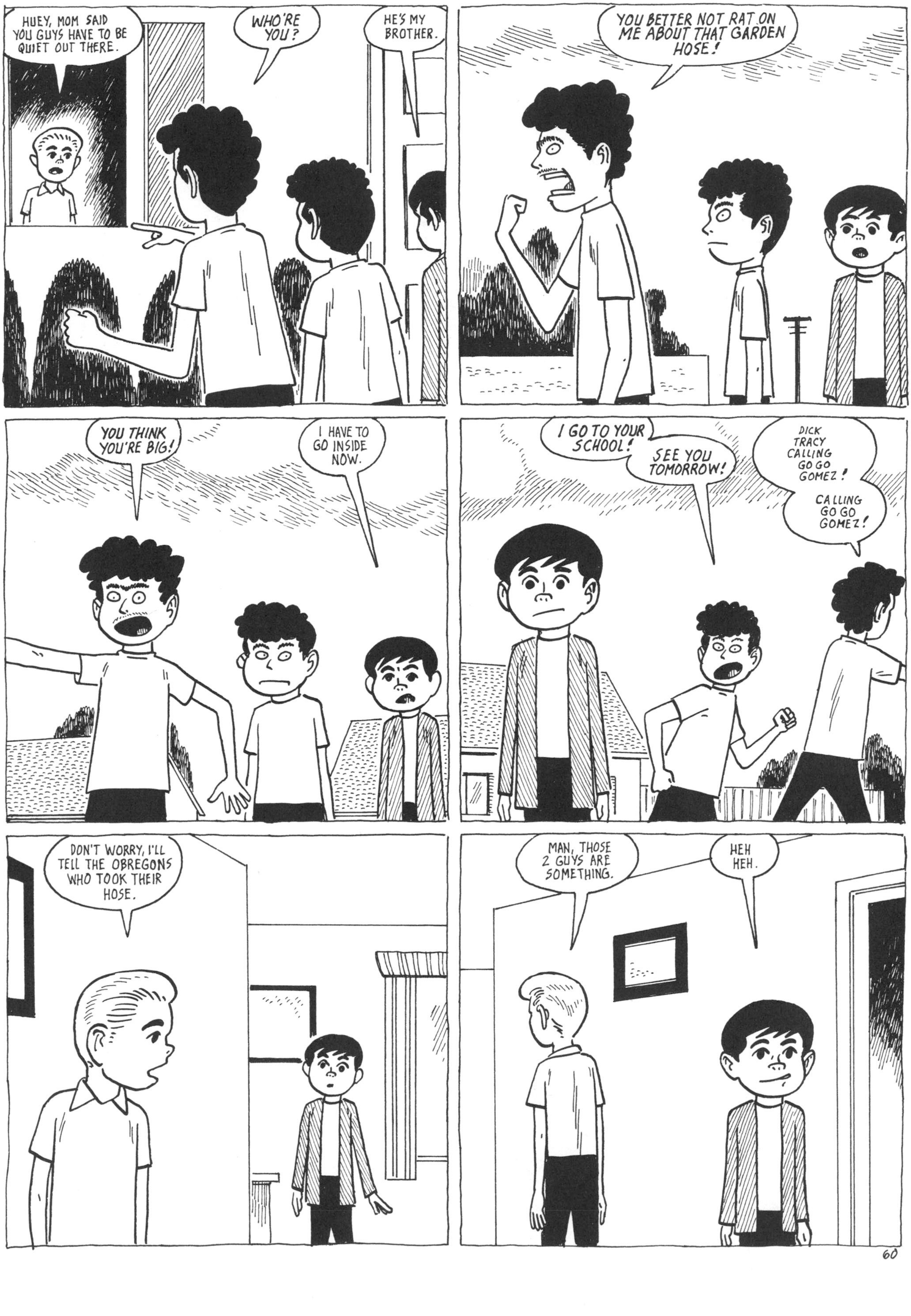
HUEY, MOM SAID YOU GUYS HAVE TO BE QUIET OUT THERE.
WHO'RE YOU?
HE'S MY BROTHER.
YOU BETTER NOT RAT ON ME ABOUT THAT GARDEN HOSE!
YOU THINK YOU'RE BIG!
I HAVE TO GO INSIDE NOW.
I GO TO YOUR SCHOOL!
SEE YOU TOMORROW!
DICK TRACY CALLING GO GO GOMEZ!
CALLING GO GO GOMEZ!
DON'T WORRY, I'LL TELL THE OBREGONS WHO TOOK THEIR HOSE.
MAN, THOSE 2 GUYS ARE SOMETHING.
HEH HEH.

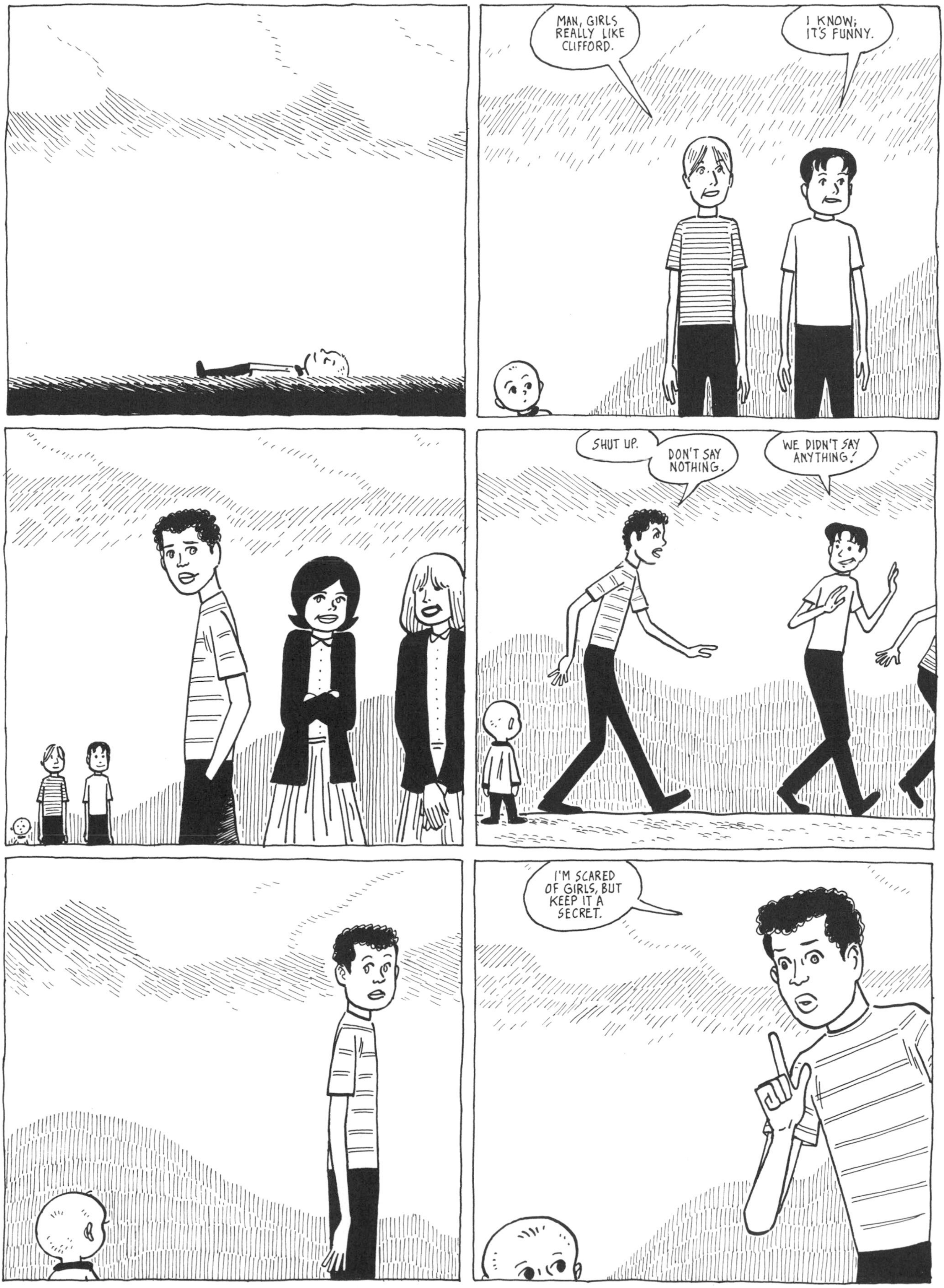

MAN, GIRLS REALLY LIKE CLIFFORD.
I KNOW; IT'S FUNNY.
SHUT UP.
DON'T SAY NOTHING.
WE DIDN'T SAY ANYTHING!
I'M SCARED OF GIRLS, BUT KEEP IT A SECRET.

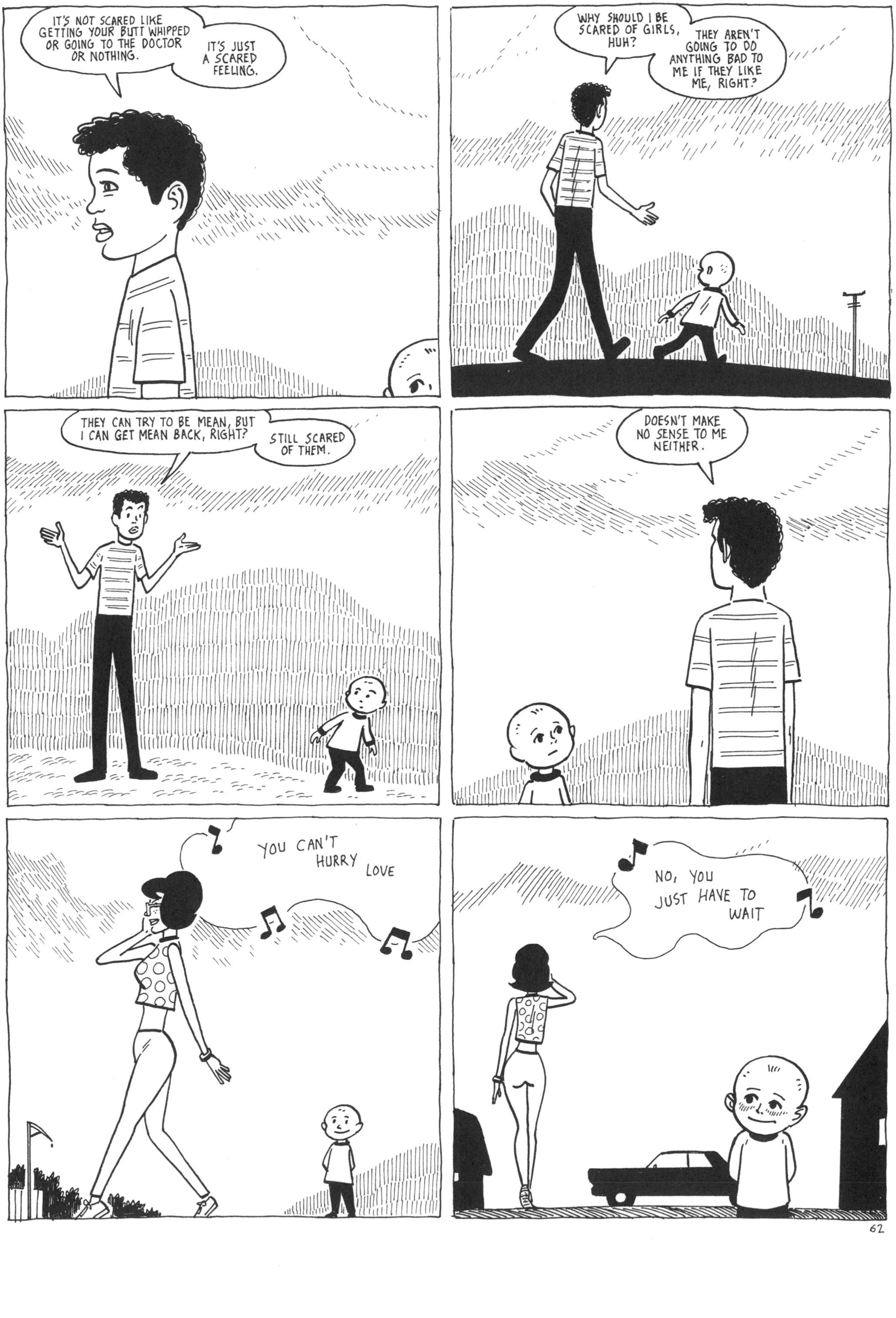
IT'S NOT SCARED LIKE GETTING YOUR BUTT WHIPPED OR GOING TO THE DOCTOR OR NOTHING.
IT'S JUST A SCARED FEELING.
WHY SHOULD I BE SCARED OF GIRLS, HUH?
THEY AREN'T GOING TO DO ANYTHING BAD TO ME IF THEY LIKE ME, RIGHT?
THEY CAN TRY TO BE MEAN, BUT I CAN GET MEAN BACK, RIGHT?
STILL SCARED OF THEM.
DOESN'T MAKE NO SENSE TO ME NEITHER.
YOU CAN'T HURRY LOVE
NO, YOU JUST HAVE TO WAIT

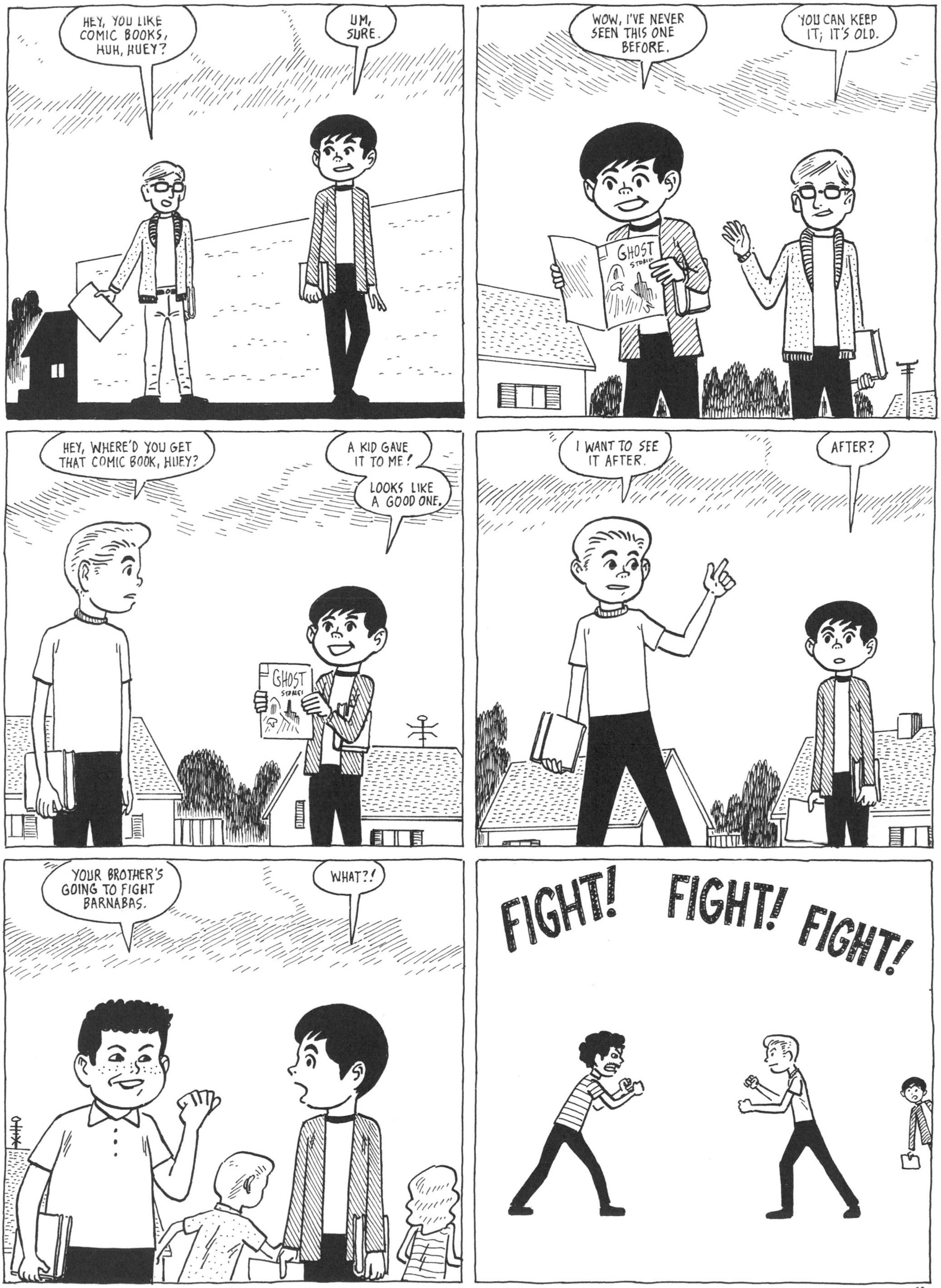
HEY, YOU LIKE COMIC BOOKS, HUH, HUEY?
UM, SURE.
WOW, I'VE NEVER SEEN THIS ONE BEFORE.
YOU CAN KEEP IT; IT'S OLD.
GHOST STORIES
HEY, WHERE'D YOU GET THAT COMIC BOOK, HUEY?
A KID GAVE IT TO ME!
LOOKS LIKE A GOOD ONE.
GHOST
I WANT TO SEE IT AFTER.
AFTER?
YOUR BROTHER'S GOING TO FIGHT BARNABAS.
WHAT?!
FIGHT! FIGHT! FIGHT!

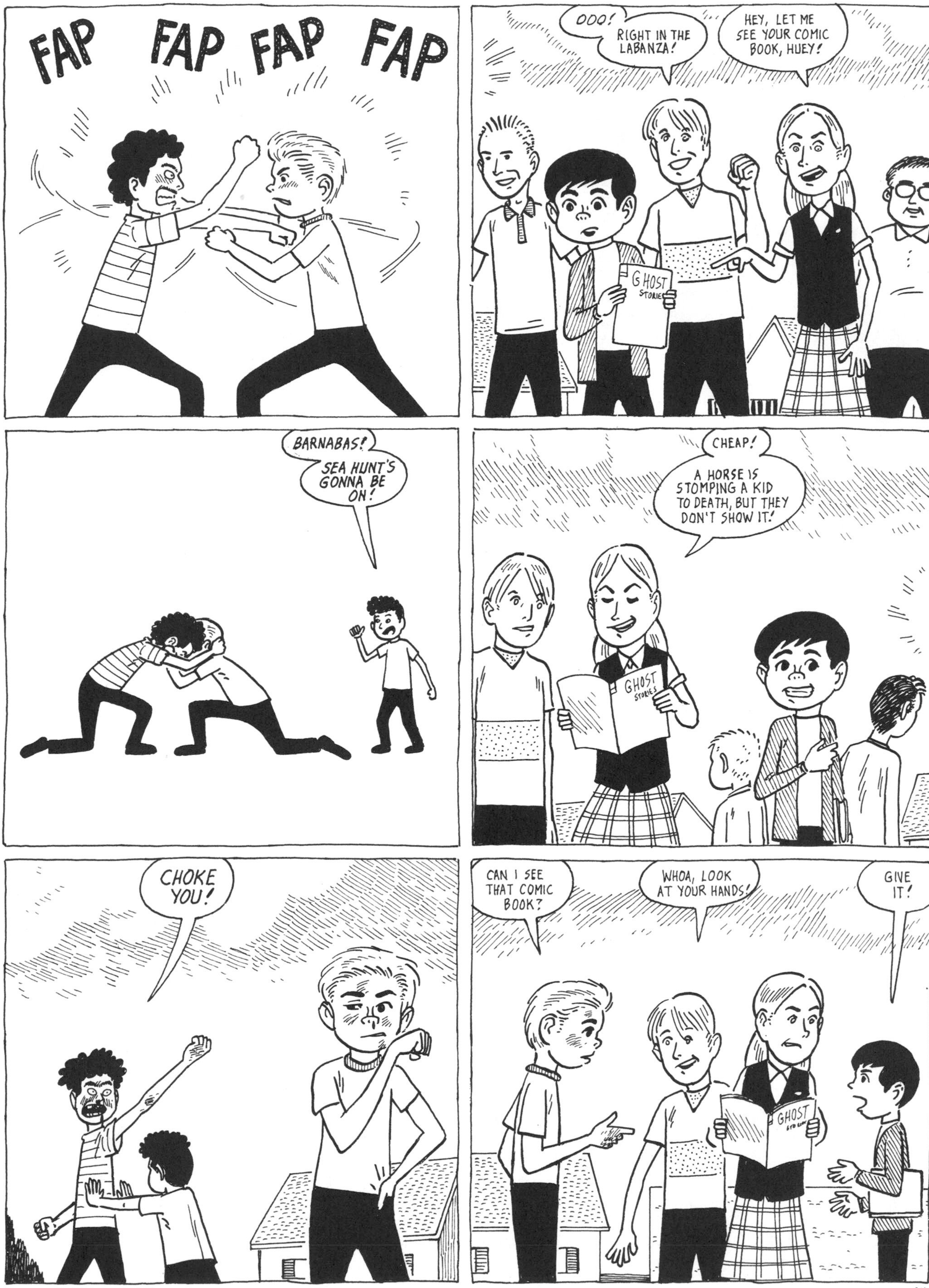
FAP FAP FAP FAP
OOO!
RIGHT IN THE LABANZA!
HEY, LET ME SEE YOUR COMIC BOOK, HUEY!
GHOST STORIES
BARNABAS!
SEA HUNT'S GONNA BE ON!
CHEAP!
A HORSE IS STOMPING A KID TO DEATH, BUT THEY DON'T SHOW IT!
GHOST STORIES
CHOKE YOU!
CAN I SEE THAT COMIC BOOK?
WHOA, LOOK AT YOUR HANDS!
GIVE IT!
GHOST

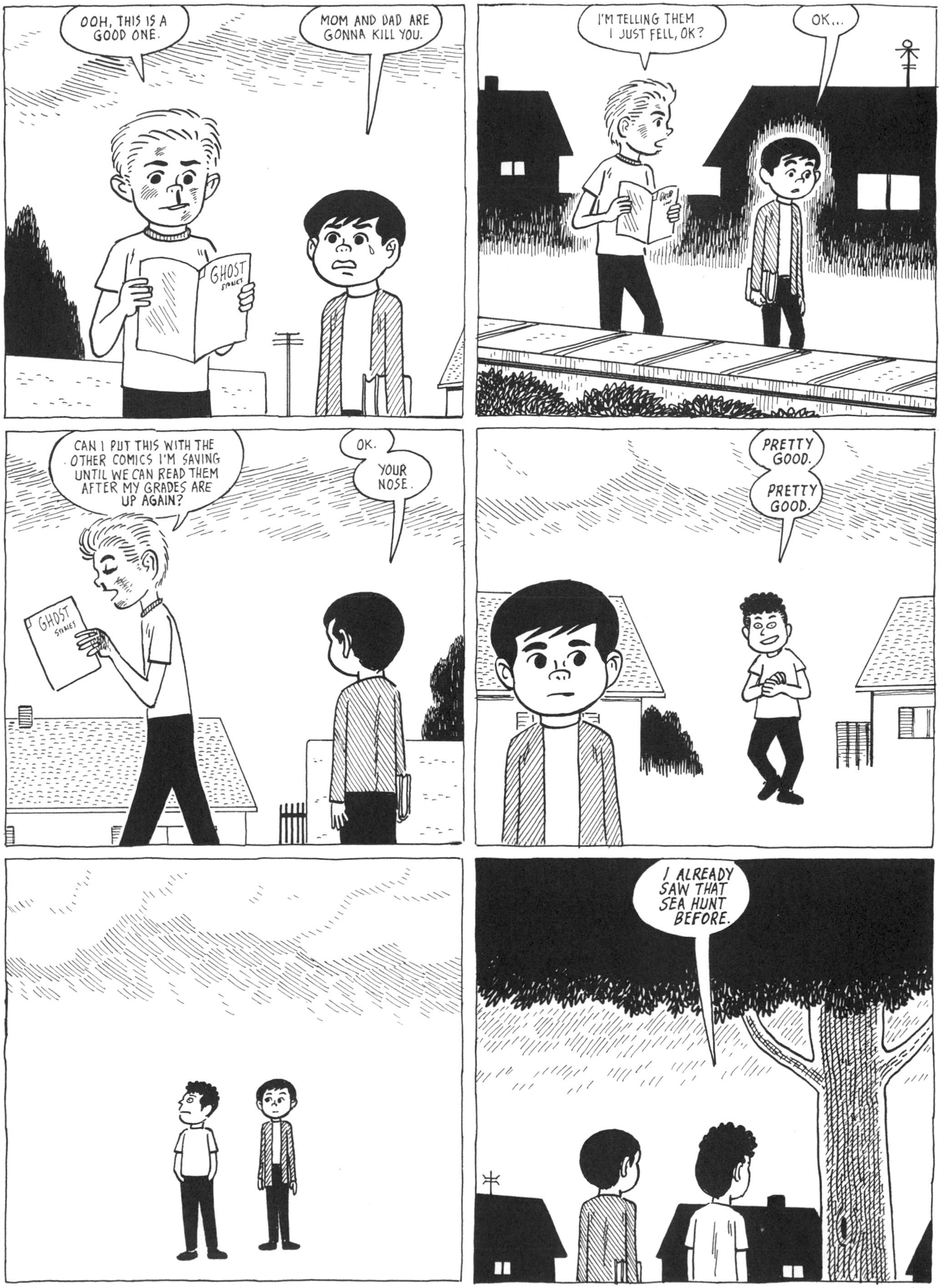
OOH, THIS IS A GOOD ONE.
MOM AND DAD ARE GONNA KILL YOU.
GHOST STORIES
I'M TELLING THEM I JUST FELL, OK?
OK...
CAN I PUT THIS WITH THE OTHER COMICS I'M SAVING UNTIL WE CAN READ THEM AFTER MY GRADES ARE UP AGAIN?
OK.
YOUR NOSE.
GHOST STORIES
PRETTY GOOD.
PRETTY GOOD.
I ALREADY SAW THAT SEA HUNT BEFORE.

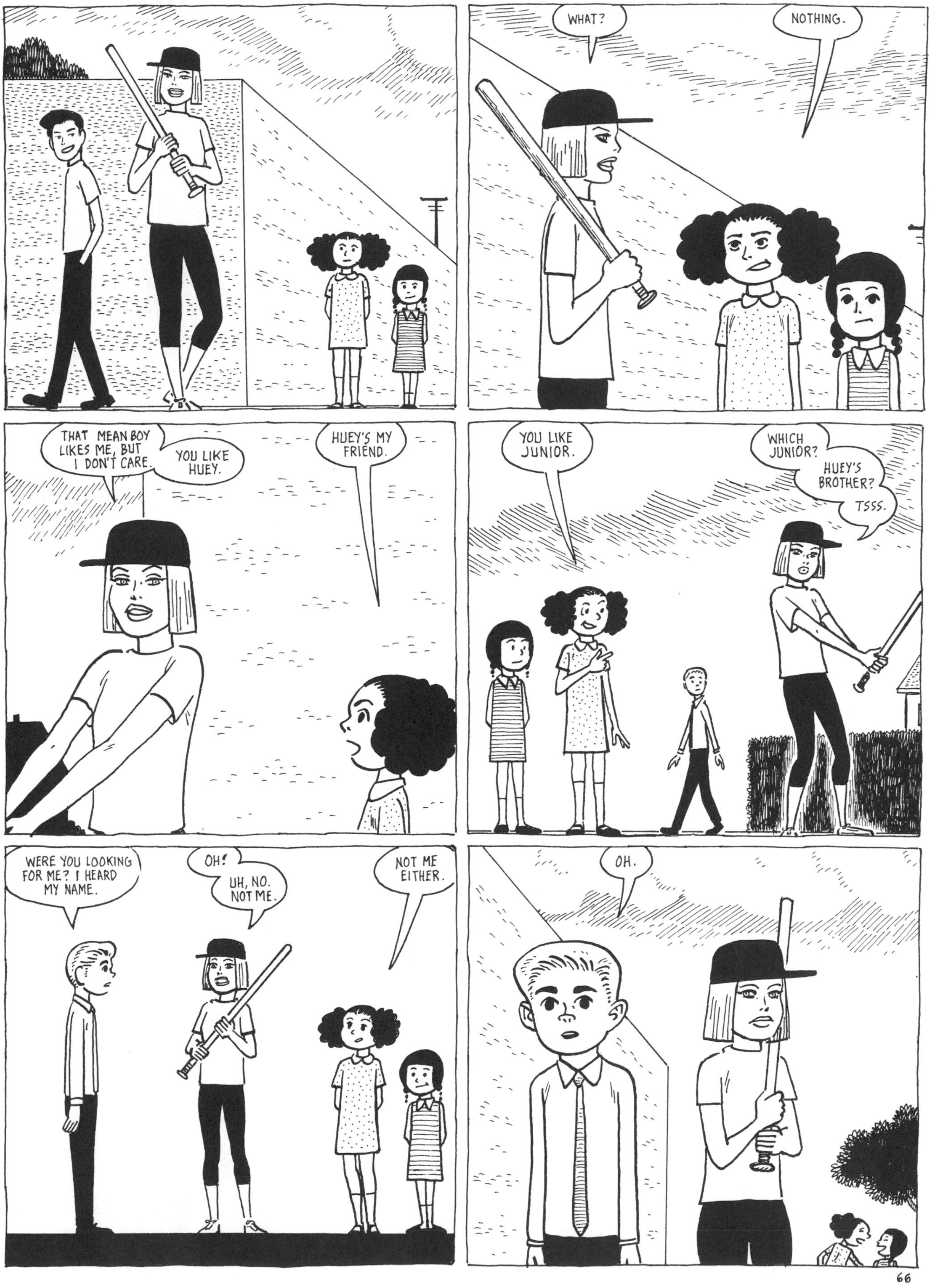
WHAT?
NOTHING.
THAT MEAN BOY LIKES ME, BUT I DON'T CARE.
YOU LIKE HUEY.
HUEY'S MY FRIEND.
YOU LIKE JUNIOR.
WHICH JUNIOR?
HUEY'S BROTHER?
TSSS.
WERE YOU LOOKING FOR ME? I HEARD MY NAME.
OH!
UH, NO. NOT ME.
NOT ME EITHER.
OH.

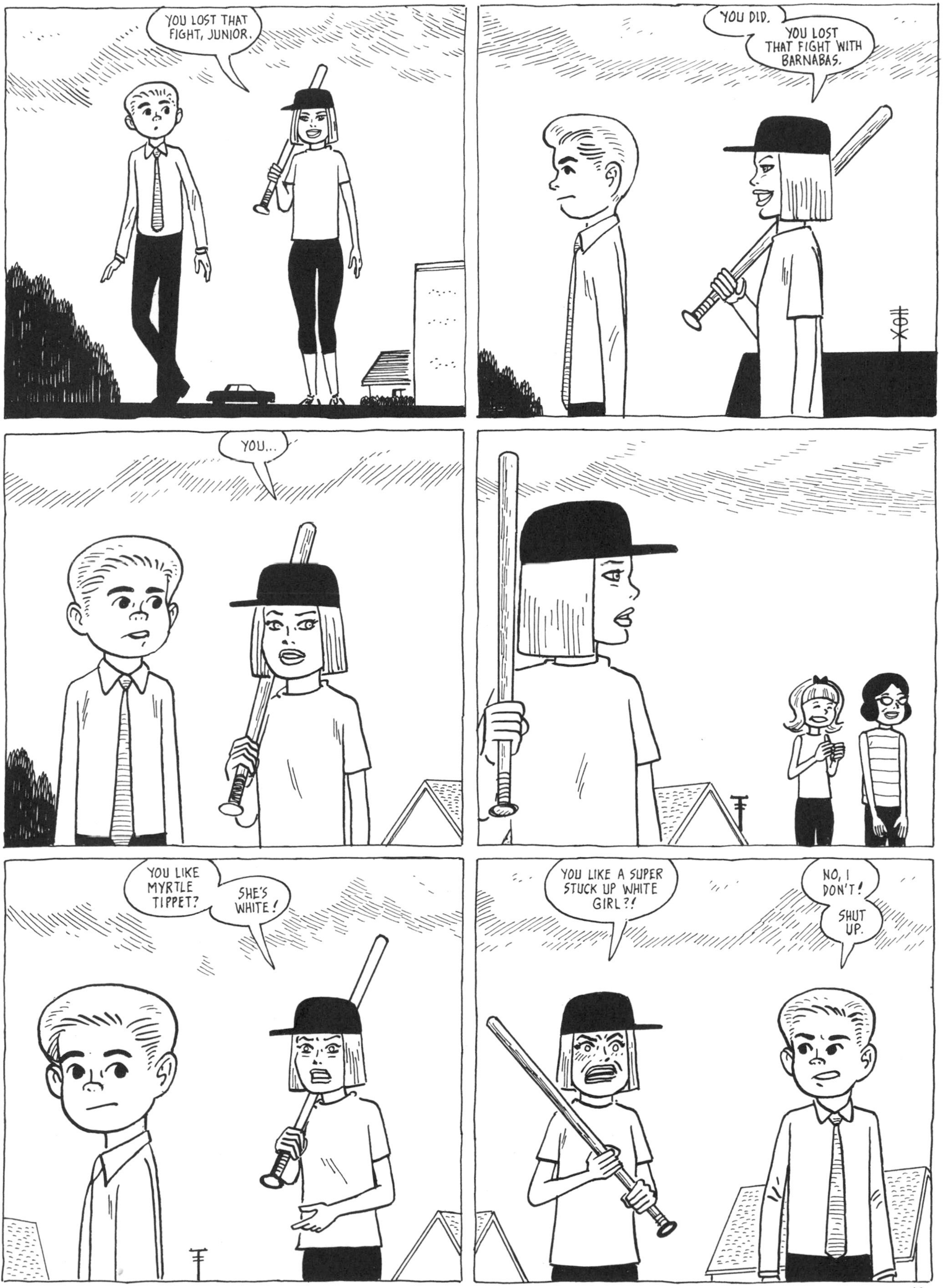
YOU LOST THAT FIGHT, JUNIOR.
YOU DID.
YOU LOST THAT FIGHT WITH BARNABAS.
YOU...
YOU LIKE MYRTLE TIPPET?
SHE'S WHITE!
YOU LIKE A SUPER STUCK UP WHITE GIRL?!
NO, I DON'T!
SHUT UP.

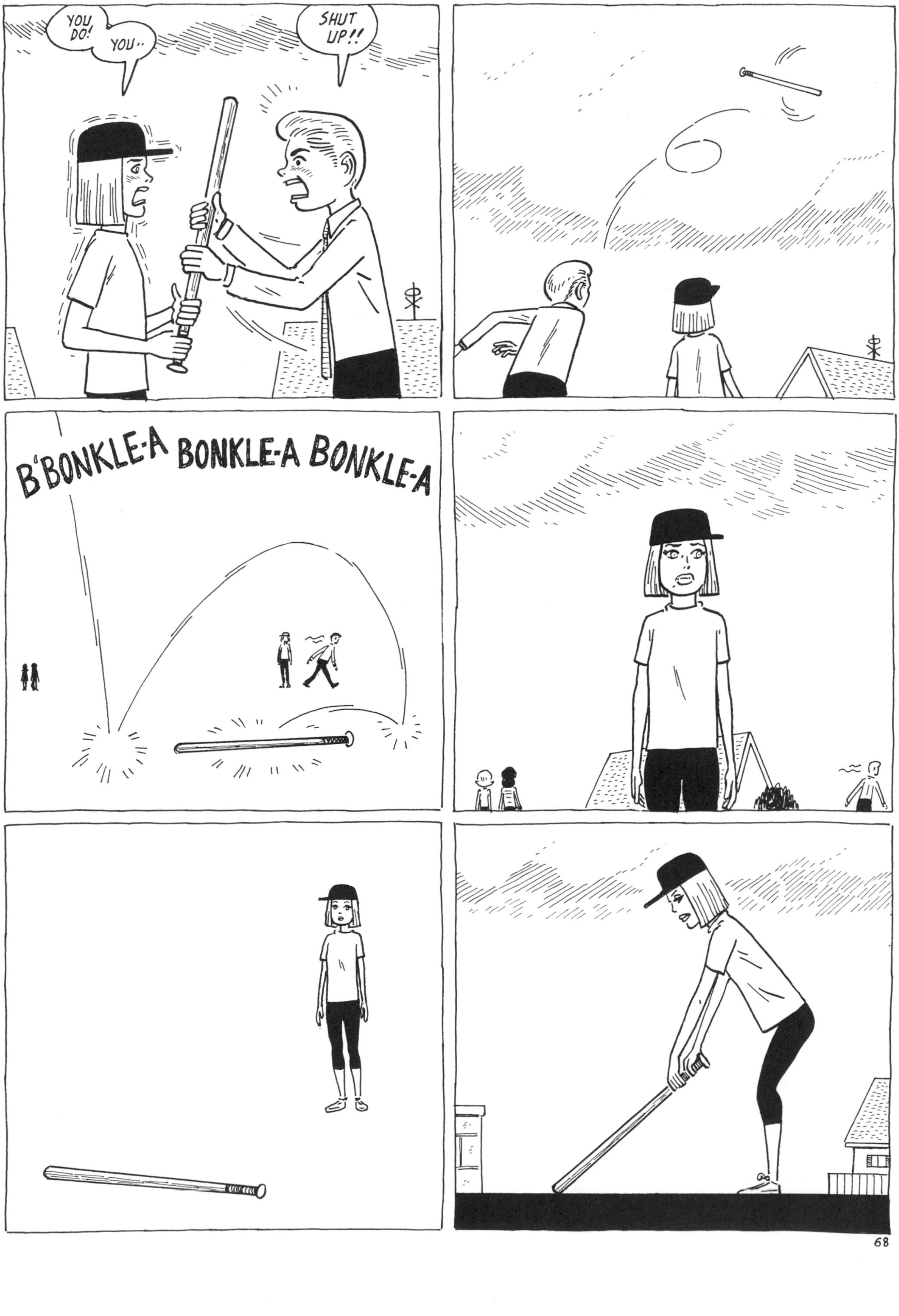
YOU DO! YOU..
SHUT UP!!
B'BONKLE-A BONKLE-A BONKLE-A

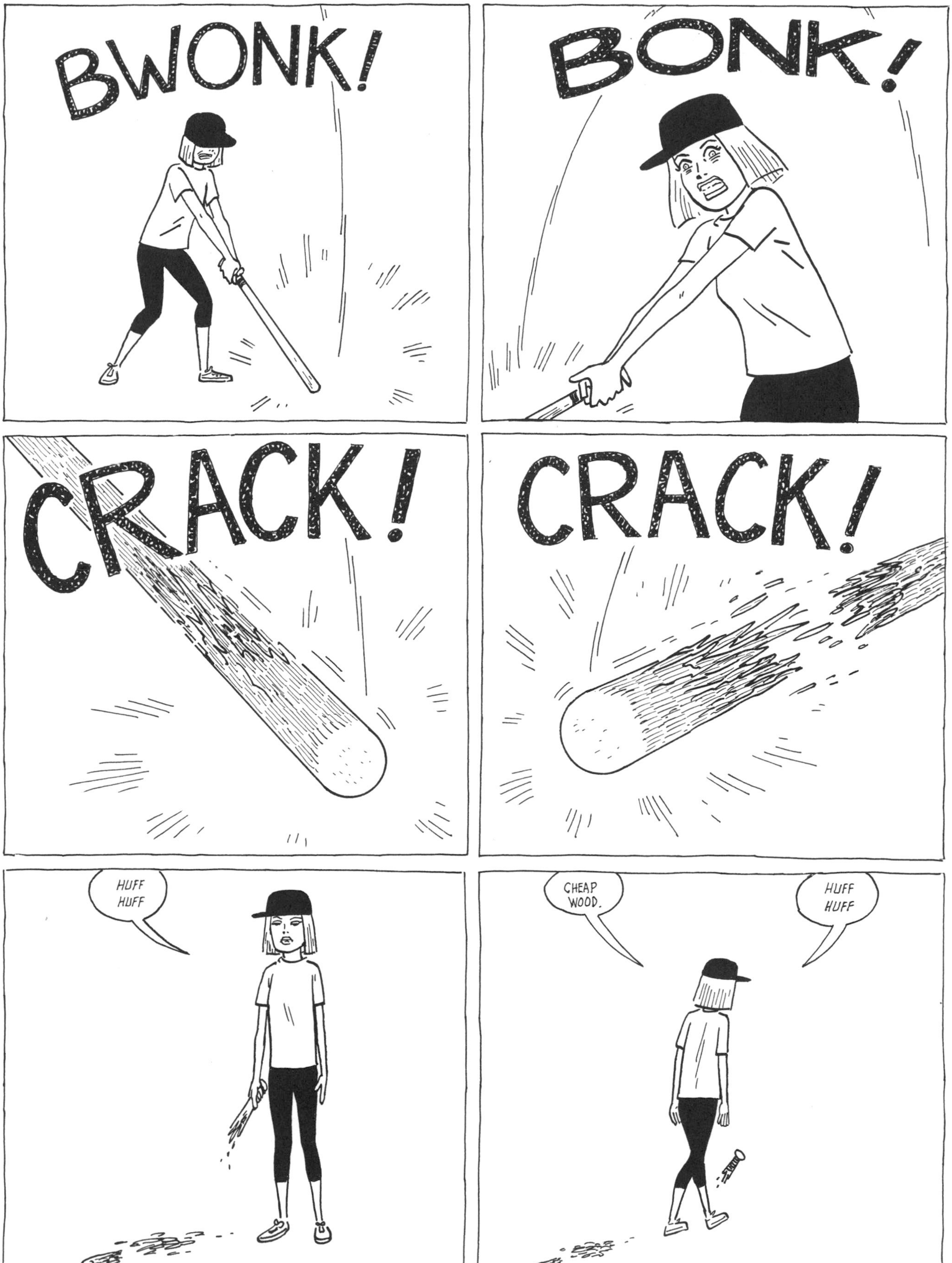
BWONK!
BONK!
CRACK!
CRACK!
HUFF HUFF
CHEAP WOOD.
HUFF HUFF

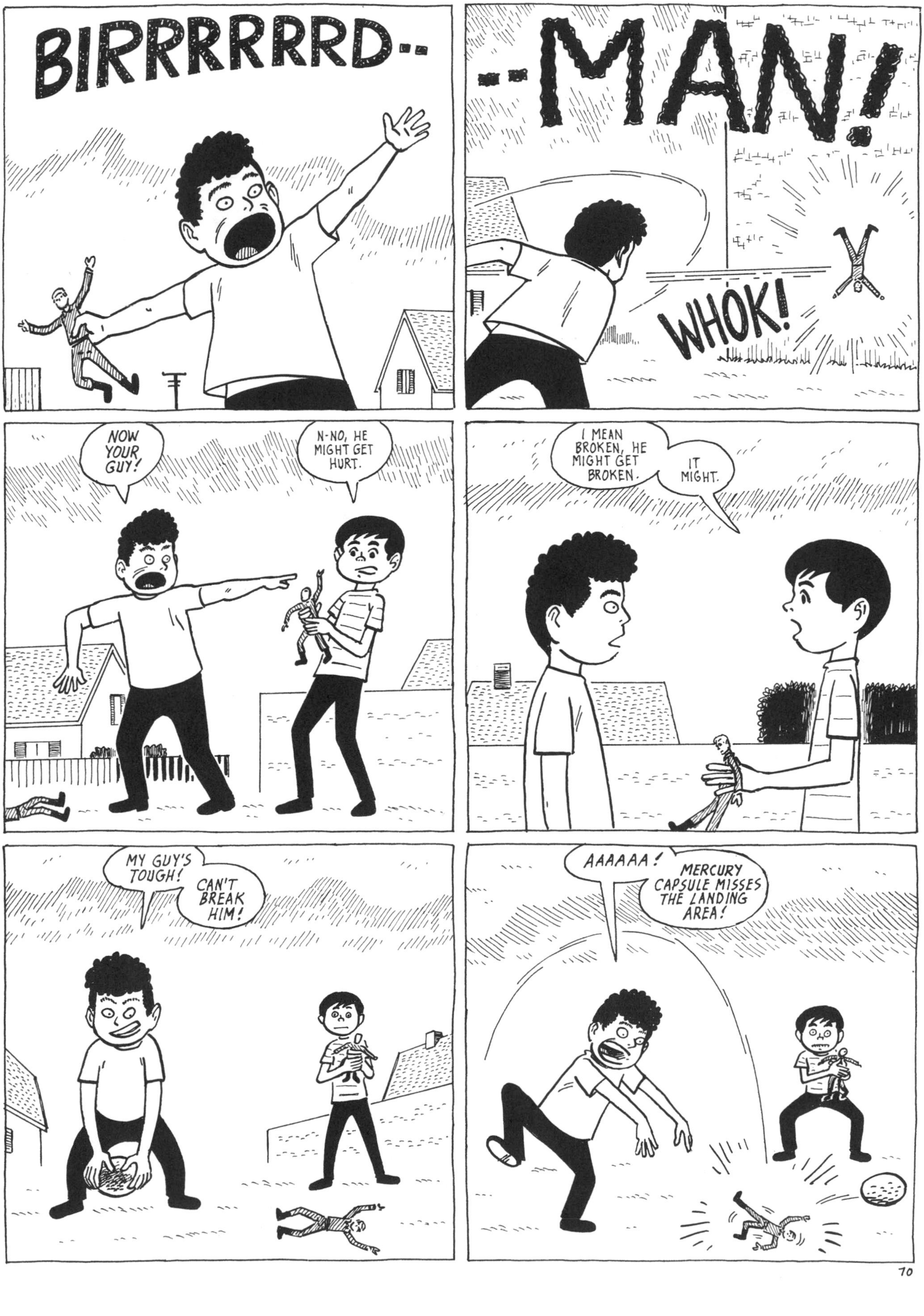
BIRRRRRRRD--
--MAN!
WHOK!
NOW YOUR GUY!
N-NO, HE MIGHT GET HURT.
I MEAN BROKEN, HE MIGHT GET BROKEN.
IT MIGHT.
MY GUY'S TOUGH!
CAN'T BREAK HIM!
AAAAAA!
MERCURY CAPSULE MISSES THE LANDING AREA!

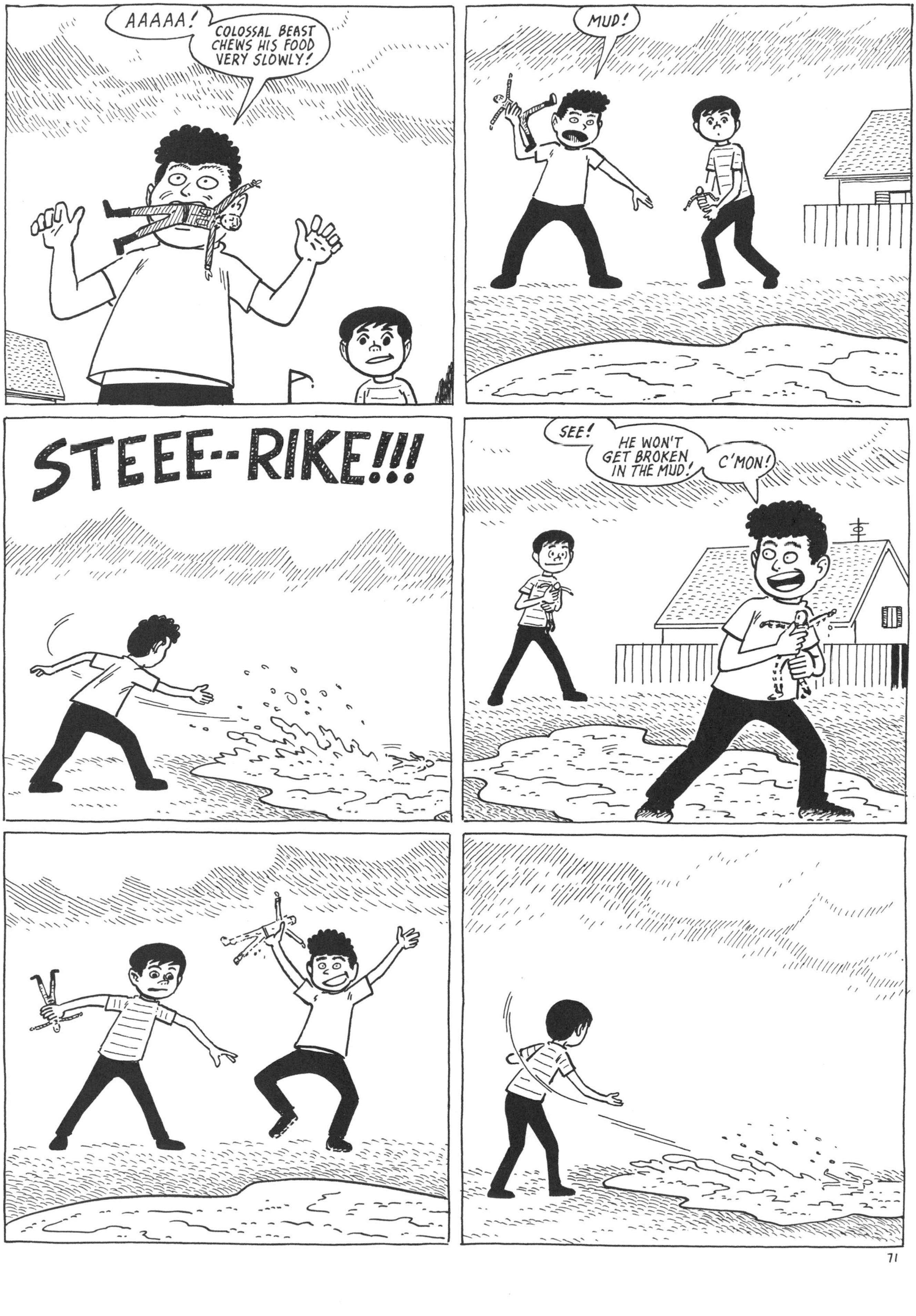
AAAAA!
COLOSSAL BEAST CHEWS HIS FOOD VERY SLOWLY!
MUD!
STEEE--RIKE!!!
SEE!
HE WON'T GET BROKEN IN THE MUD!
C'MON!

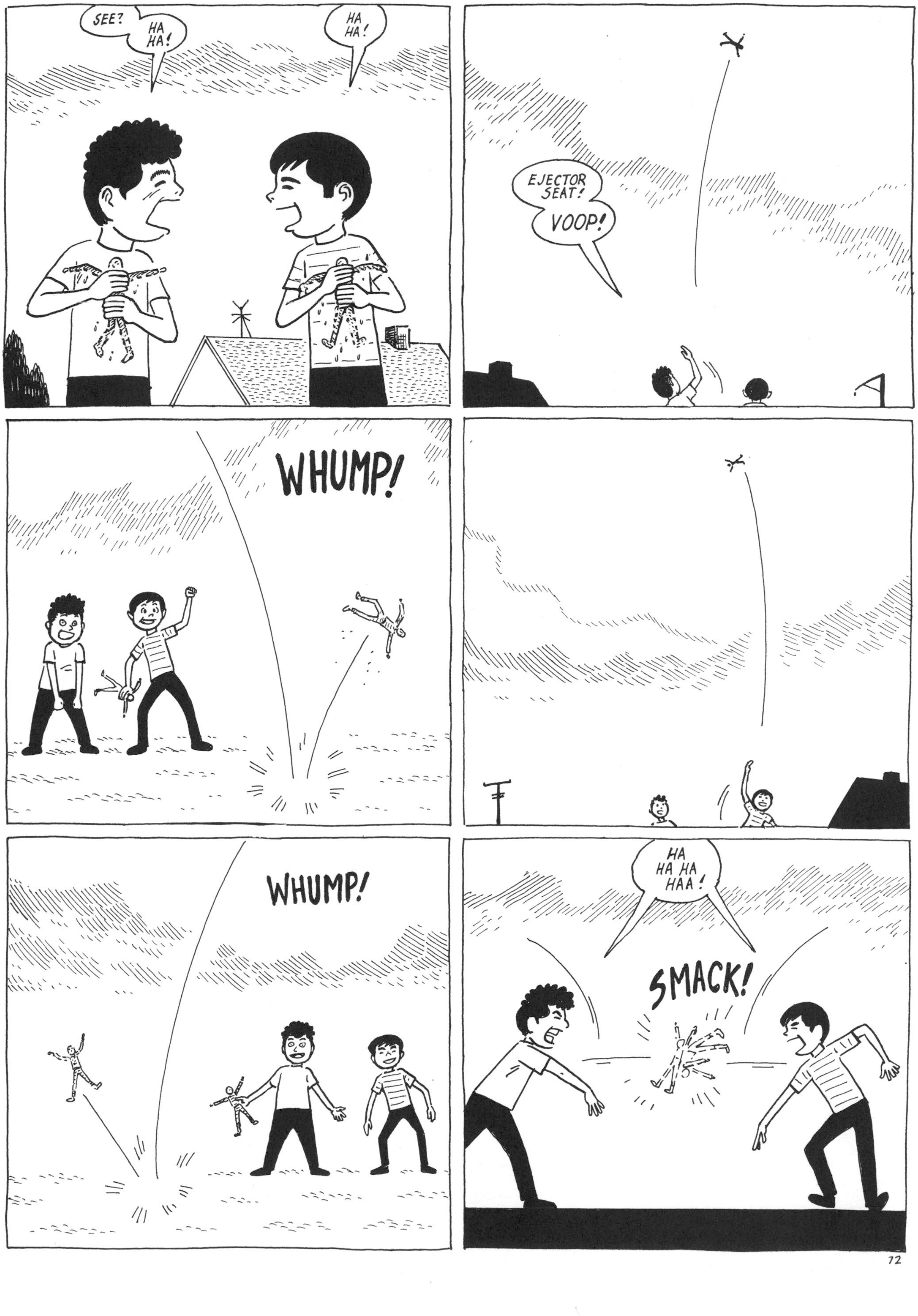
SEE?
HA HA!
HA HA!
EJECTOR SEAT!
VOOP!
WHUMP!
WHUMP!
HA HA HA HAA!
SMACK!

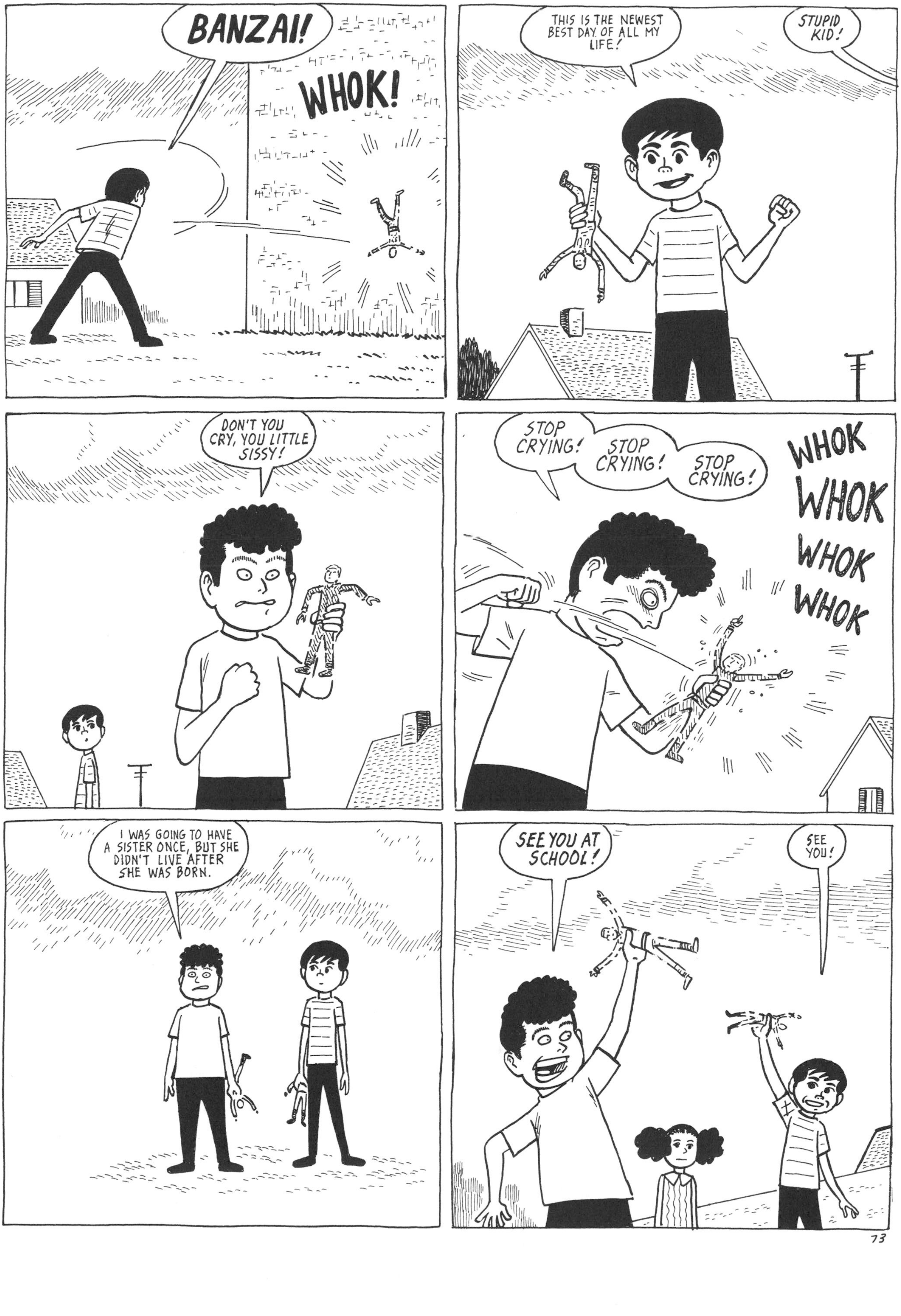

BANZAI!
WHOK!
THIS IS THE NEWEST BEST DAY OF ALL MY LIFE!
STUPID KID!
DON'T YOU CRY, YOU LITTLE SISSY!
STOP CRYING!
STOP CRYING!
STOP CRYING!
WHOK
WHOK
WHOK
WHOK
I WAS GOING TO HAVE A SISTER ONCE, BUT SHE DIDN'T LIVE AFTER SHE WAS BORN.
SEE YOU AT SCHOOL!
SEE YOU!

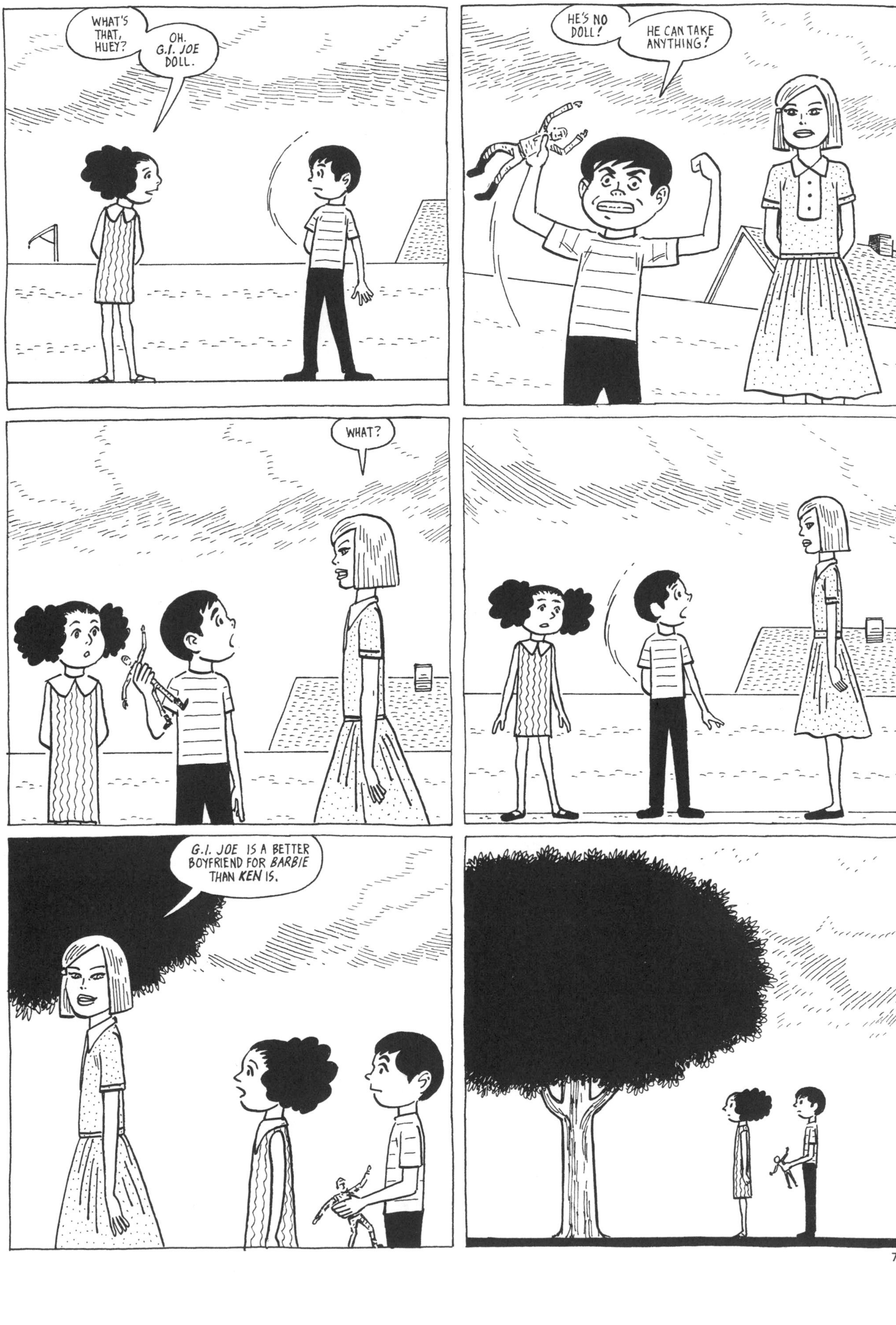
WHAT'S THAT, HUEY?
OH. G.I. JOE DOLL.
HE'S NO DOLL!
HE CAN TAKE ANYTHING!
WHAT?
G.I. JOE IS A BETTER BOYFRIEND FOR BARBIE THAN KEN IS.

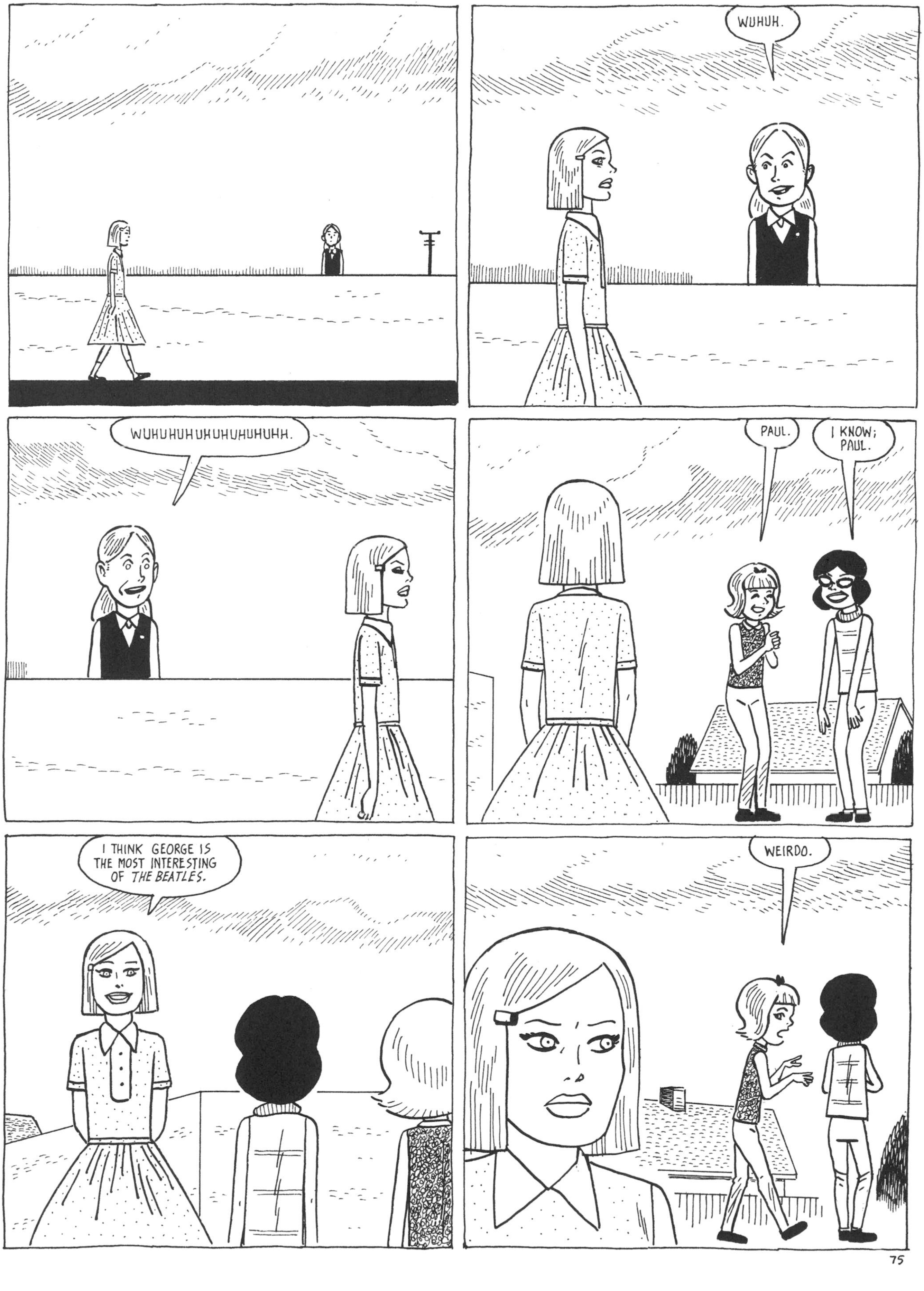
WUHUH.
WUHUHUHUHUHUHUHUHH.
PAUL.
I KNOW; PAUL.
I THINK GEORGE IS THE MOST INTERESTING OF *THE BEATLES.*
WEIRDO.

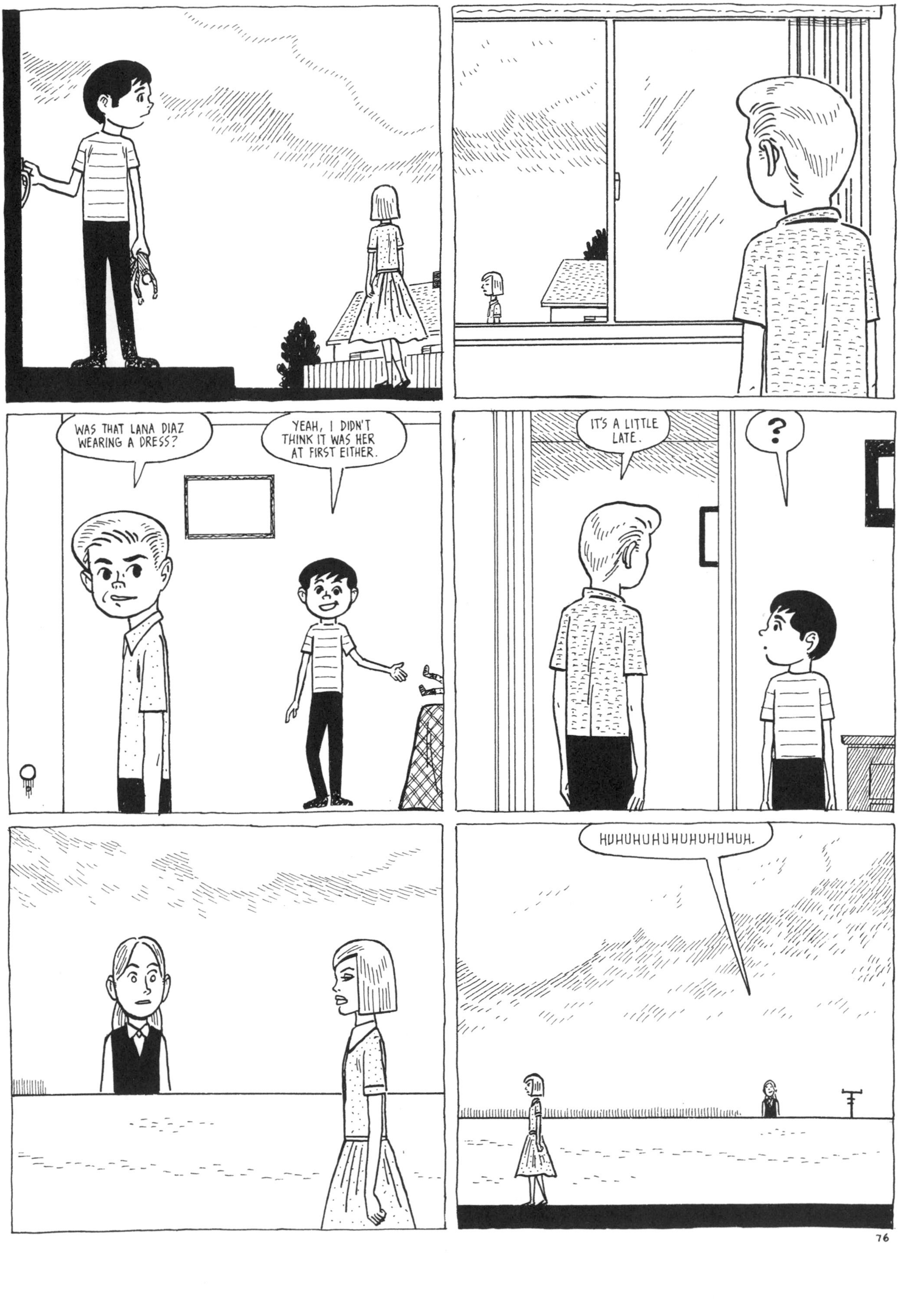
WAS THAT LANA DIAZ WEARING A DRESS?
YEAH, I DIDN'T THINK IT WAS HER AT FIRST EITHER.
IT'S A LITTLE LATE.
?
HUHUHUHUHUHUHUHUH.

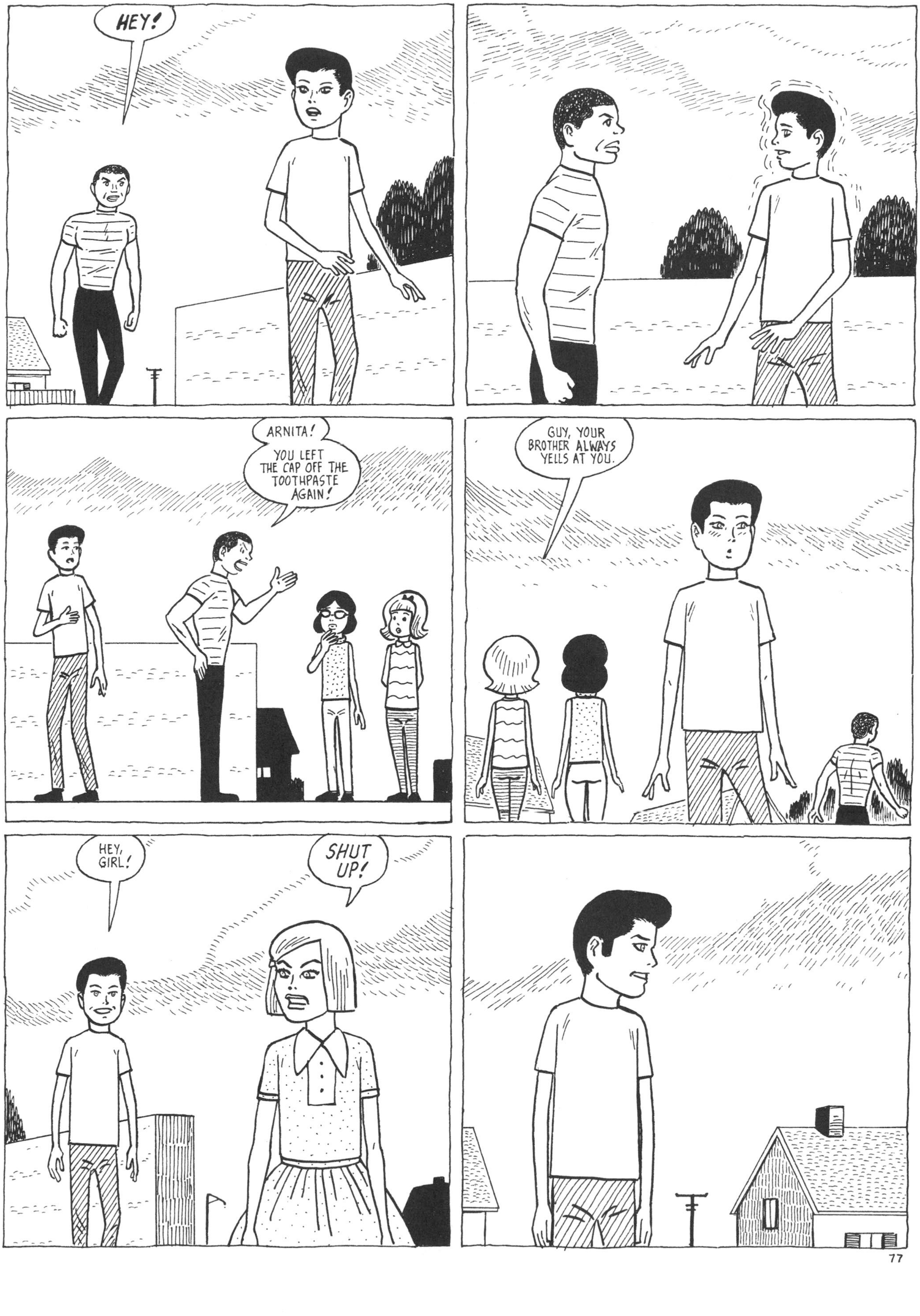
HEY!
ARNITA!
YOU LEFT THE CAP OFF THE TOOTHPASTE AGAIN!
GUY, YOUR BROTHER ALWAYS YELLS AT YOU.
HEY, GIRL!
SHUT UP!

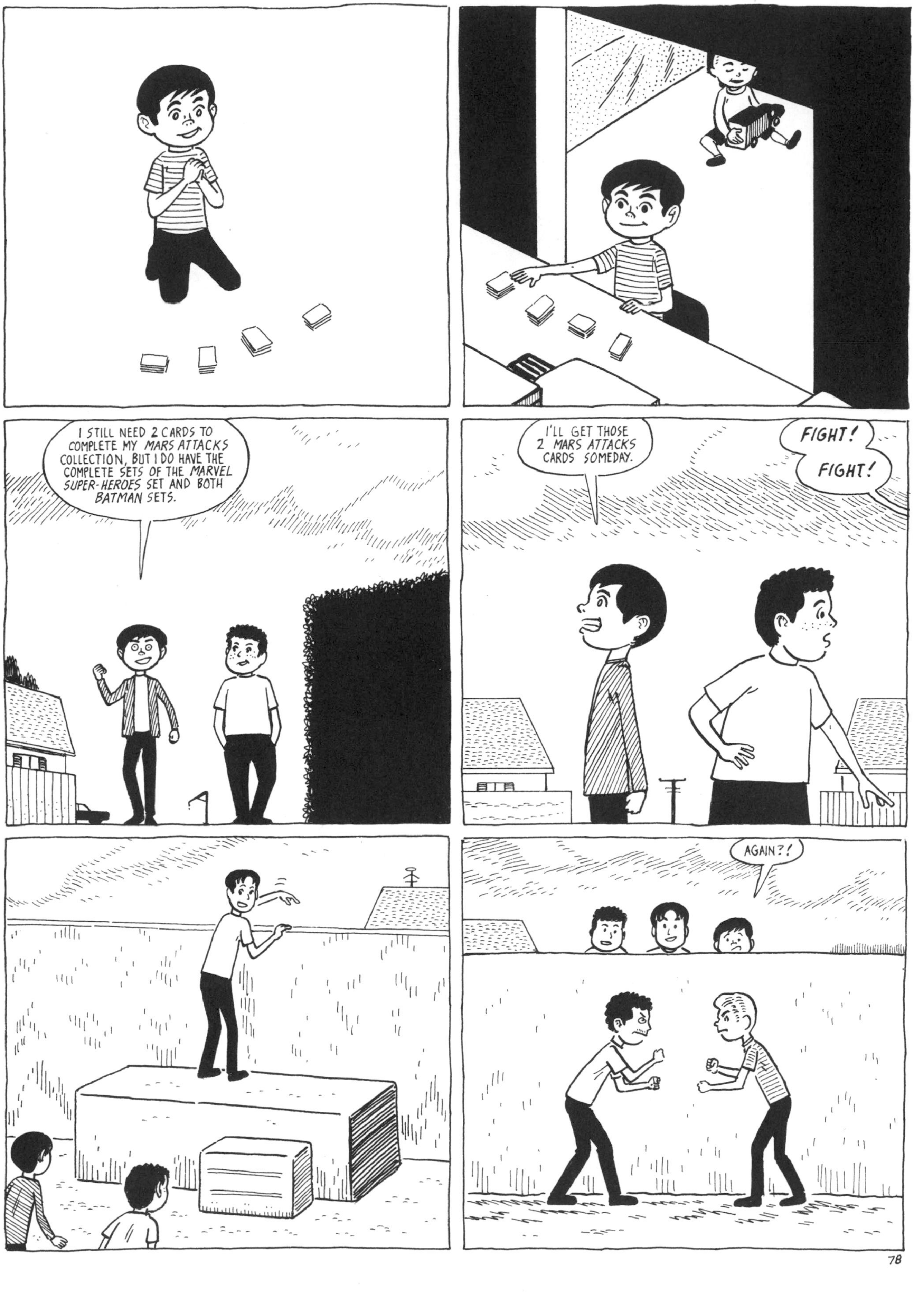
I STILL NEED 2 CARDS TO COMPLETE MY MARS ATTACKS COLLECTION, BUT I DO HAVE THE COMPLETE SETS OF THE MARVEL SUPER-HEROES SET AND BOTH BATMAN SETS.
I'LL GET THOSE 2 MARS ATTACKS CARDS SOMEDAY.
FIGHT!
FIGHT!
AGAIN?!

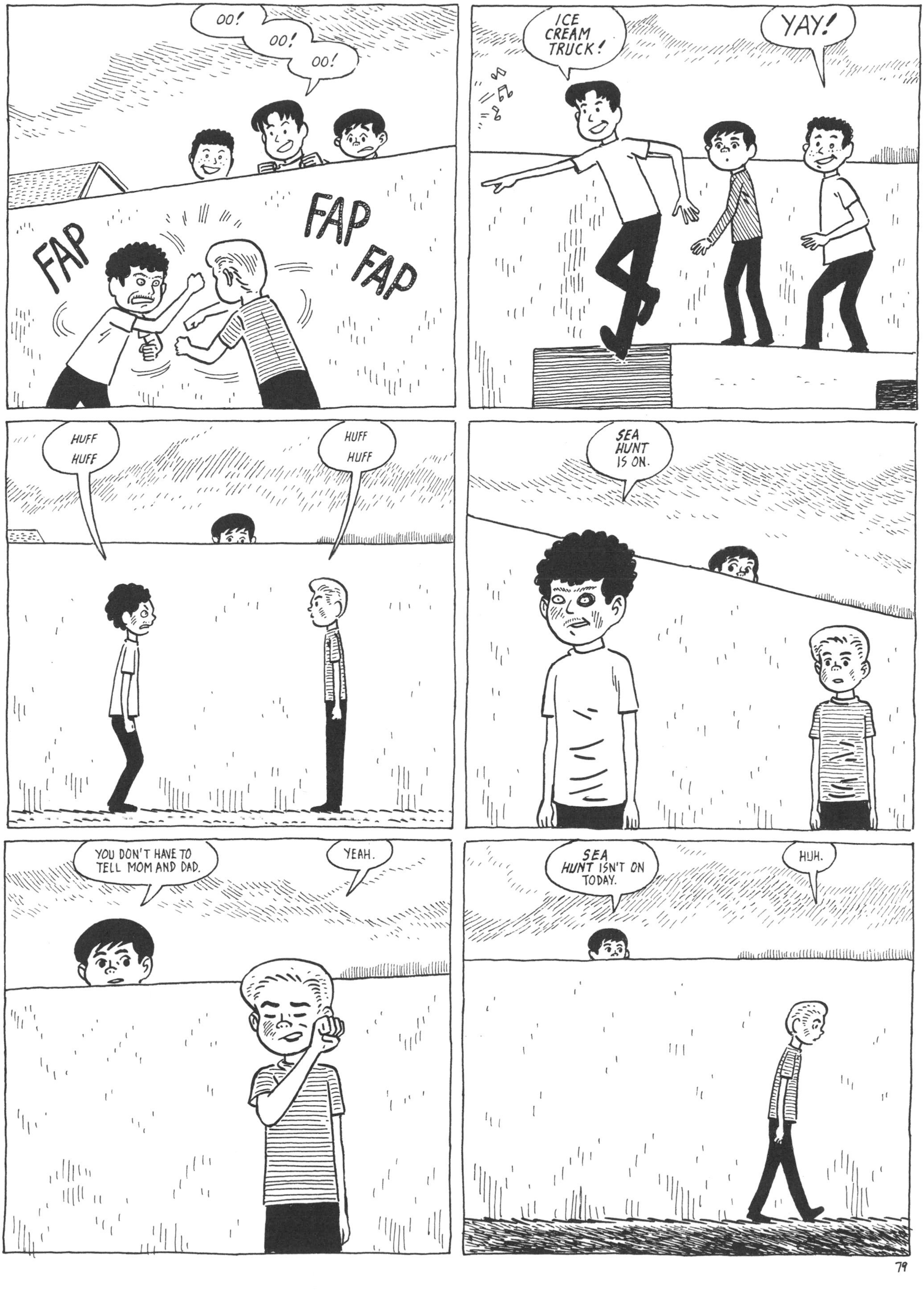

OO!
OO!
OO!
FAP
FAP
FAP
ICE CREAM TRUCK!
YAY!
HUFF HUFF
HUFF HUFF
SEA HUNT IS ON.
YOU DON'T HAVE TO TELL MOM AND DAD.
YEAH.
SEA HUNT ISN'T ON TODAY.
HUH.

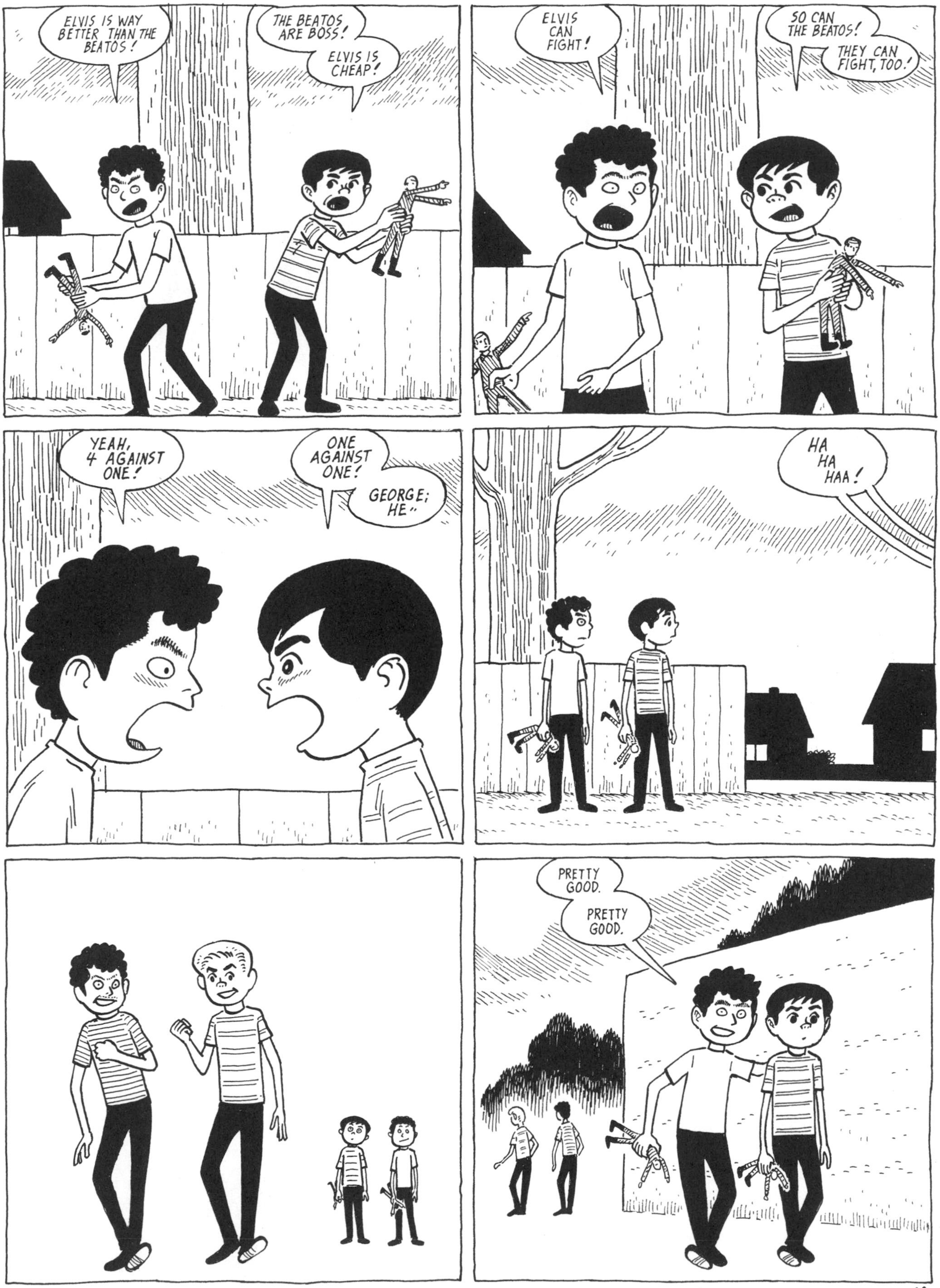
ELVIS IS WAY BETTER THAN THE BEATOS!
THE BEATOS ARE BOSS!
ELVIS IS CHEAP!
ELVIS CAN FIGHT!
SO CAN THE BEATOS!
THEY CAN FIGHT, TOO!
YEAH, 4 AGAINST ONE!
ONE AGAINST ONE!
GEORGE; HE--
HA HA HAA!
PRETTY GOOD.
PRETTY GOOD.

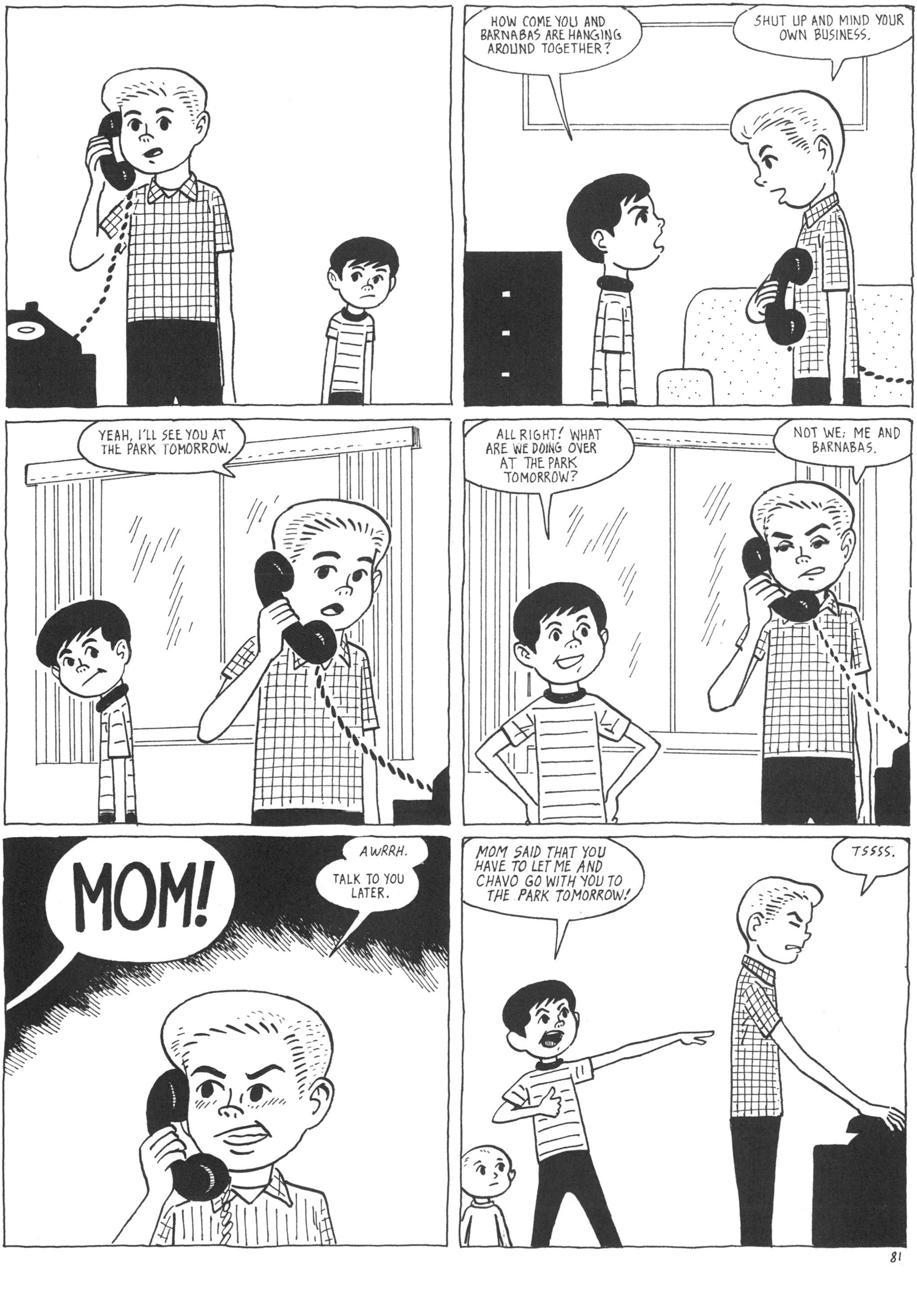
HOW COME YOU AND BARNABAS ARE HANGING AROUND TOGETHER?
SHUT UP AND MIND YOUR OWN BUSINESS.
YEAH, I'LL SEE YOU AT THE PARK TOMORROW.
ALL RIGHT! WHAT ARE WE DOING OVER AT THE PARK TOMORROW?
NOT WE; ME AND BARNABAS.
MOM!
AWRRH.
TALK TO YOU LATER.
MOM SAID THAT YOU HAVE TO LET ME AND CHAVO GO WITH YOU TO THE PARK TOMORROW!
TSSSS.

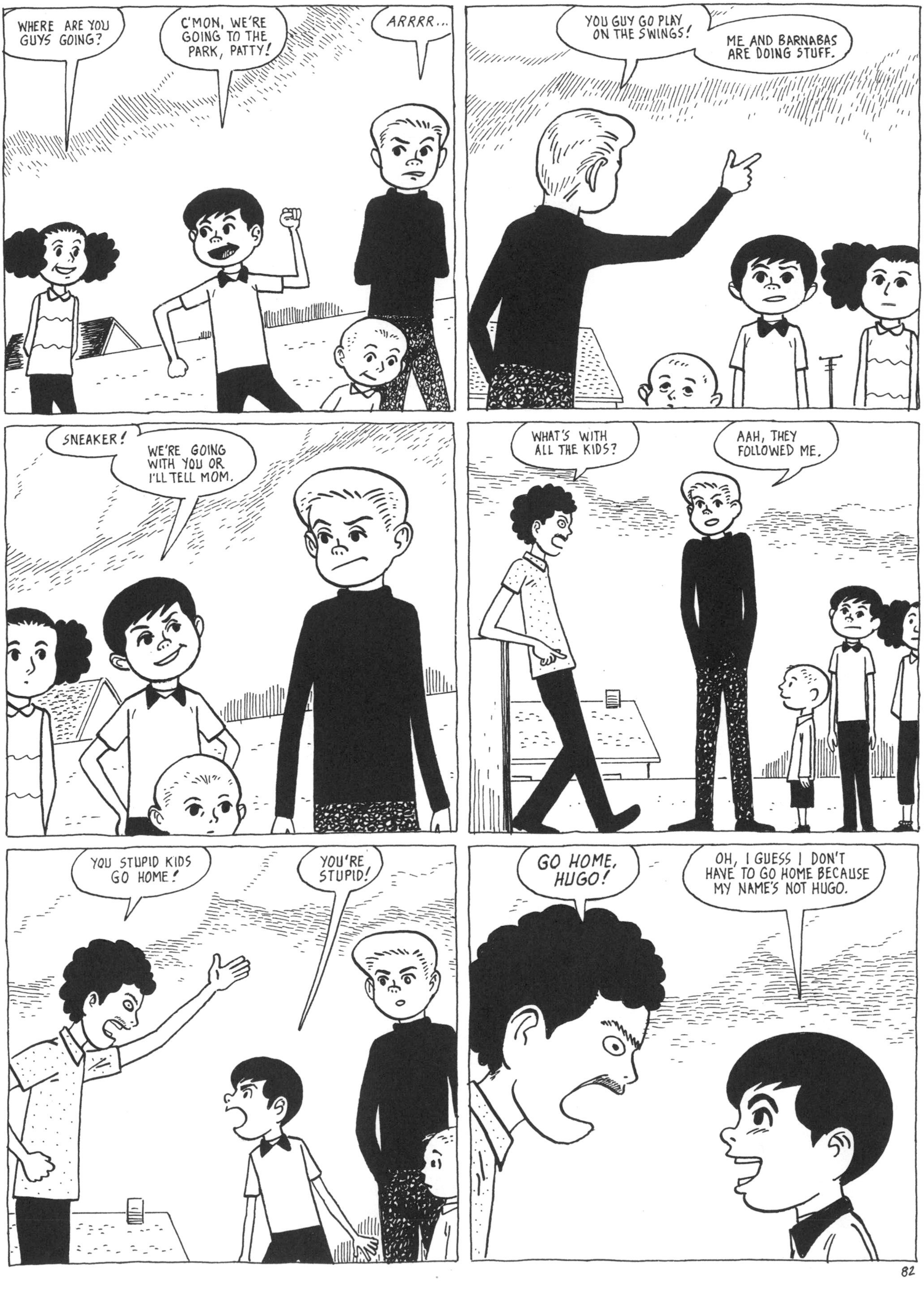
WHERE ARE YOU GUYS GOING?
C'MON, WE'RE GOING TO THE PARK, PATTY!
ARRRR...
YOU GUY GO PLAY ON THE SWINGS!
ME AND BARNABAS ARE DOING STUFF.
SNEAKER!
WE'RE GOING WITH YOU OR I'LL TELL MOM.
WHAT'S WITH ALL THE KIDS?
AAH, THEY FOLLOWED ME.
YOU STUPID KIDS GO HOME!
YOU'RE STUPID!
GO HOME, HUGO!
OH, I GUESS I DON'T HAVE TO GO HOME BECAUSE MY NAME'S NOT HUGO.

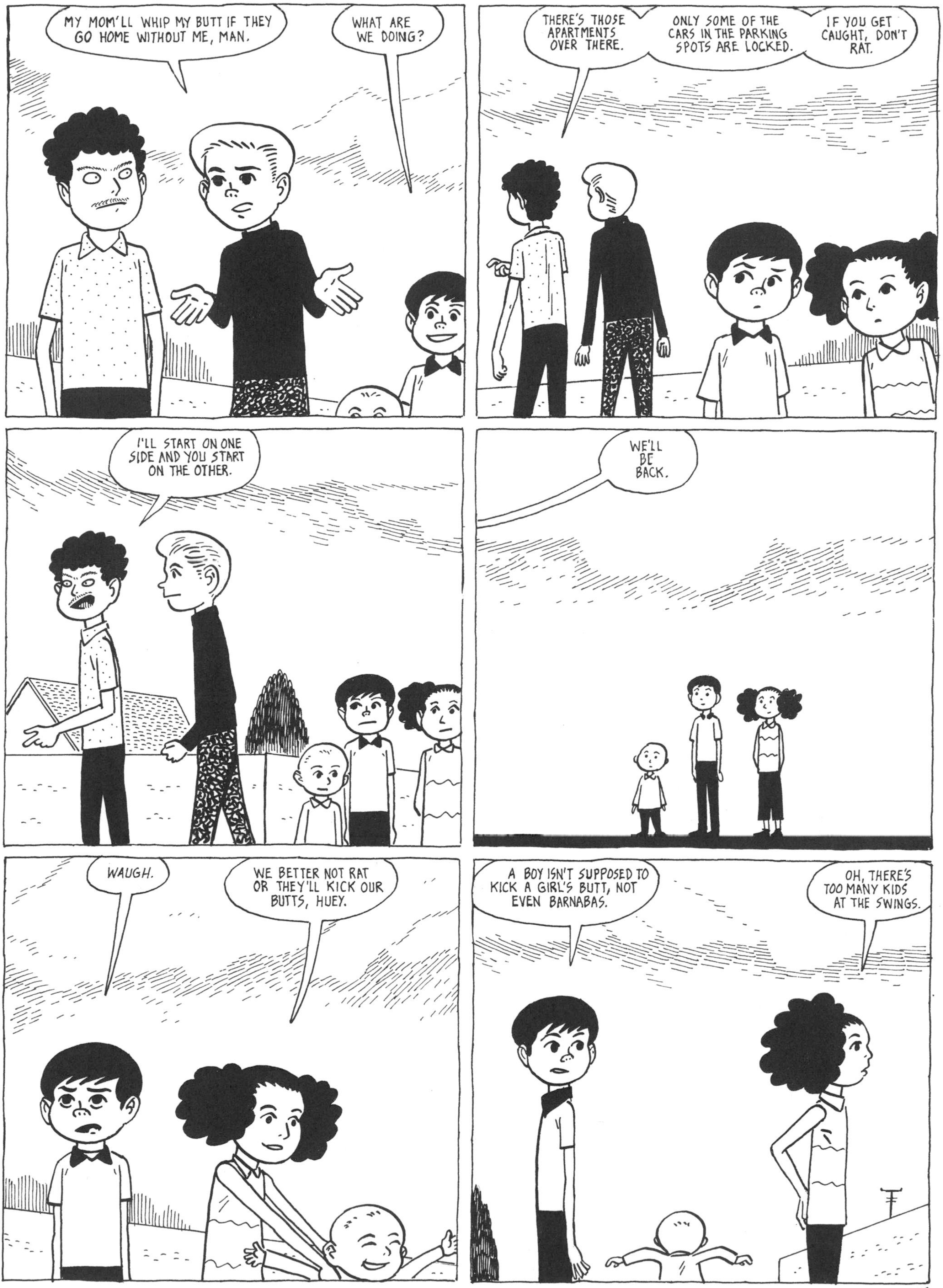
MY MOM'LL WHIP MY BUTT IF THEY GO HOME WITHOUT ME, MAN.
WHAT ARE WE DOING?
THERE'S THOSE APARTMENTS OVER THERE.
ONLY SOME OF THE CARS IN THE PARKING SPOTS ARE LOCKED.
IF YOU GET CAUGHT, DON'T RAT.
I'LL START ON ONE SIDE AND YOU START ON THE OTHER.
WE'LL BE BACK.
WAUGH.
WE BETTER NOT RAT OR THEY'LL KICK OUR BUTTS, HUEY.
A BOY ISN'T SUPPOSED TO KICK A GIRL'S BUTT, NOT EVEN BARNABAS.
OH, THERE'S TOO MANY KIDS AT THE SWINGS.

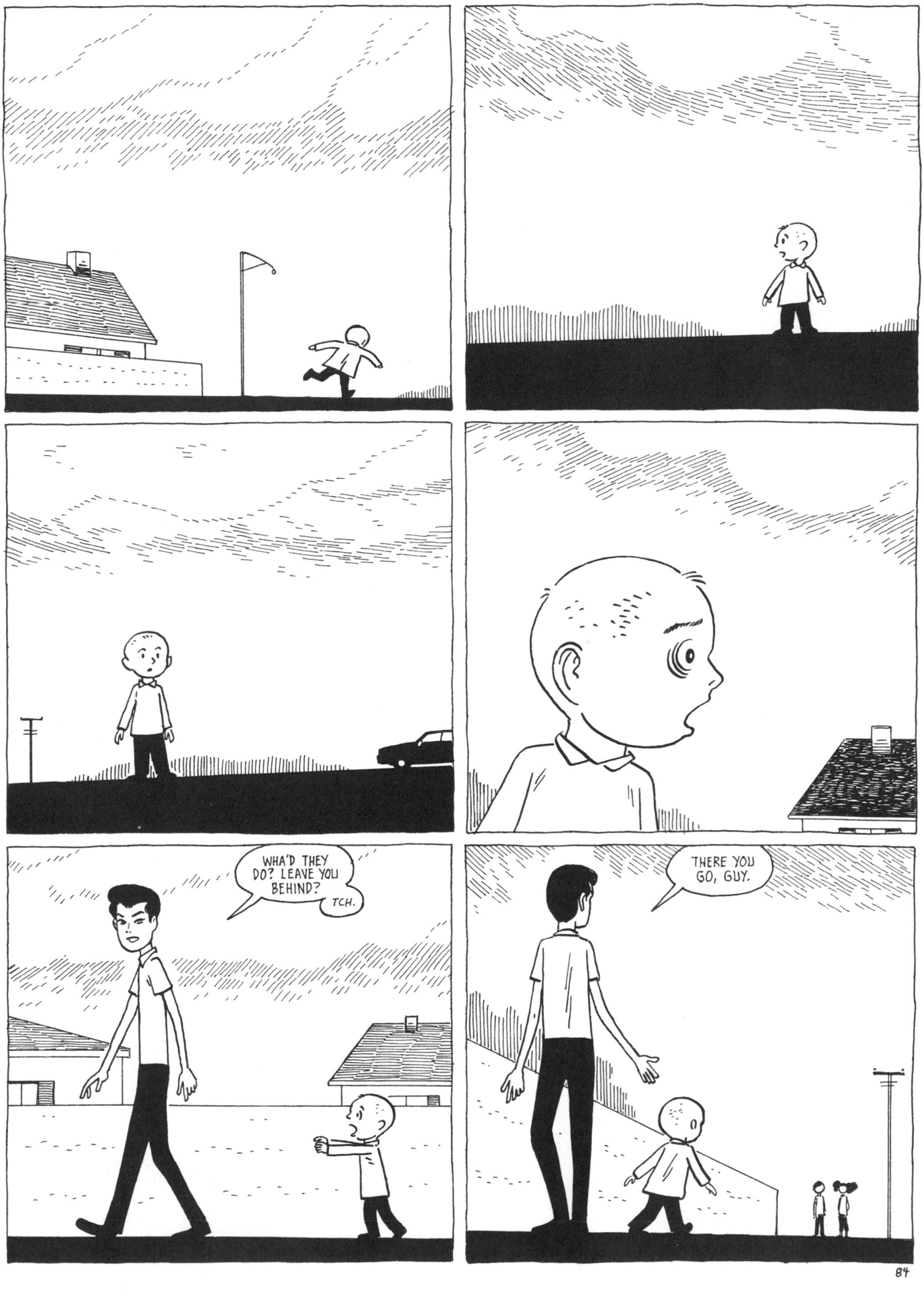
WHA'D THEY DO? LEAVE YOU BEHIND?
TCH.
THERE YOU GO, GUY.

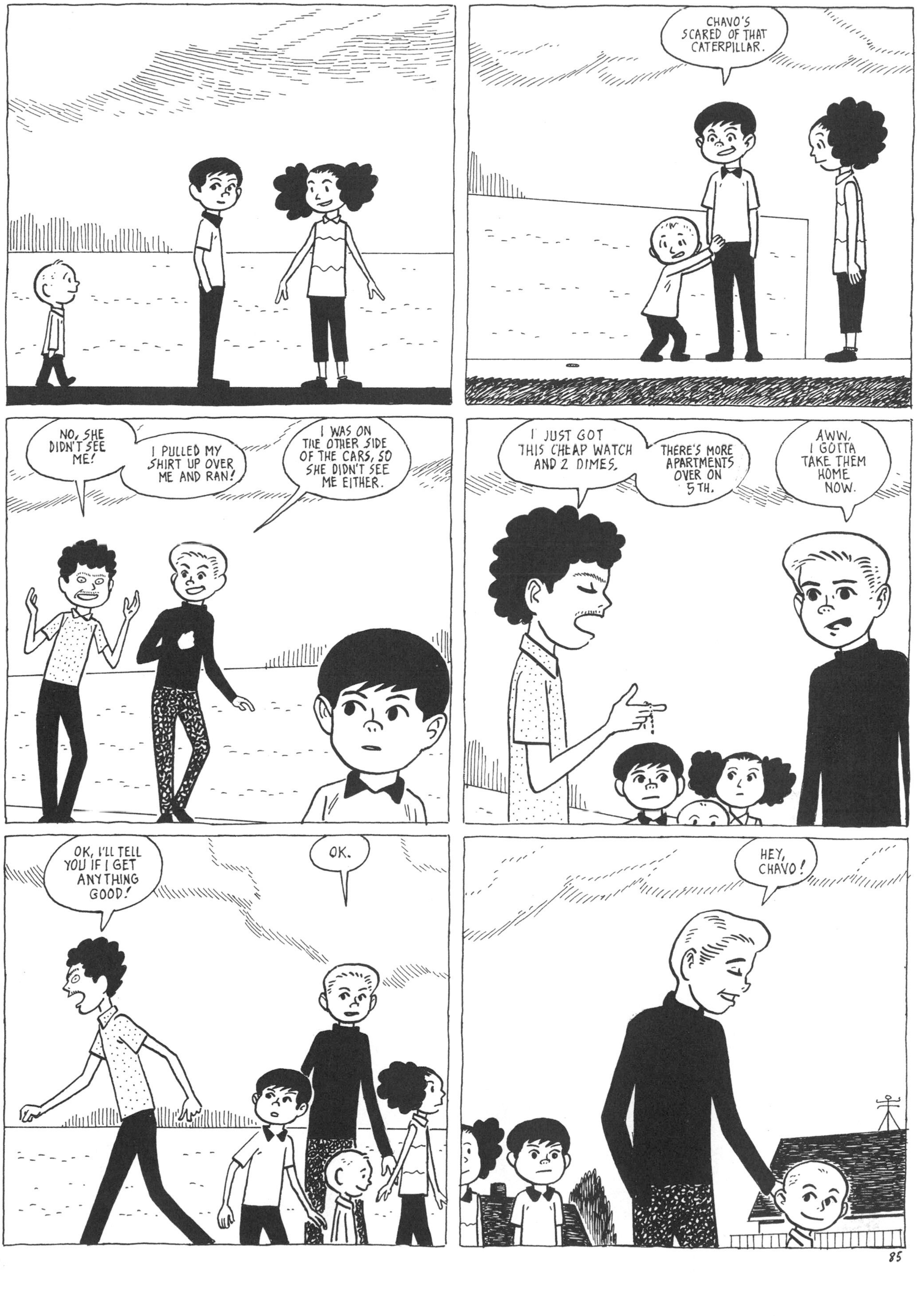
CHAVO'S SCARED OF THAT CATERPILLAR.
NO, SHE DIDN'T SEE ME!
I PULLED MY SHIRT UP OVER ME AND RAN!
I WAS ON THE OTHER SIDE OF THE CARS, SO SHE DIDN'T SEE ME EITHER.
I JUST GOT THIS CHEAP WATCH AND 2 DIMES.
THERE'S MORE APARTMENTS OVER ON 5TH.
AWW, I GOTTA TAKE THEM HOME NOW.
OK, I'LL TELL YOU IF I GET ANYTHING GOOD!
OK.
HEY, CHAVO!

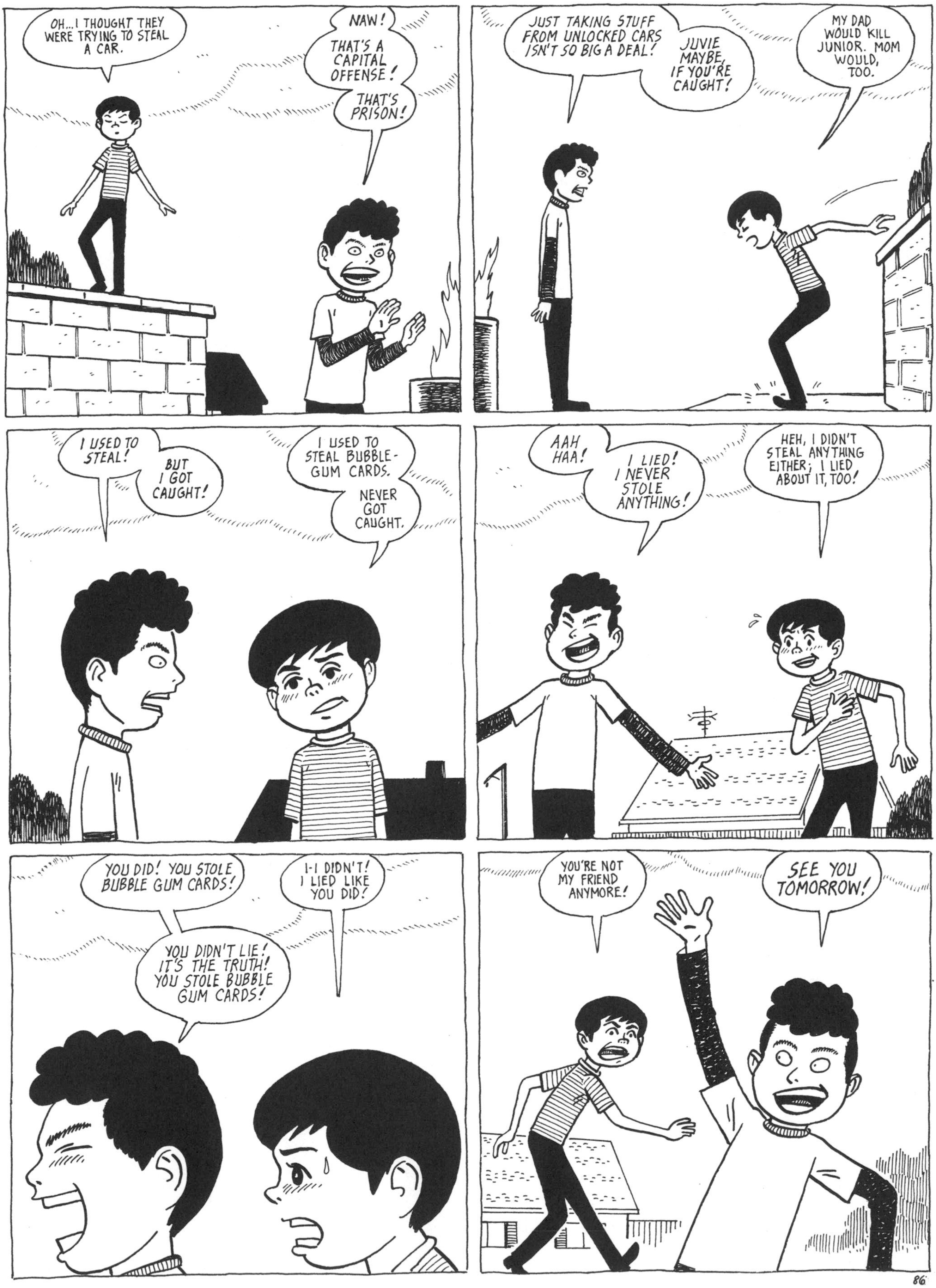

OH... I THOUGHT THEY WERE TRYING TO STEAL A CAR.
NAW! THAT'S A CAPITAL OFFENSE! THAT'S PRISON!
JUST TAKING STUFF FROM UNLOCKED CARS ISN'T SO BIG A DEAL!
JUVIE MAYBE, IF YOU'RE CAUGHT!
MY DAD WOULD KILL JUNIOR. MOM WOULD, TOO.
I USED TO STEAL!
BUT I GOT CAUGHT!
I USED TO STEAL BUBBLE-GUM CARDS.
NEVER GOT CAUGHT.
AAH HAA!
I LIED! I NEVER STOLE ANYTHING!
HEH, I DIDN'T STEAL ANYTHING EITHER; I LIED ABOUT IT, TOO!
YOU DID! YOU STOLE BUBBLE GUM CARDS!
YOU DIDN'T LIE! IT'S THE TRUTH! YOU STOLE BUBBLE GUM CARDS!
I-I DIDN'T! I LIED LIKE YOU DID!
YOU'RE NOT MY FRIEND ANYMORE!
SEE YOU TOMORROW!

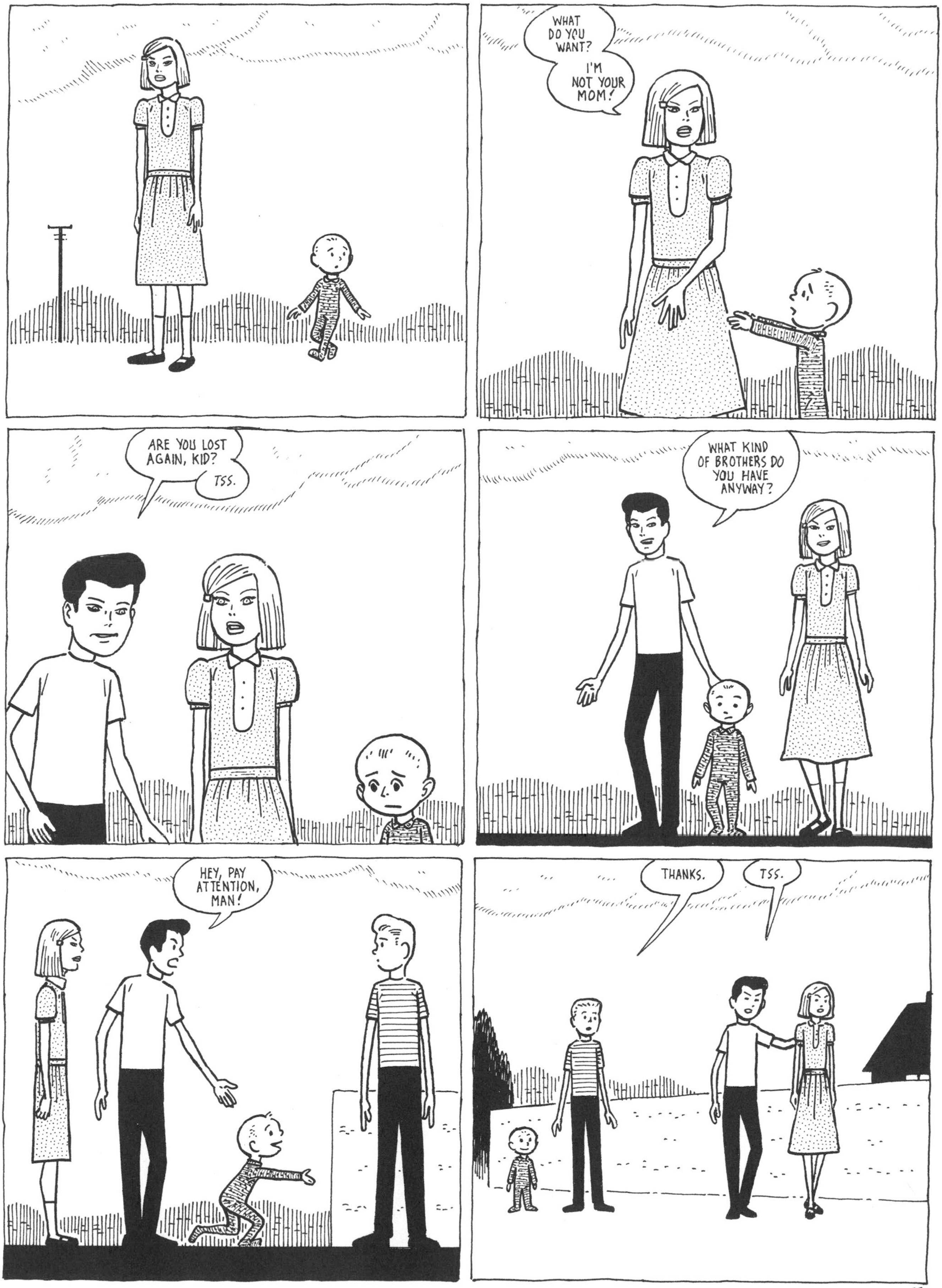
WHAT DO YOU WANT?
I'M NOT YOUR MOM!
ARE YOU LOST AGAIN, KID?
TSS.
WHAT KIND OF BROTHERS DO YOU HAVE ANYWAY?
HEY, PAY ATTENTION, MAN!
THANKS.
TSS.

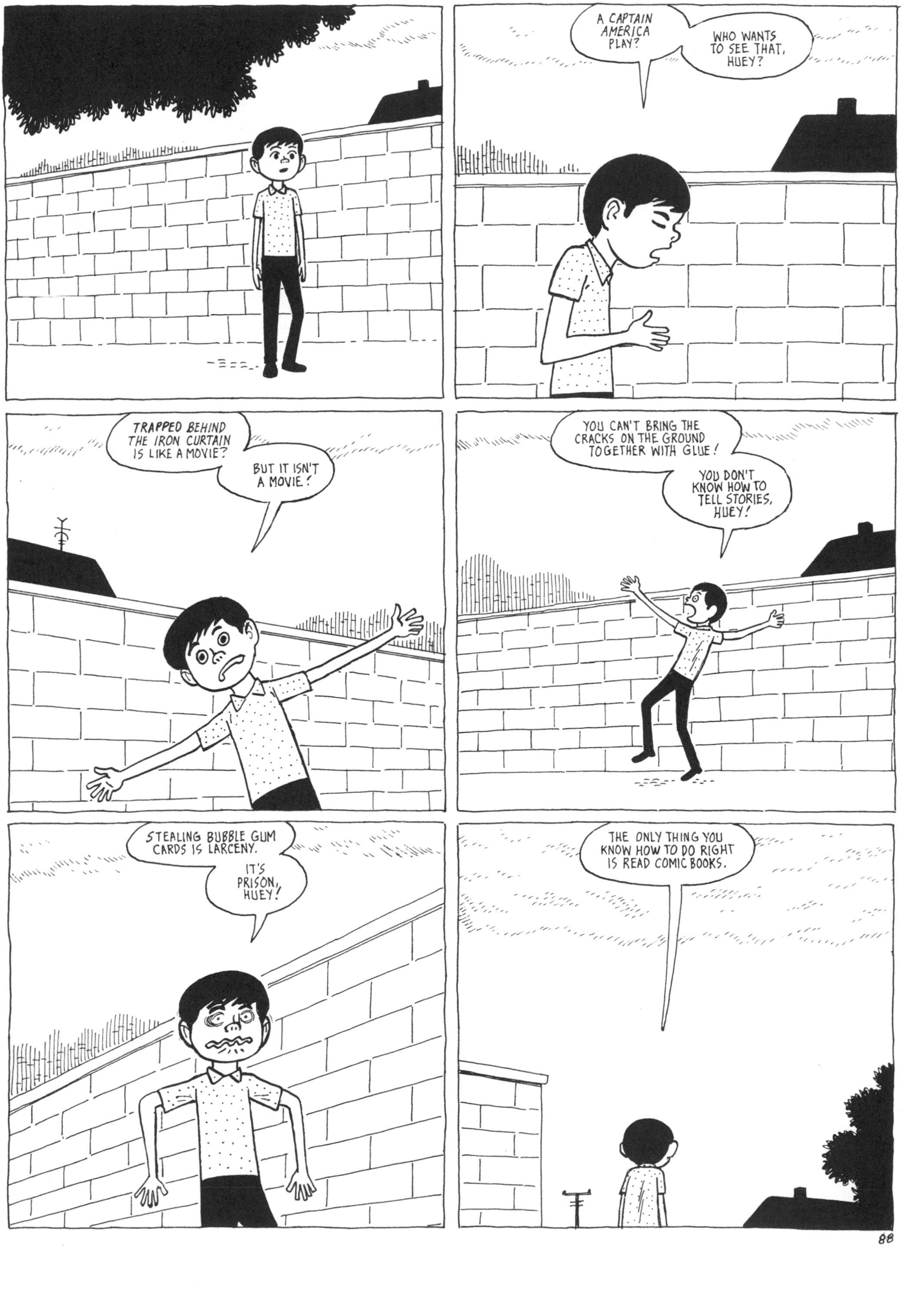
A CAPTAIN AMERICA PLAY?
WHO WANTS TO SEE THAT, HUEY?
TRAPPED BEHIND THE IRON CURTAIN IS LIKE A MOVIE?
BUT IT ISN'T A MOVIE!
YOU CAN'T BRING THE CRACKS ON THE GROUND TOGETHER WITH GLUE!
YOU DON'T KNOW HOW TO TELL STORIES, HUEY!
STEALING BUBBLE GUM CARDS IS LARCENY.
IT'S PRISON, HUEY!
THE ONLY THING YOU KNOW HOW TO DO RIGHT IS READ COMIC BOOKS.

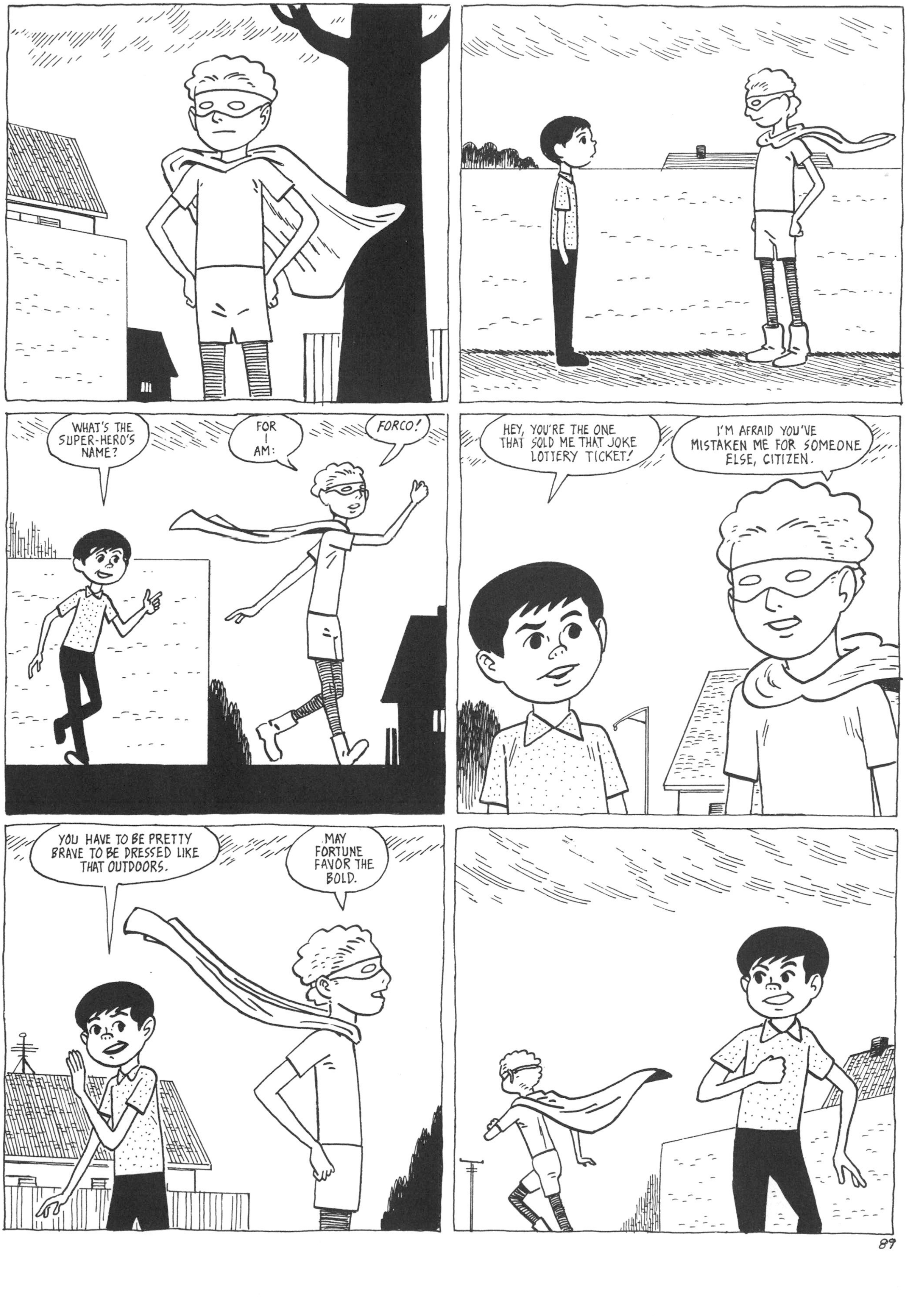
WHAT'S THE SUPER-HERO'S NAME?
FOR I AM:
FORCO!
HEY, YOU'RE THE ONE THAT SOLD ME THAT JOKE LOTTERY TICKET!
I'M AFRAID YOU'VE MISTAKEN ME FOR SOMEONE ELSE, CITIZEN.
YOU HAVE TO BE PRETTY BRAVE TO BE DRESSED LIKE THAT OUTDOORS.
MAY FORTUNE FAVOR THE BOLD.

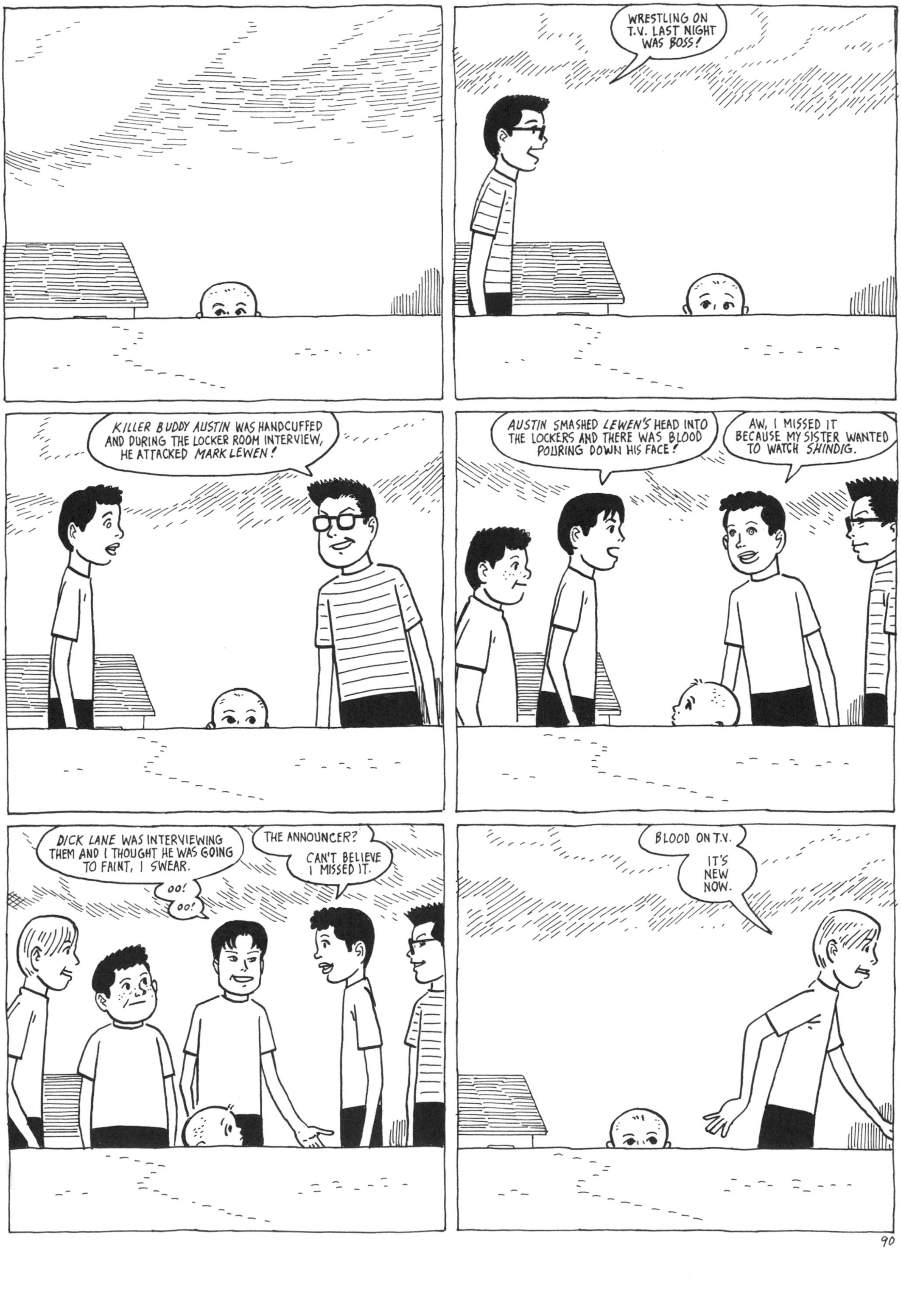
WRESTLING ON T.V. LAST NIGHT WAS BOSS!
KILLER BUDDY AUSTIN WAS HANDCUFFED AND DURING THE LOCKER ROOM INTERVIEW, HE ATTACKED MARK LEWEN!
AUSTIN SMASHED LEWEN'S HEAD INTO THE LOCKERS AND THERE WAS BLOOD POURING DOWN HIS FACE!
AW, I MISSED IT BECAUSE MY SISTER WANTED TO WATCH SHINDIG.
DICK LANE WAS INTERVIEWING THEM AND I THOUGHT HE WAS GOING TO FAINT, I SWEAR.
OO!
OO!
THE ANNOUNCER?
CAN'T BELIEVE I MISSED IT.
BLOOD ON T.V.
IT'S NEW NOW.

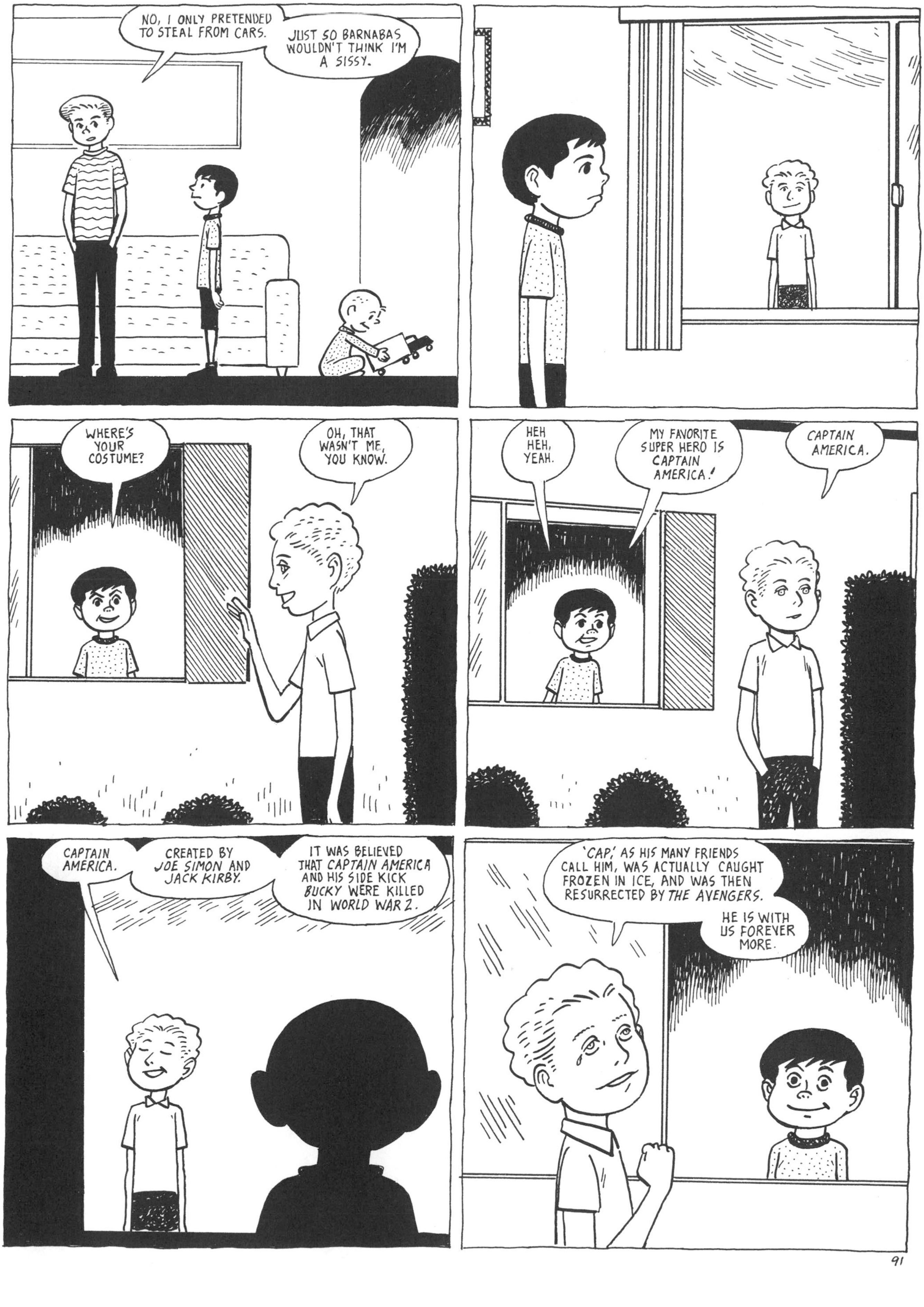
NO, I ONLY PRETENDED TO STEAL FROM CARS.
JUST SO BARNABAS WOULDN'T THINK I'M A SISSY.
WHERE'S YOUR COSTUME?
OH, THAT WASN'T ME, YOU KNOW.
HEH HEH, YEAH.
MY FAVORITE SUPER HERO IS CAPTAIN AMERICA!
CAPTAIN AMERICA.
CAPTAIN AMERICA.
CREATED BY JOE SIMON AND JACK KIRBY.
IT WAS BELIEVED THAT CAPTAIN AMERICA AND HIS SIDE KICK BUCKY WERE KILLED IN WORLD WAR 2.
'CAP,' AS HIS MANY FRIENDS CALL HIM, WAS ACTUALLY CAUGHT FROZEN IN ICE, AND WAS THEN RESURRECTED BY THE AVENGERS.
HE IS WITH US FOREVER MORE.

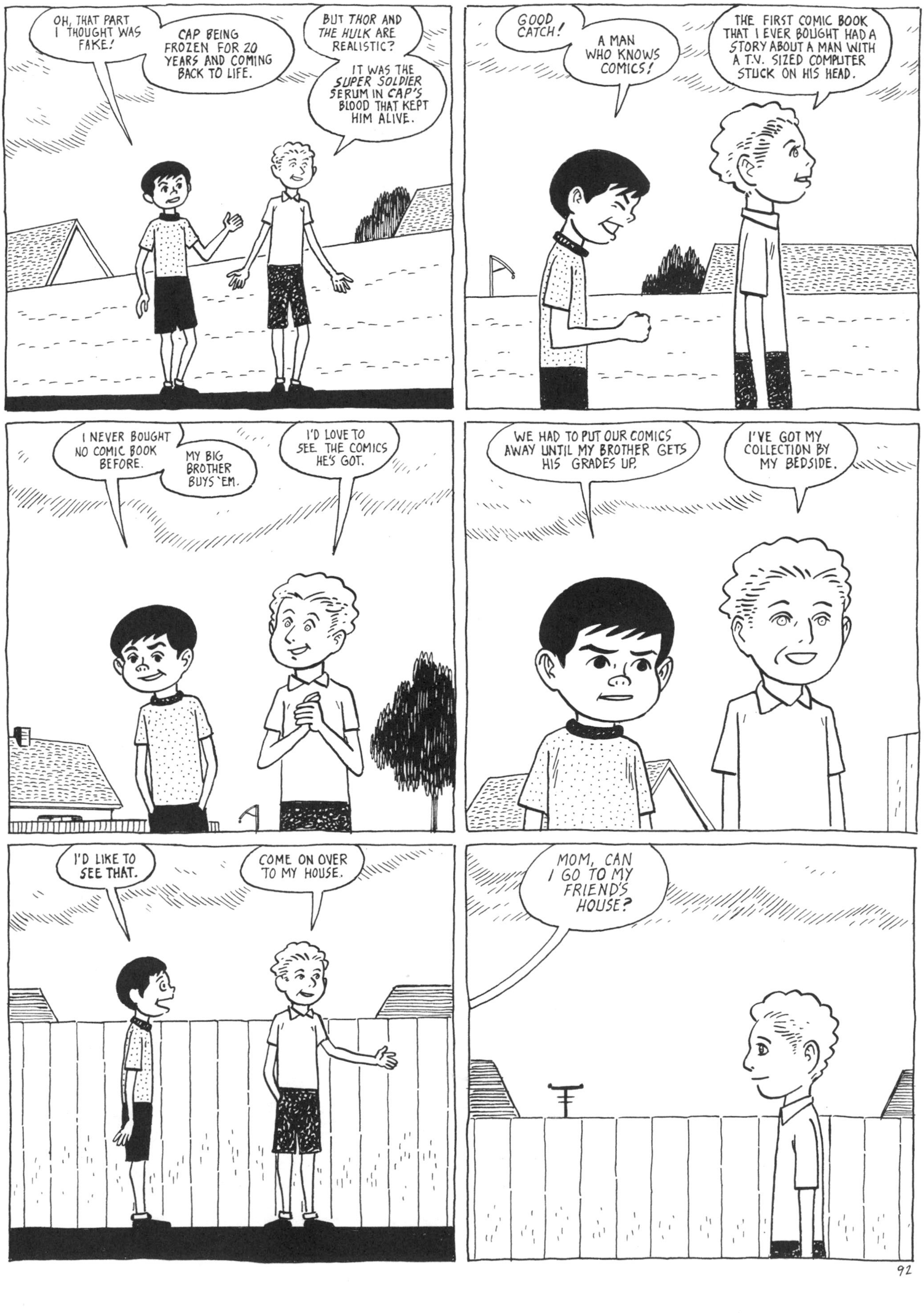
OH, THAT PART I THOUGHT WAS FAKE!
CAP BEING FROZEN FOR 20 YEARS AND COMING BACK TO LIFE.
BUT THOR AND THE HULK ARE REALISTIC?
IT WAS THE SUPER SOLDIER SERUM IN CAP'S BLOOD THAT KEPT HIM ALIVE.
GOOD CATCH!
A MAN WHO KNOWS COMICS!
THE FIRST COMIC BOOK THAT I EVER BOUGHT HAD A STORY ABOUT A MAN WITH A T.V. SIZED COMPUTER STUCK ON HIS HEAD.
I NEVER BOUGHT NO COMIC BOOK BEFORE.
MY BIG BROTHER BUYS 'EM.
I'D LOVE TO SEE THE COMICS HE'S GOT.
WE HAD TO PUT OUR COMICS AWAY UNTIL MY BROTHER GETS HIS GRADES UP.
I'VE GOT MY COLLECTION BY MY BEDSIDE.
I'D LIKE TO SEE THAT.
COME ON OVER TO MY HOUSE.
MOM, CAN I GO TO MY FRIEND'S HOUSE?

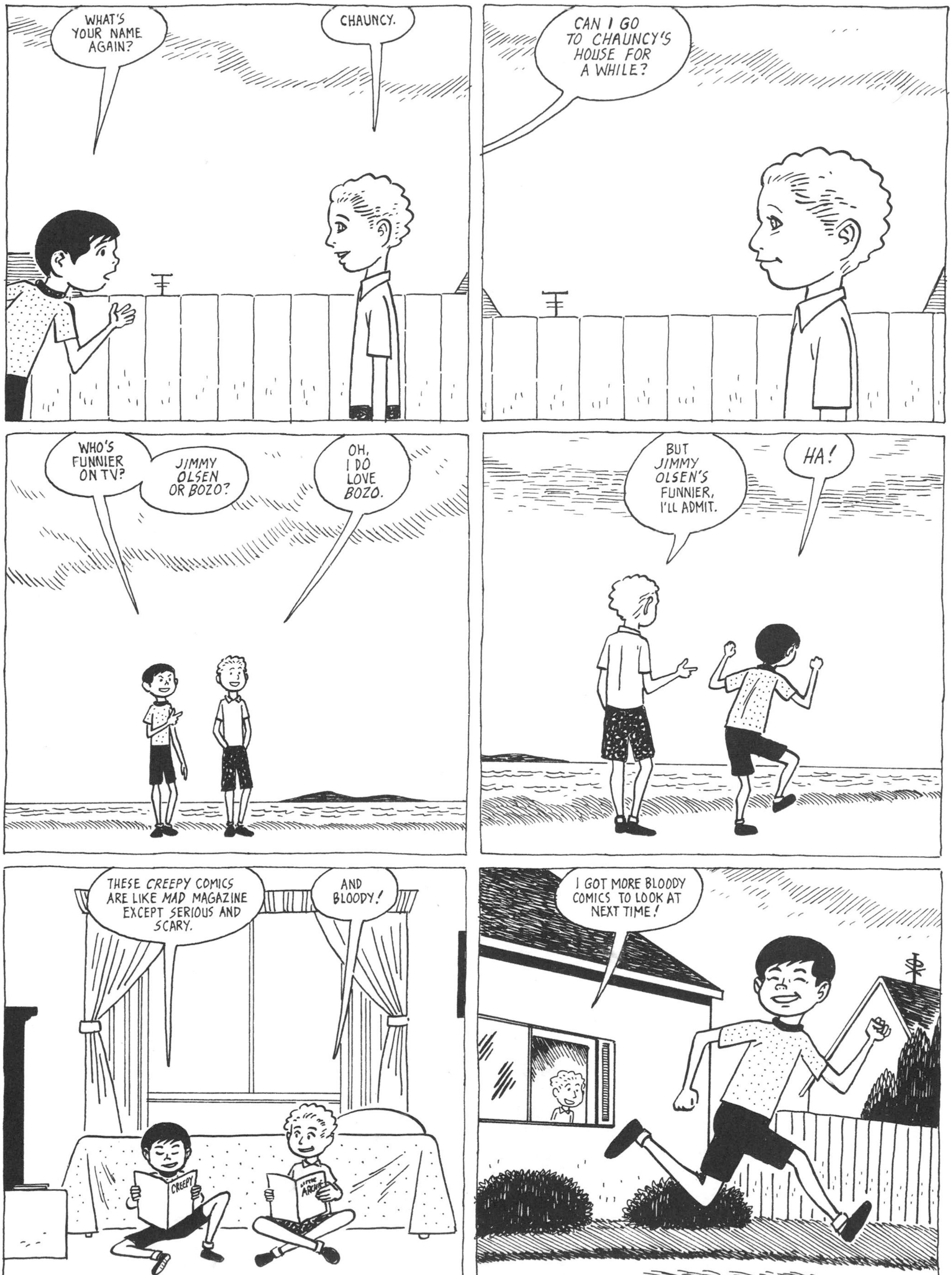
WHAT'S YOUR NAME AGAIN?
CHAUNCY.
CAN I GO TO CHAUNCY'S HOUSE FOR A WHILE?
WHO'S FUNNIER ON TV?
JIMMY OLSEN OR BOZO?
OH, I DO LOVE BOZO.
BUT JIMMY OLSEN'S FUNNIER, I'LL ADMIT.
HA!
THESE CREEPY COMICS ARE LIKE MAD MAGAZINE EXCEPT SERIOUS AND SCARY.
AND BLOODY!
CREEPY
I GOT MORE BLOODY COMICS TO LOOK AT NEXT TIME!

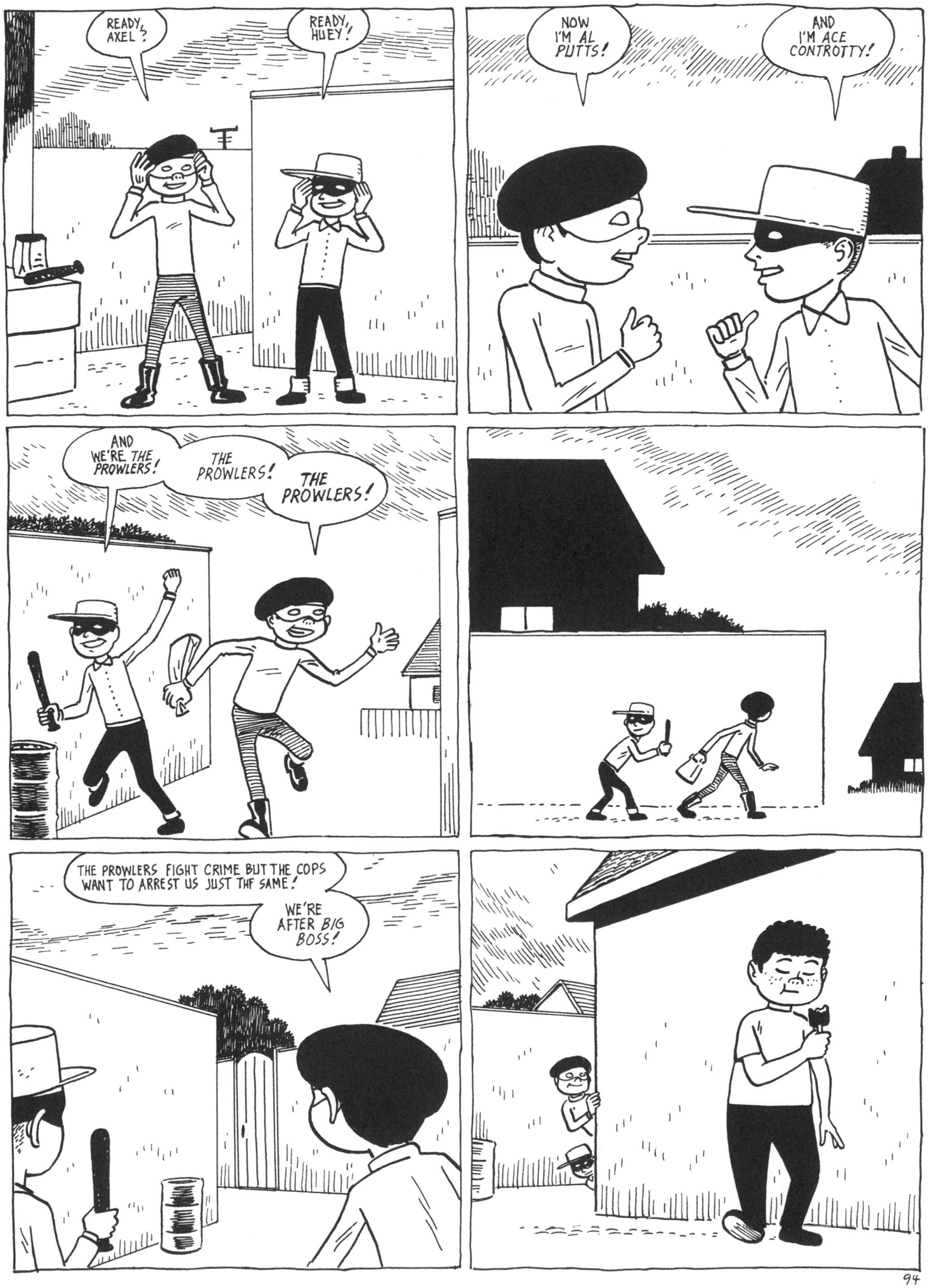
READY, AXEL?
READY, HUEY!
NOW I'M AL PUTTS!
AND I'M ACE CONTROTTY!
AND WE'RE THE PROWLERS!
THE PROWLERS!
THE PROWLERS!
THE PROWLERS FIGHT CRIME BUT THE COPS WANT TO ARREST US JUST THE SAME!
WE'RE AFTER BIG BOSS!

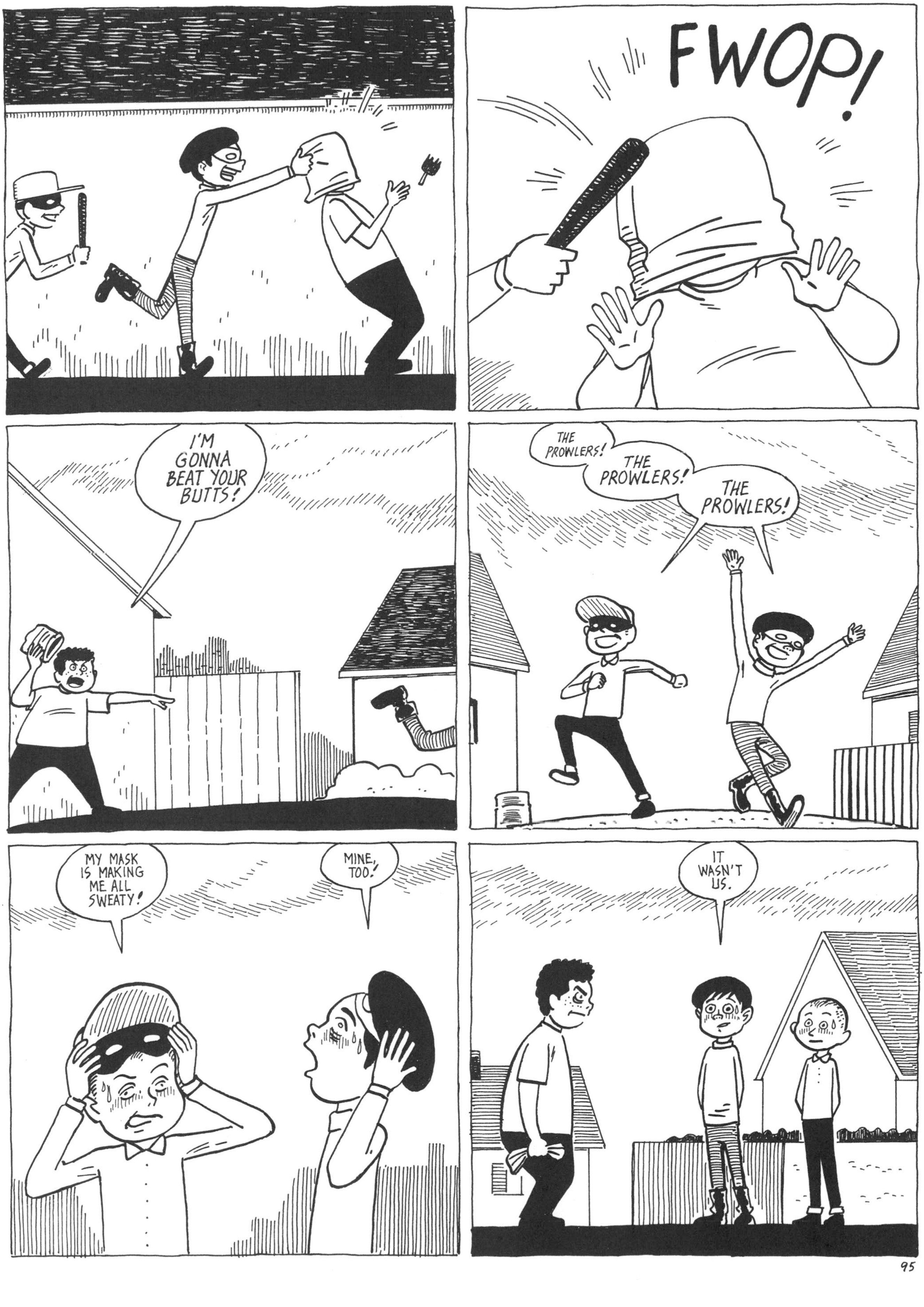
FWOP!
I'M GONNA BEAT YOUR BUTTS!
THE PROWLERS!
THE PROWLERS!
THE PROWLERS!
MY MASK IS MAKING ME ALL SWEATY!
MINE, TOO!
IT WASN'T US.

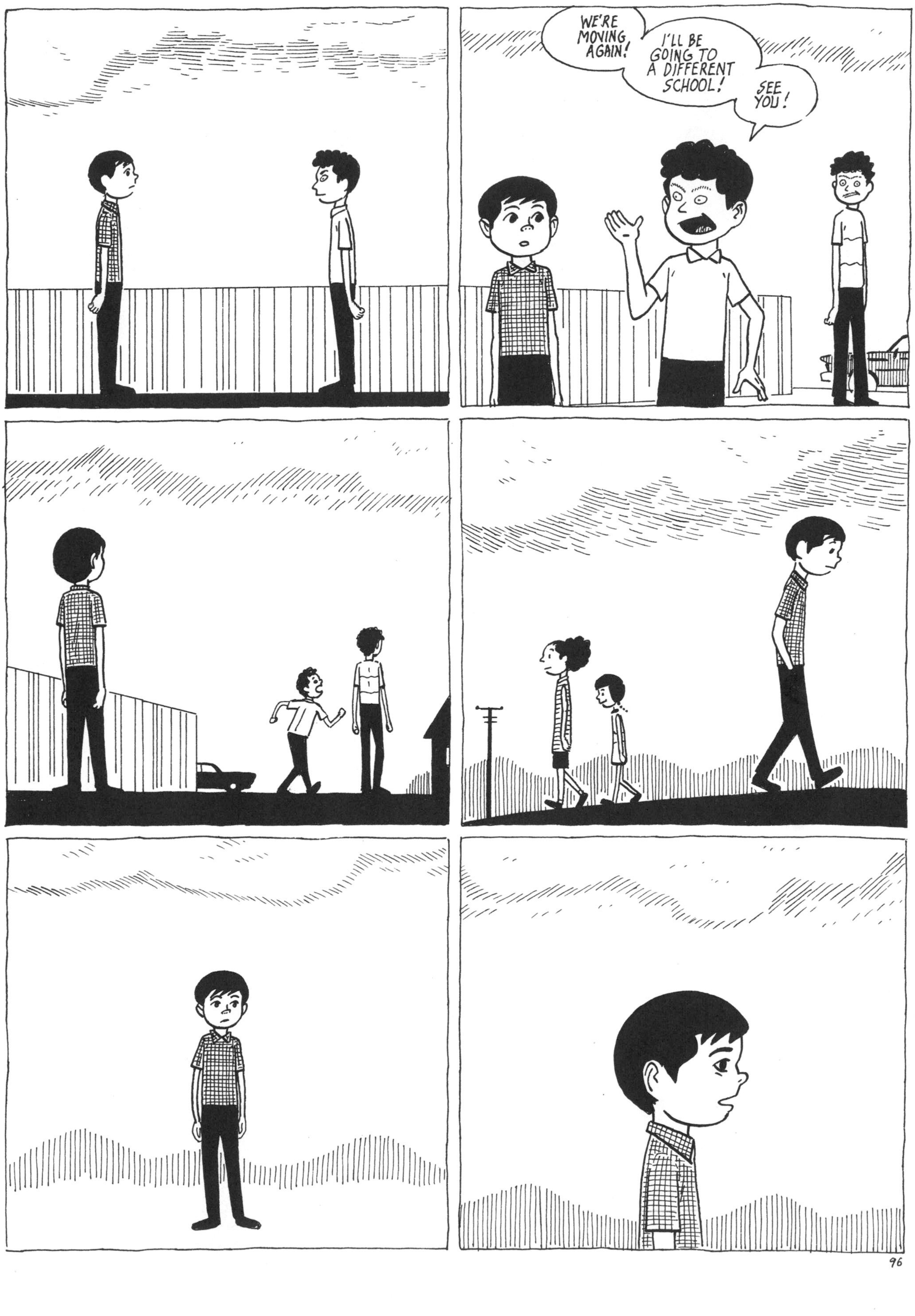
WE'RE MOVING AGAIN!
I'LL BE GOING TO A DIFFERENT SCHOOL!
SEE YOU!

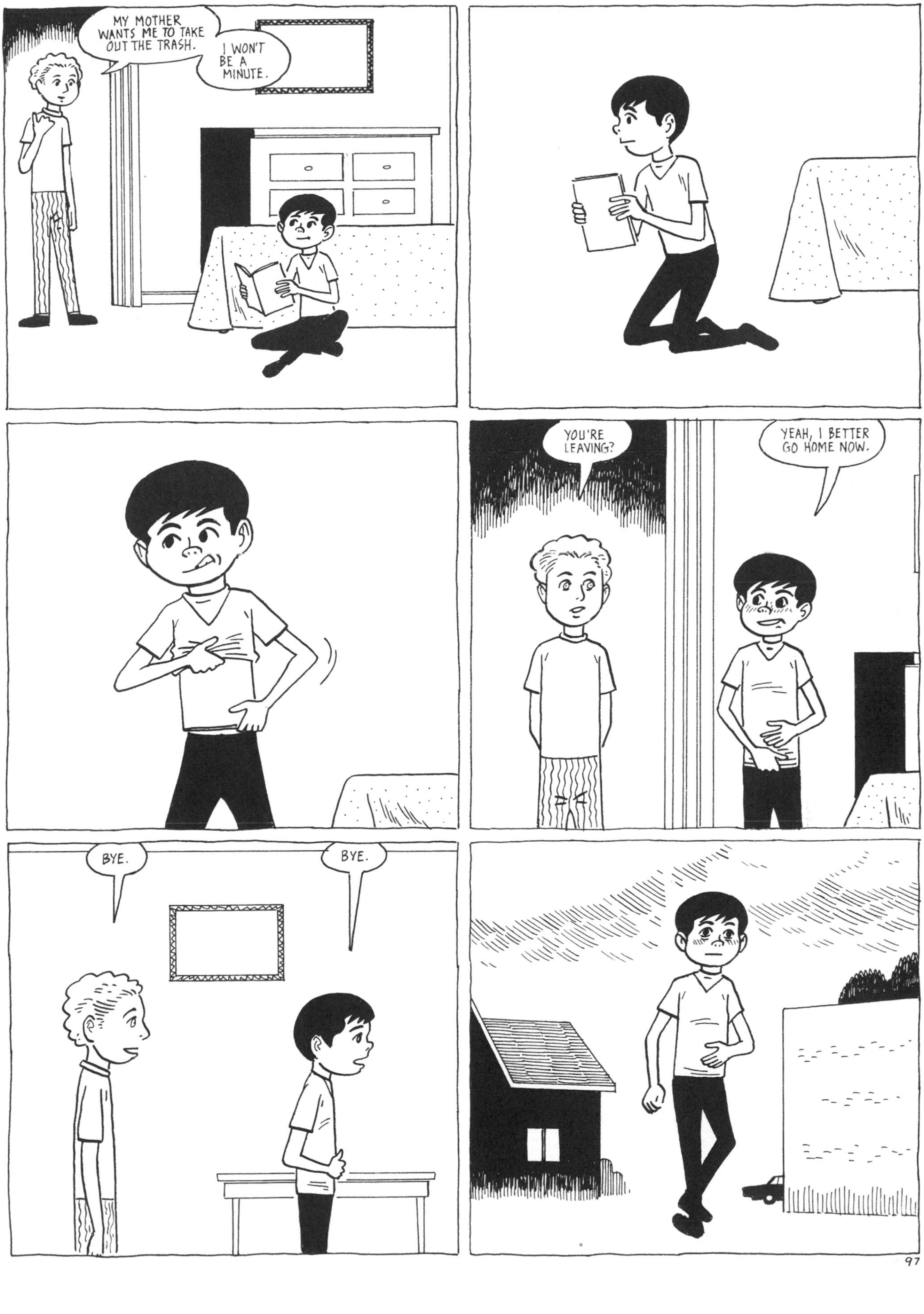
MY MOTHER WANTS ME TO TAKE OUT THE TRASH.
I WON'T BE A MINUTE.
YOU'RE LEAVING?
YEAH, I BETTER GO HOME NOW.
BYE.
BYE.

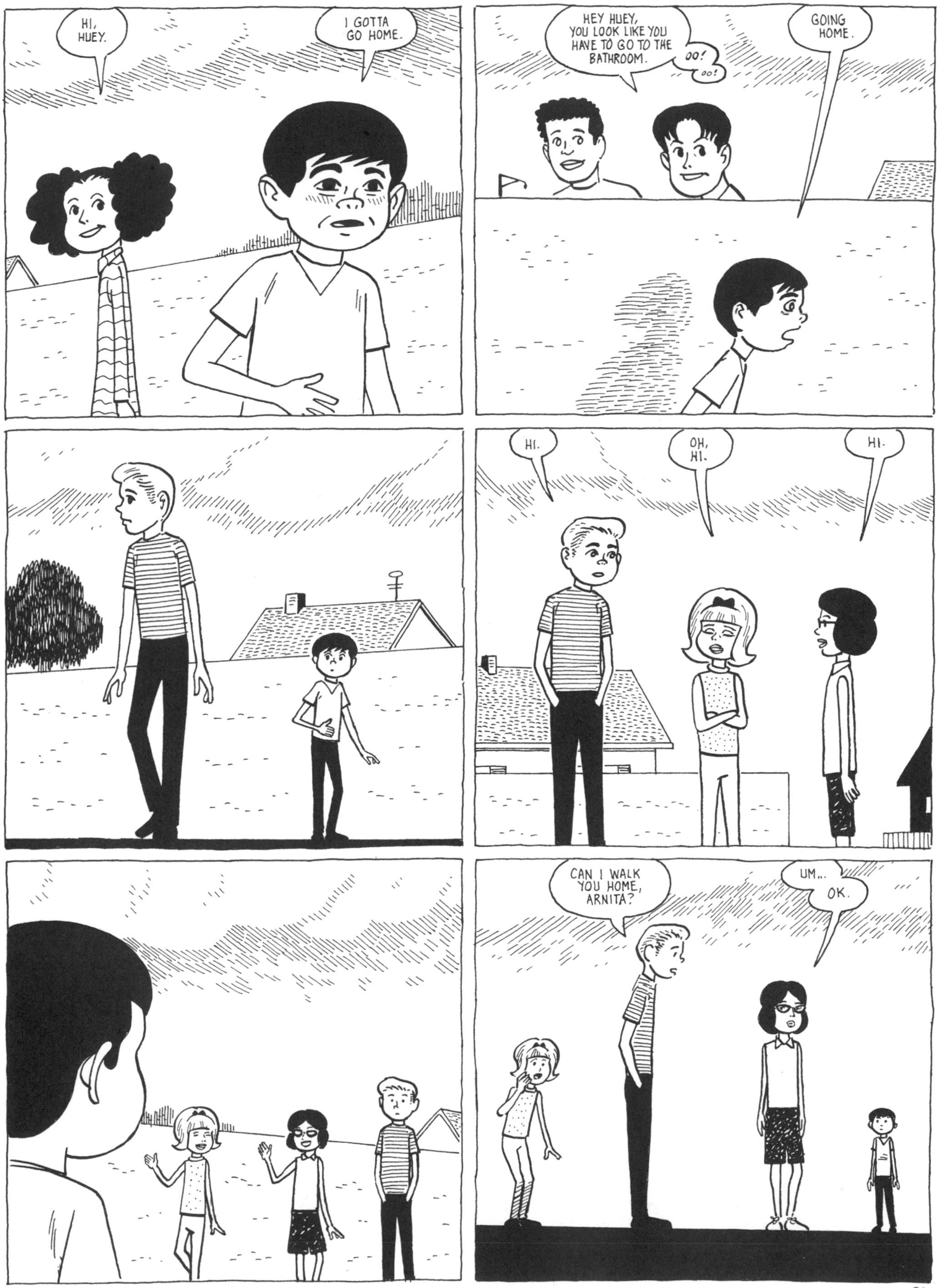

HI, HUEY.
I GOTTA GO HOME.
HEY HUEY, YOU LOOK LIKE YOU HAVE TO GO TO THE BATHROOM.
OO! OO!
GOING HOME.
HI.
OH, HI.
HI.
CAN I WALK YOU HOME, ARNITA?
UM... OK.

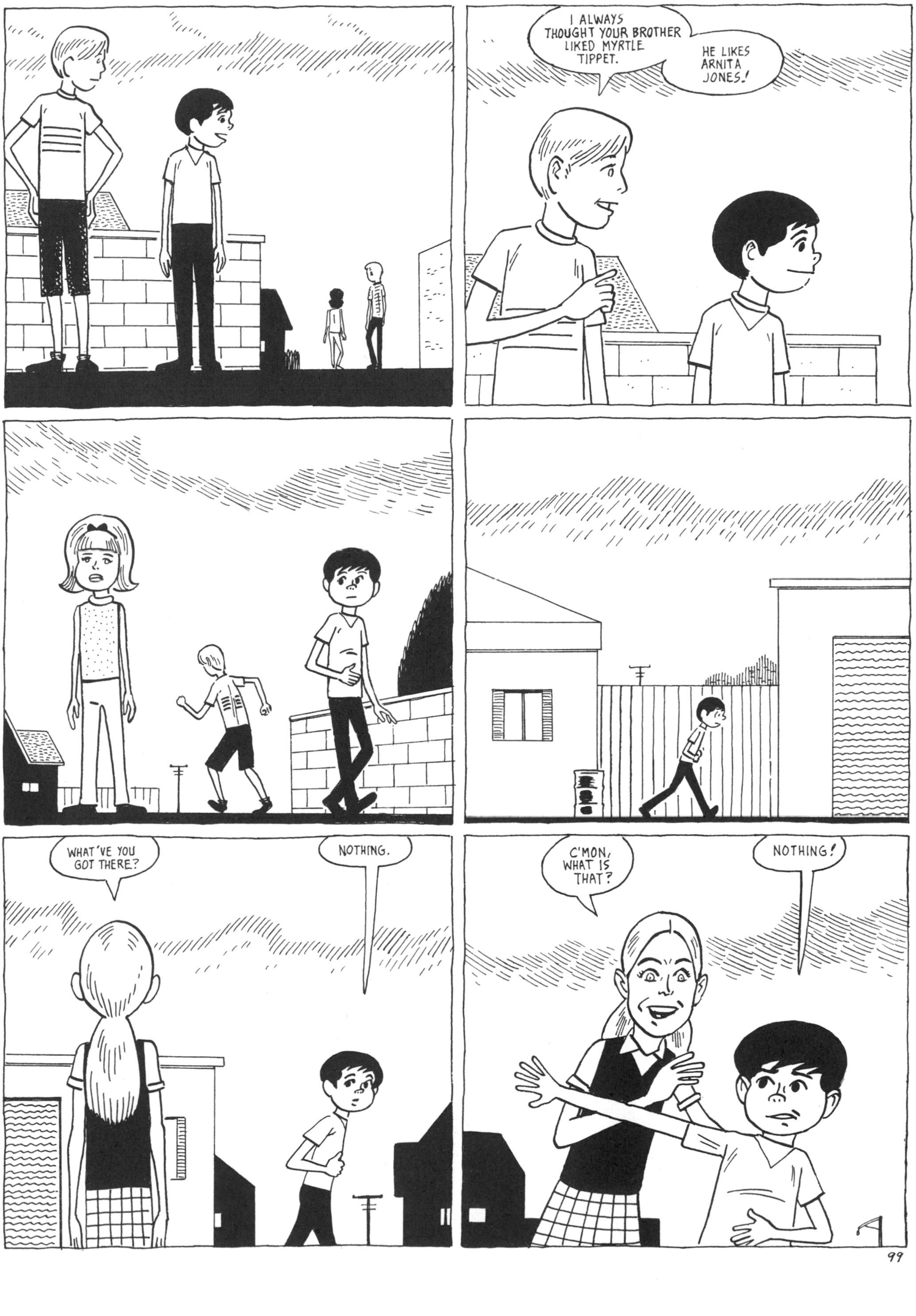
I ALWAYS THOUGHT YOUR BROTHER LIKED MYRTLE TIPPET.
HE LIKES ARNITA JONES!
WHAT'VE YOU GOT THERE?
NOTHING.
C'MON, WHAT IS THAT?
NOTHING!

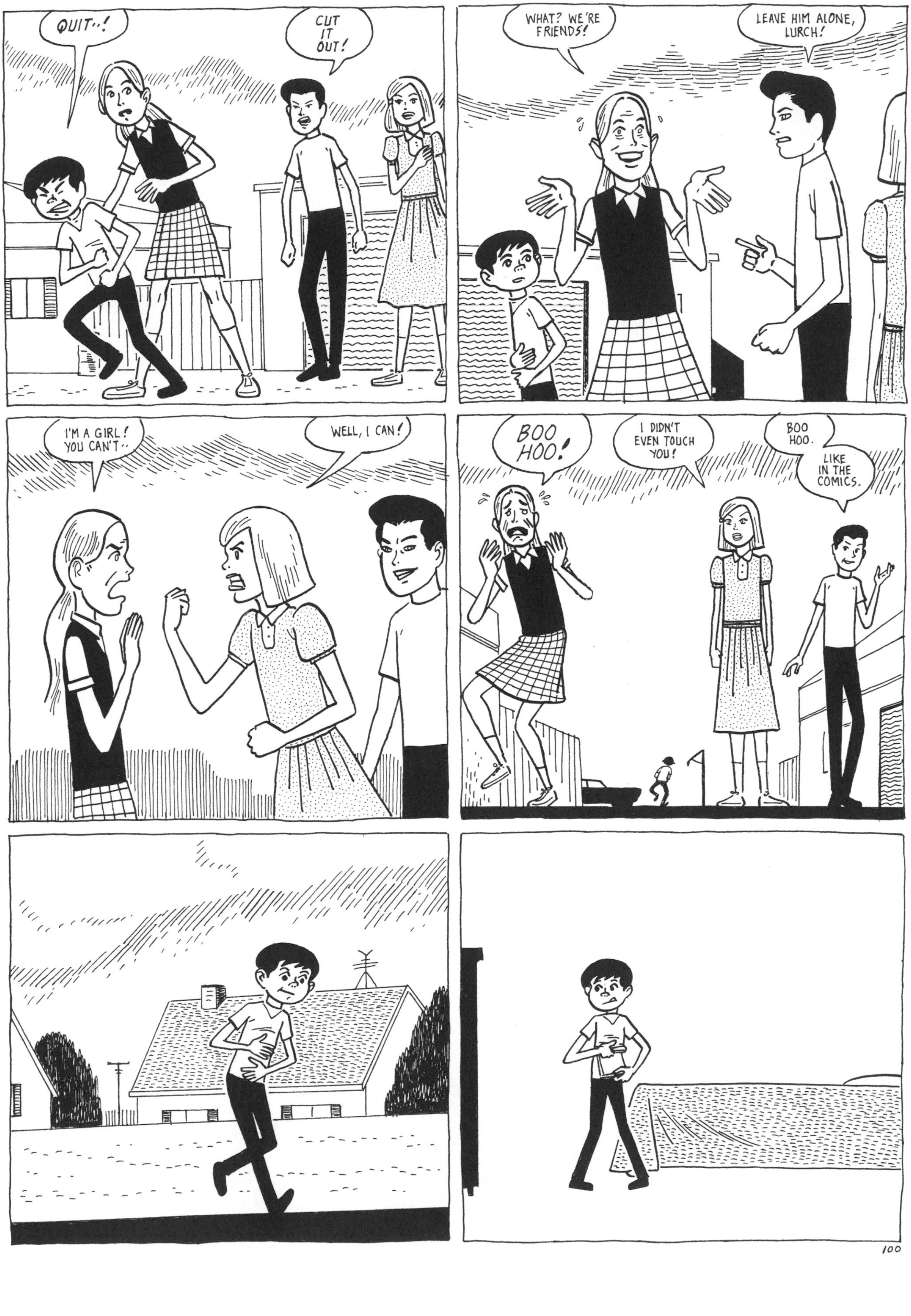
QUIT..!
CUT IT OUT!
WHAT? WE'RE FRIENDS!
LEAVE HIM ALONE, LURCH!
I'M A GIRL! YOU CAN'T..
WELL, I CAN!
BOO HOO!
I DIDN'T EVEN TOUCH YOU!
BOO HOO.
LIKE IN THE COMICS.

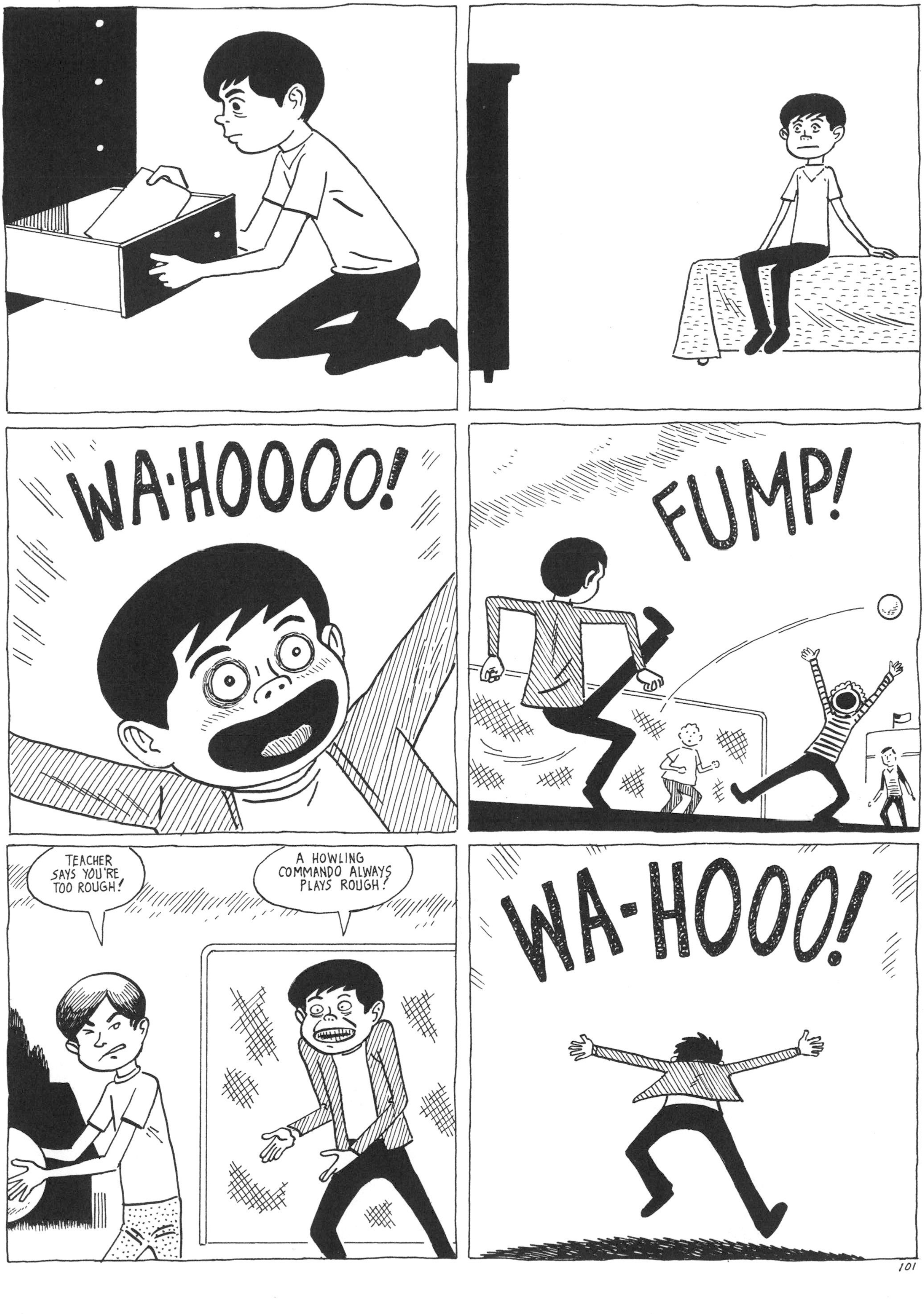
WA-HOOOO!
FUMP!
TEACHER SAYS YOU'RE TOO ROUGH!
A HOWLING COMMANDO ALWAYS PLAYS ROUGH!
WA-HOOO!

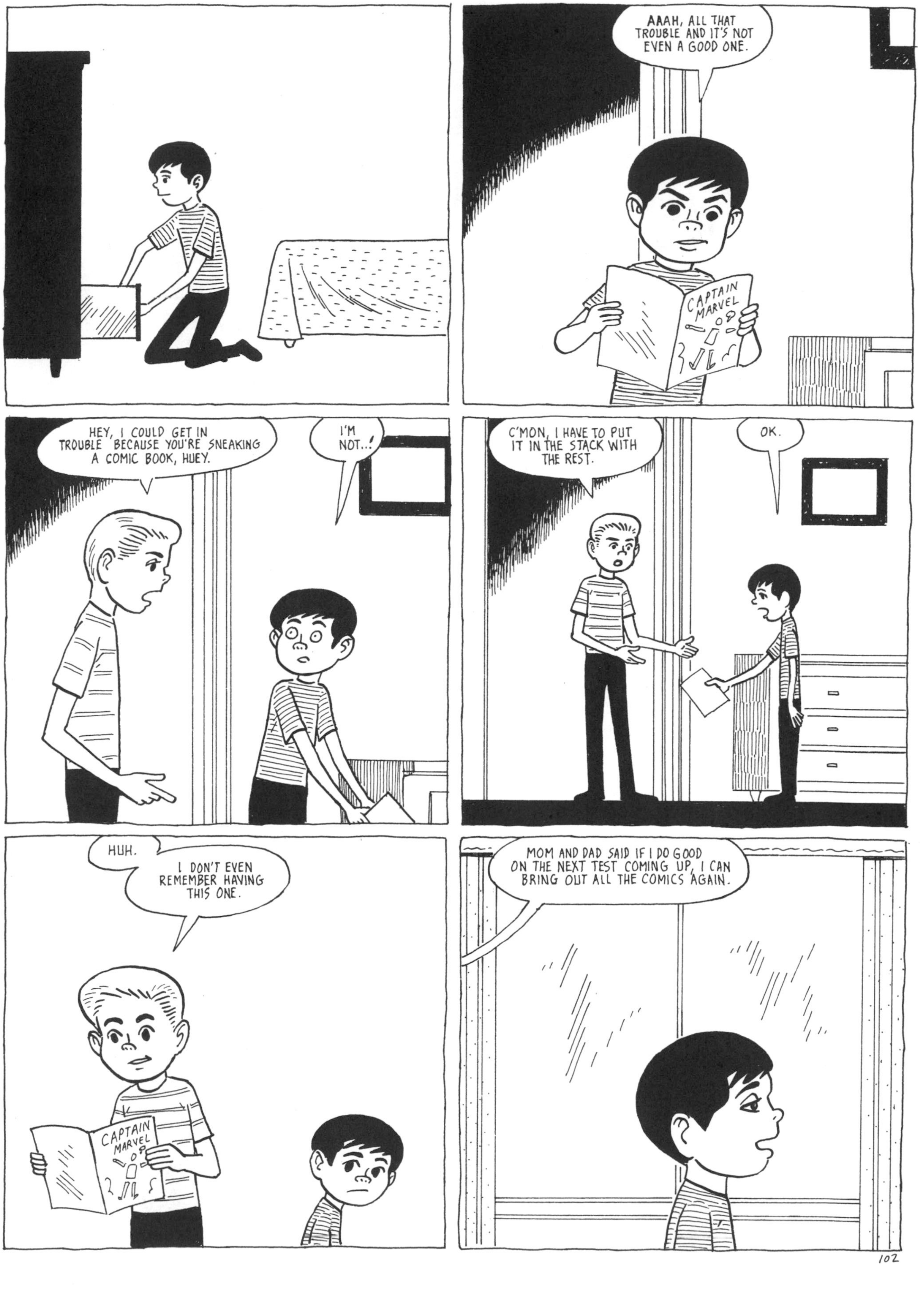
AAAH, ALL THAT TROUBLE AND IT'S NOT EVEN A GOOD ONE.
CAPTAIN MARVEL
HEY, I COULD GET IN TROUBLE BECAUSE YOU'RE SNEAKING A COMIC BOOK, HUEY.
I'M NOT...!
C'MON, I HAVE TO PUT IT IN THE STACK WITH THE REST.
OK.
HUH.
I DON'T EVEN REMEMBER HAVING THIS ONE.
CAPTAIN MARVEL
MOM AND DAD SAID IF I DO GOOD ON THE NEXT TEST COMING UP, I CAN BRING OUT ALL THE COMICS AGAIN.

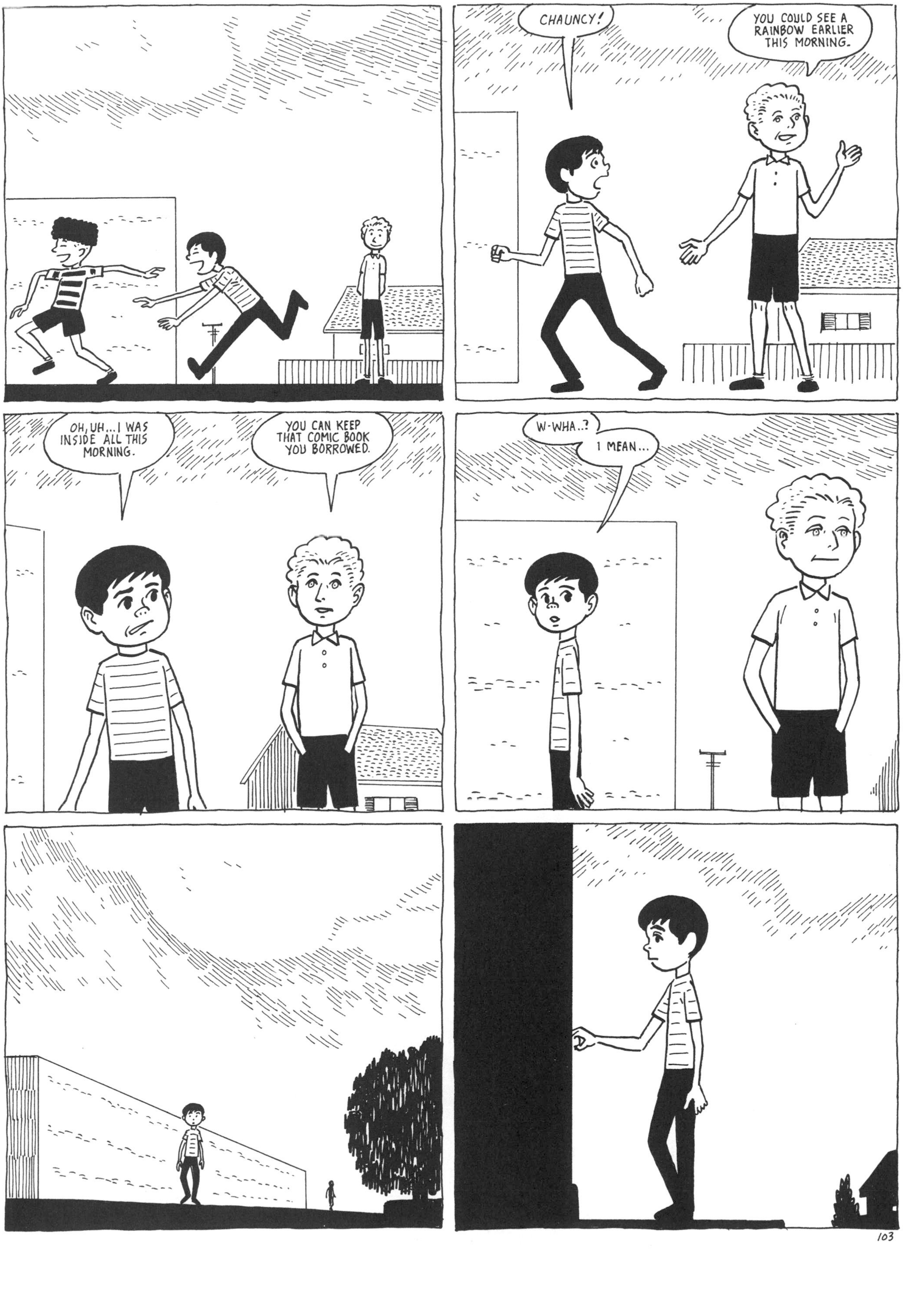
CHAUNCY!
YOU COULD SEE A RAINBOW EARLIER THIS MORNING.
OH, UH...I WAS INSIDE ALL THIS MORNING.
YOU CAN KEEP THAT COMIC BOOK YOU BORROWED.
W-WHA..?
I MEAN...

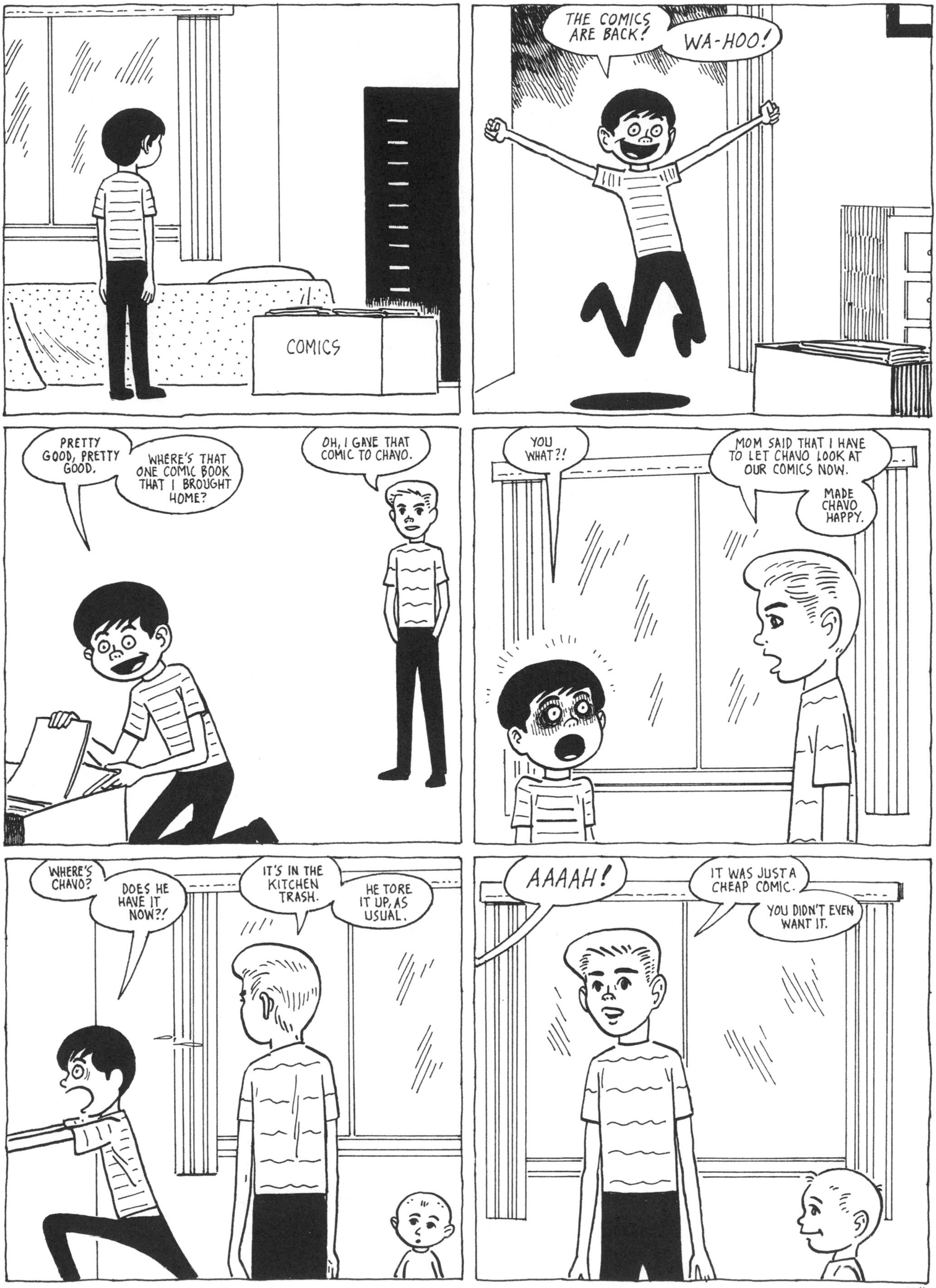

COMICS
THE COMICS ARE BACK!
WA-HOO!
PRETTY GOOD, PRETTY GOOD.
WHERE'S THAT ONE COMIC BOOK THAT I BROUGHT HOME?
OH, I GAVE THAT COMIC TO CHAVO.
YOU WHAT?!
MOM SAID THAT I HAVE TO LET CHAVO LOOK AT OUR COMICS NOW.
MADE CHAVO HAPPY.
WHERE'S CHAVO?
DOES HE HAVE IT NOW?!
IT'S IN THE KITCHEN TRASH.
HE TORE IT UP, AS USUAL.
AAAAH!
IT WAS JUST A CHEAP COMIC.
YOU DIDN'T EVEN WANT IT.

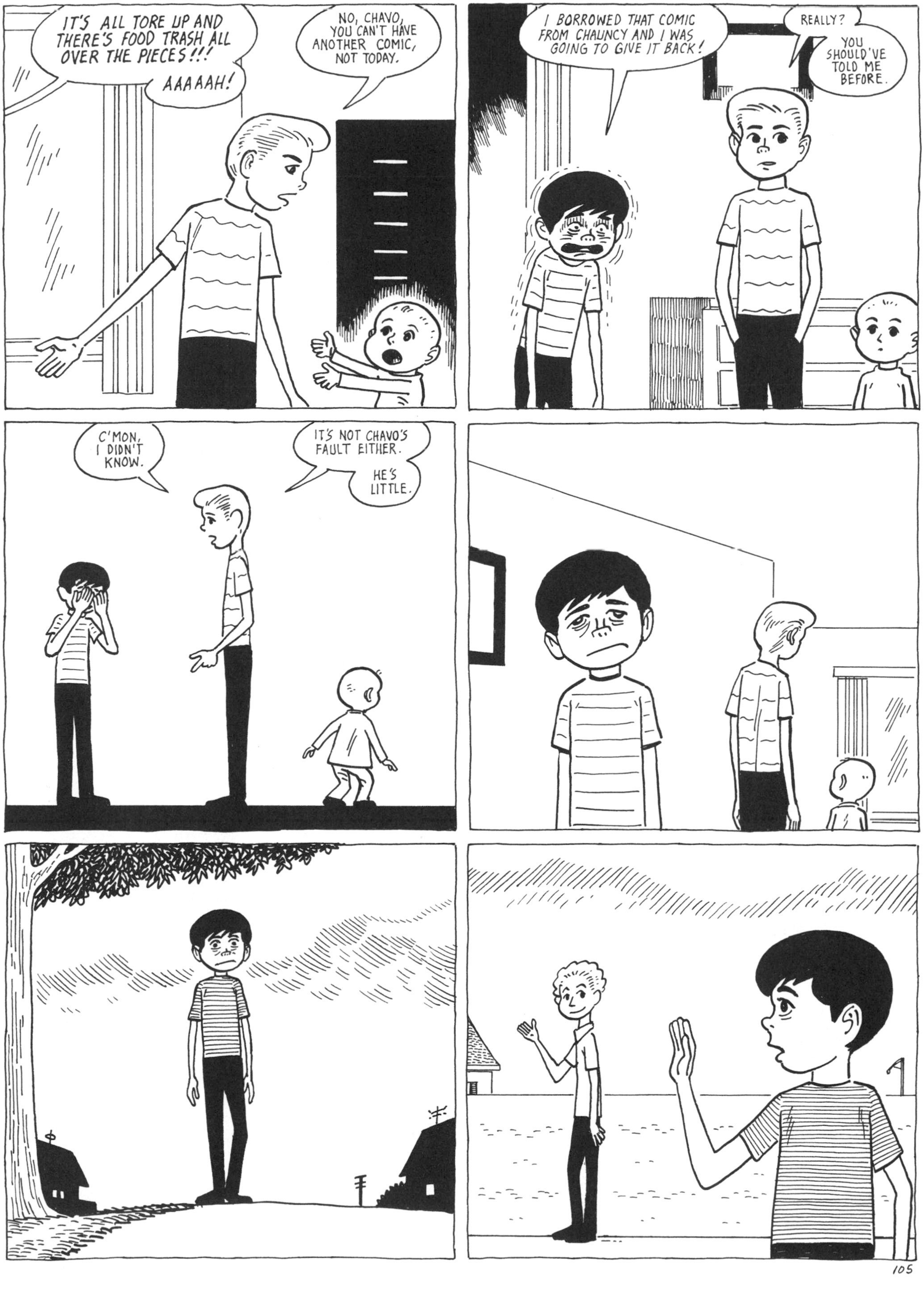

IT'S ALL TORE UP AND THERE'S FOOD TRASH ALL OVER THE PIECES!!!
AAAAAH!
NO, CHAVO, YOU CAN'T HAVE ANOTHER COMIC, NOT TODAY.
I BORROWED THAT COMIC FROM CHAUNCY AND I WAS GOING TO GIVE IT BACK!
REALLY?
YOU SHOULD'VE TOLD ME BEFORE.
C'MON, I DIDN'T KNOW.
IT'S NOT CHAVO'S FAULT EITHER.
HE'S LITTLE.

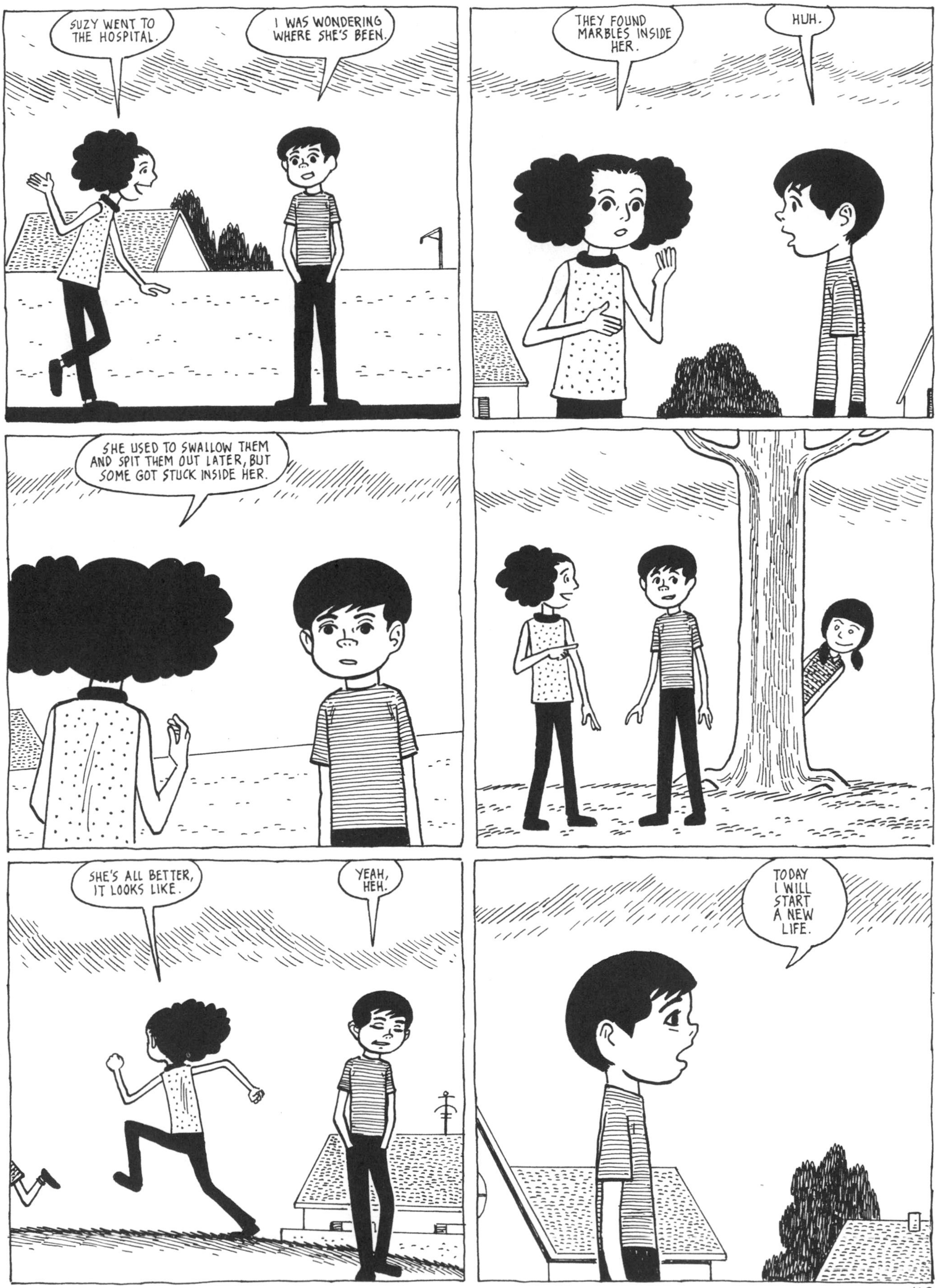
SUZY WENT TO THE HOSPITAL.
I WAS WONDERING WHERE SHE'S BEEN.
THEY FOUND MARBLES INSIDE HER.
HUH.
SHE USED TO SWALLOW THEM AND SPIT THEM OUT LATER, BUT SOME GOT STUCK INSIDE HER.
SHE'S ALL BETTER, IT LOOKS LIKE.
YEAH, HEH.
TODAY I WILL START A NEW LIFE.

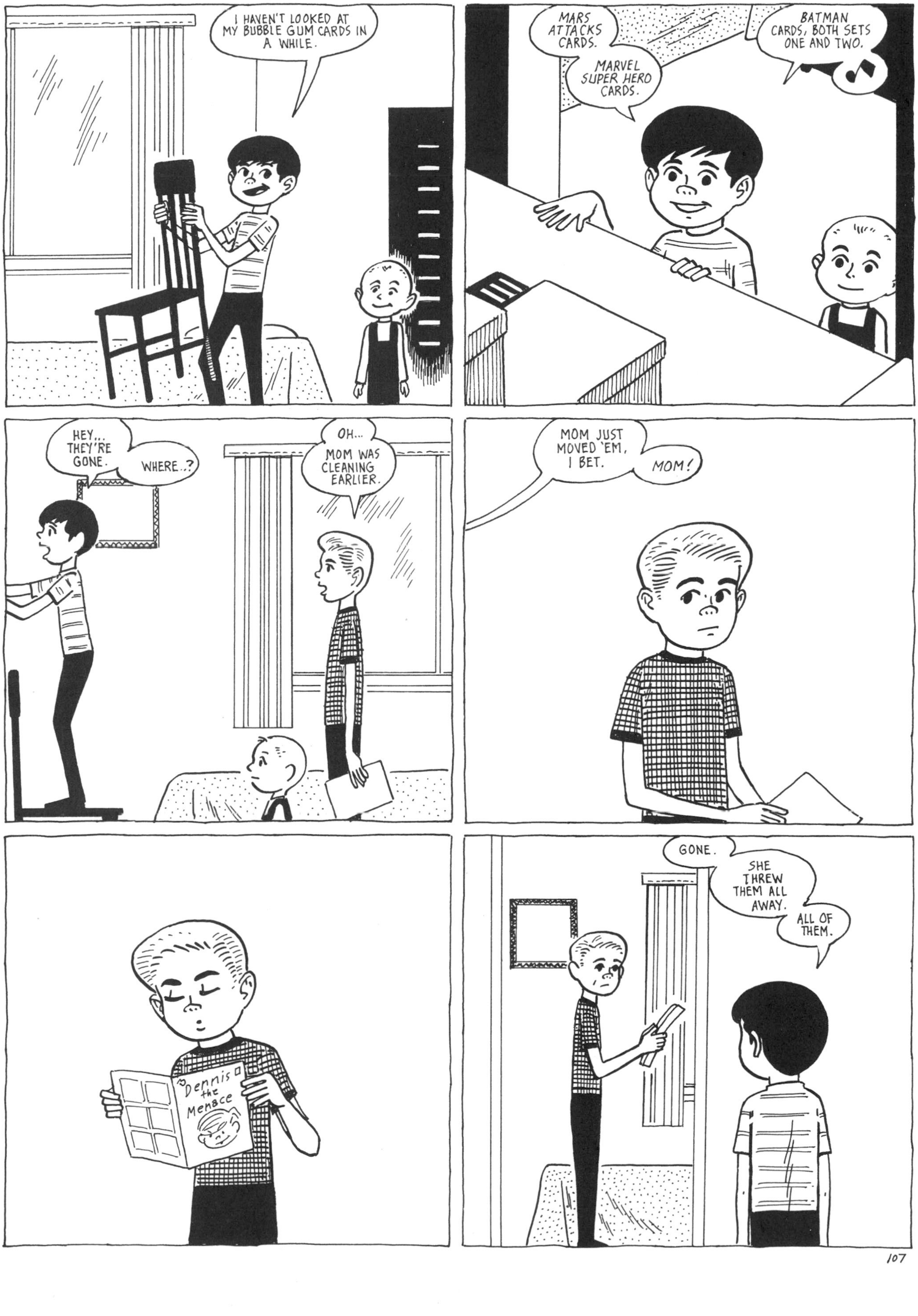
I HAVEN'T LOOKED AT MY BUBBLE GUM CARDS IN A WHILE.
MARS ATTACKS CARDS.
MARVEL SUPER HERO CARDS.
BATMAN CARDS, BOTH SETS ONE AND TWO.
HEY... THEY'RE GONE.
WHERE..?
OH... MOM WAS CLEANING EARLIER.
MOM JUST MOVED 'EM, I BET.
MOM!
Dennis the Menace
GONE.
SHE THREW THEM ALL AWAY.
ALL OF THEM.

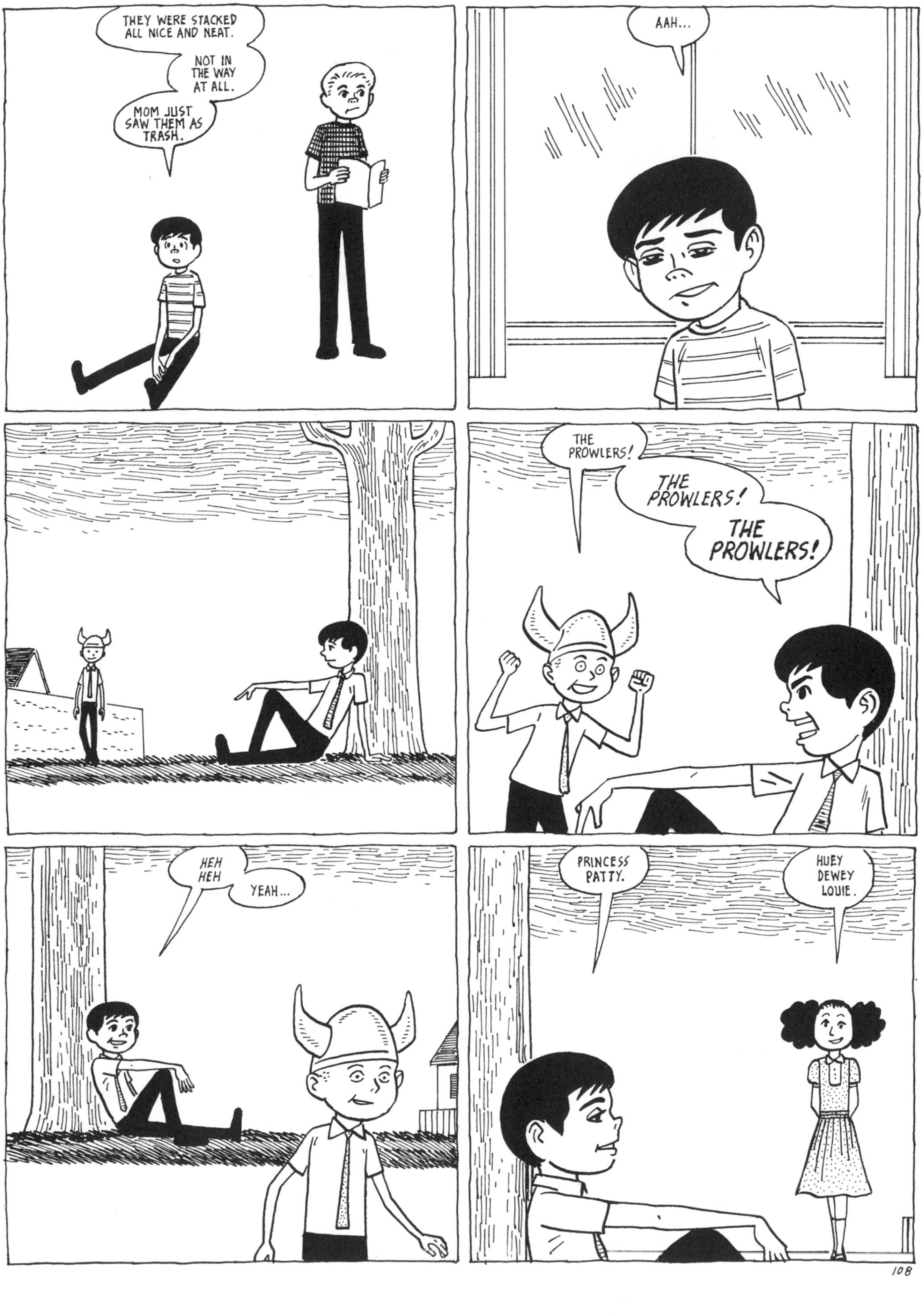
THEY WERE STACKED ALL NICE AND NEAT.
NOT IN THE WAY AT ALL.
MOM JUST SAW THEM AS TRASH.
AAH...
THE PROWLERS!
THE PROWLERS!
THE PROWLERS!
HEH HEH
YEAH...
PRINCESS PATTY.
HUEY DEWEY LOUIE.

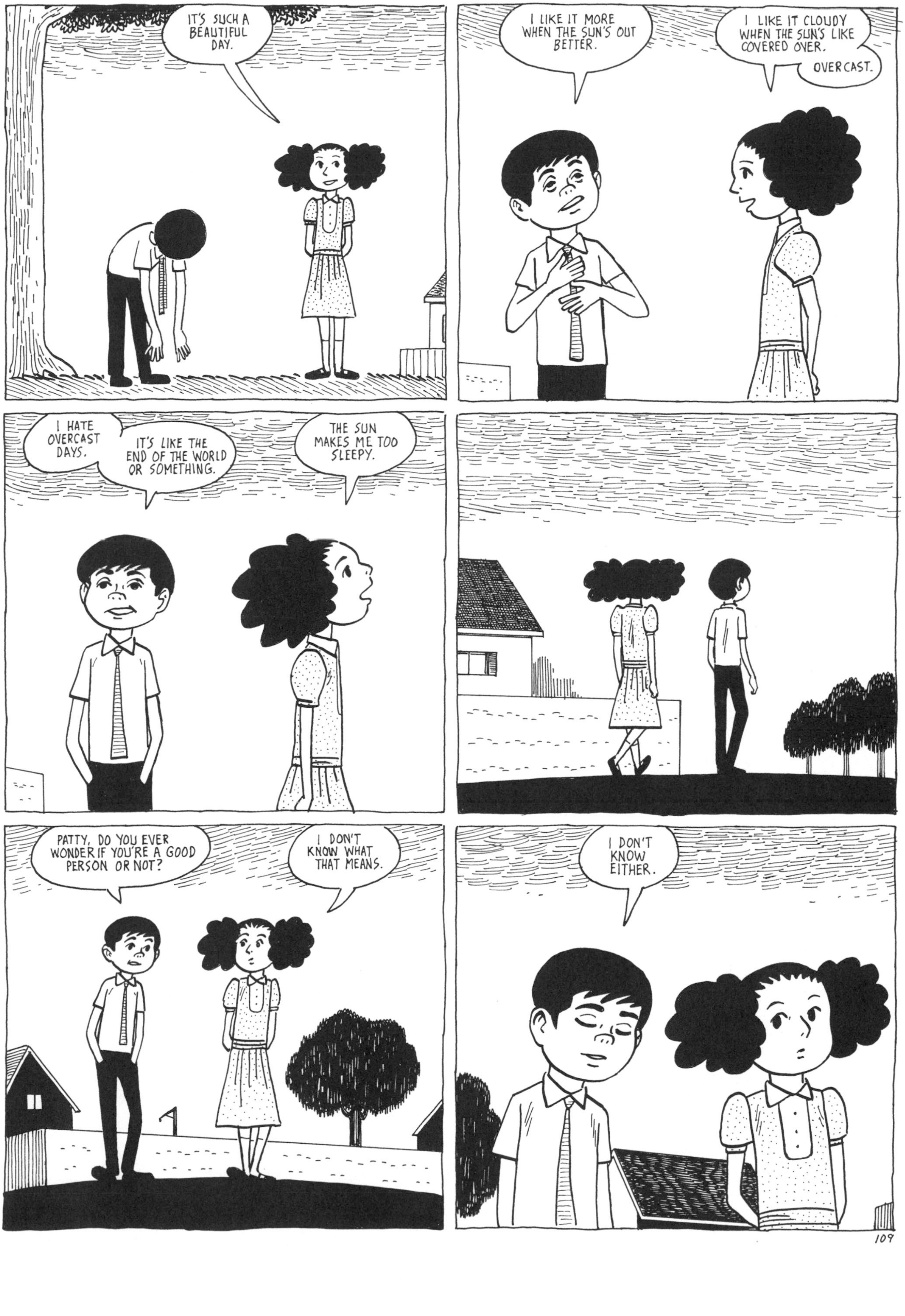
IT'S SUCH A BEAUTIFUL DAY.
I LIKE IT MORE WHEN THE SUN'S OUT BETTER.
I LIKE IT CLOUDY WHEN THE SUN'S LIKE COVERED OVER.
OVERCAST.
I HATE OVERCAST DAYS.
IT'S LIKE THE END OF THE WORLD OR SOMETHING.
THE SUN MAKES ME TOO SLEEPY.
PATTY, DO YOU EVER WONDER IF YOU'RE A GOOD PERSON OR NOT?
I DON'T KNOW WHAT THAT MEANS.
I DON'T KNOW EITHER.

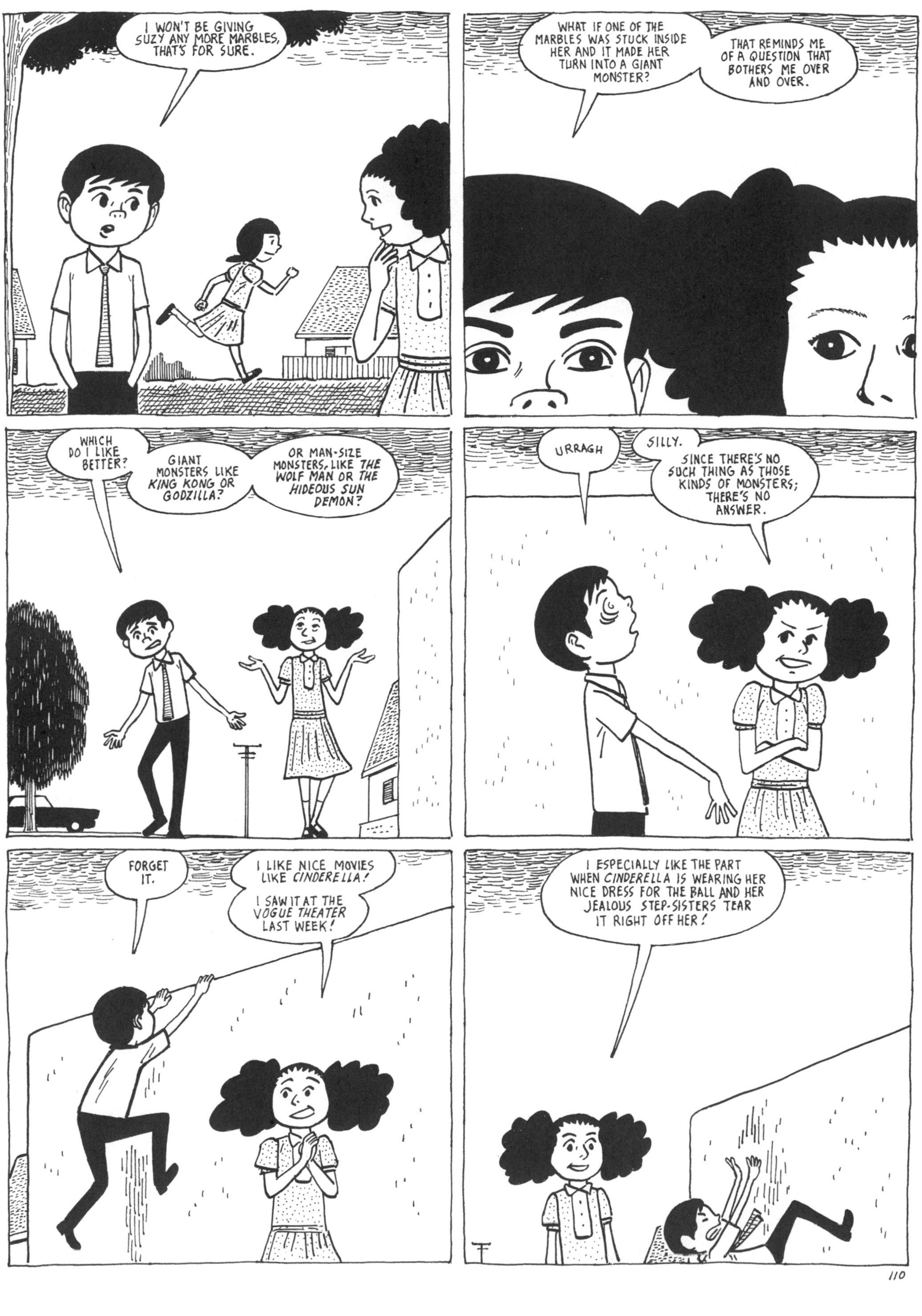
I WON'T BE GIVING SUZY ANY MORE MARBLES, THAT'S FOR SURE.
WHAT IF ONE OF THE MARBLES WAS STUCK INSIDE HER AND IT MADE HER TURN INTO A GIANT MONSTER?
THAT REMINDS ME OF A QUESTION THAT BOTHERS ME OVER AND OVER.
WHICH DO I LIKE BETTER?
GIANT MONSTERS LIKE KING KONG OR GODZILLA?
OR MAN-SIZE MONSTERS, LIKE THE WOLF MAN OR THE HIDEOUS SUN DEMON?
URRAGH
SILLY.
SINCE THERE'S NO SUCH THING AS THOSE KINDS OF MONSTERS; THERE'S NO ANSWER.
FORGET IT.
I LIKE NICE MOVIES LIKE CINDERELLA!
I SAW IT AT THE VOGUE THEATER LAST WEEK!
I ESPECIALLY LIKE THE PART WHEN CINDERELLA IS WEARING HER NICE DRESS FOR THE BALL AND HER JEALOUS STEP-SISTERS TEAR IT RIGHT OFF HER!

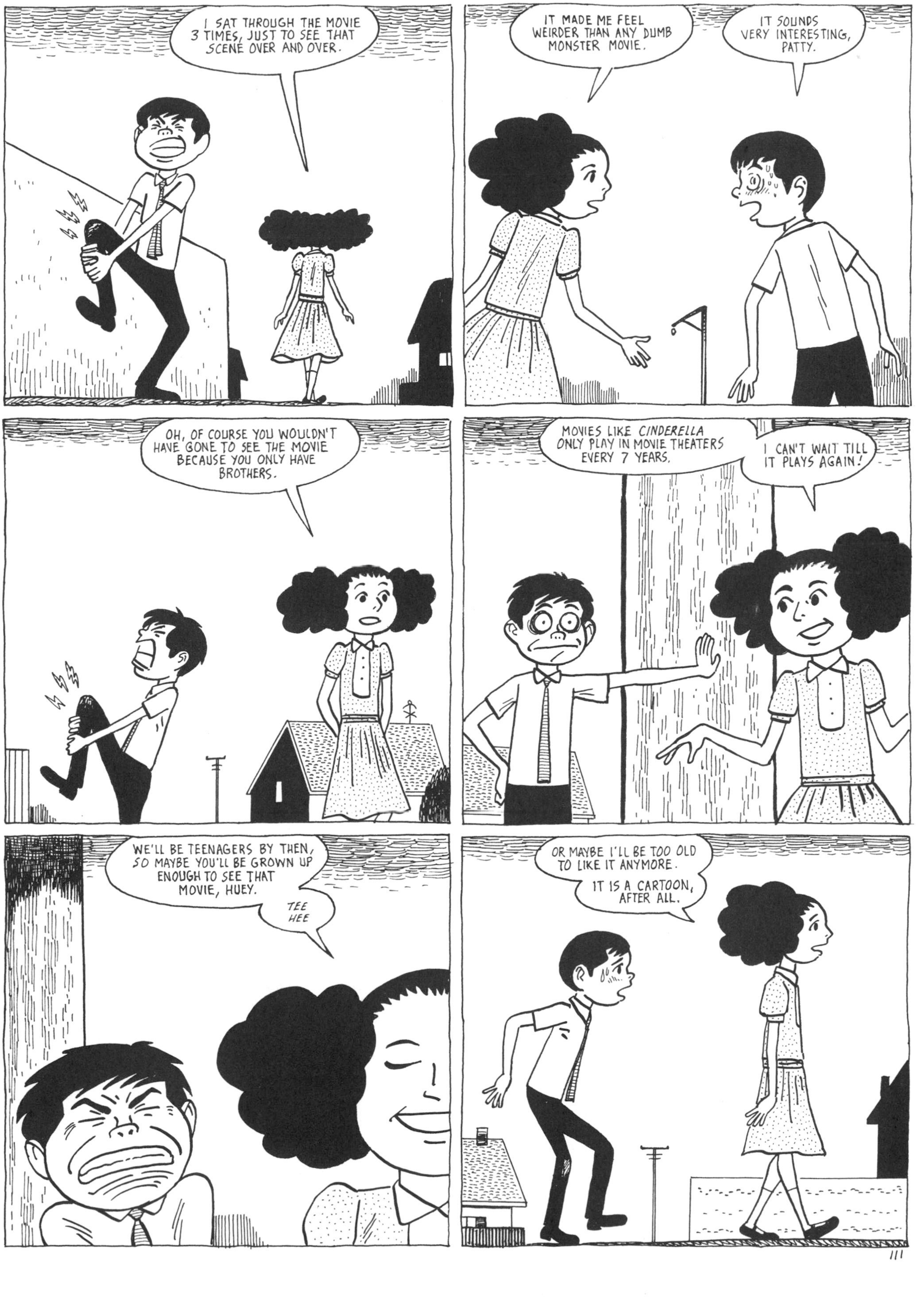
I SAT THROUGH THE MOVIE 3 TIMES, JUST TO SEE THAT SCENE OVER AND OVER.
IT MADE ME FEEL WEIRDER THAN ANY DUMB MONSTER MOVIE.
IT SOUNDS VERY INTERESTING, PATTY.
OH, OF COURSE YOU WOULDN'T HAVE GONE TO SEE THE MOVIE BECAUSE YOU ONLY HAVE BROTHERS.
MOVIES LIKE CINDERELLA ONLY PLAY IN MOVIE THEATERS EVERY 7 YEARS.
I CAN'T WAIT TILL IT PLAYS AGAIN!
WE'LL BE TEENAGERS BY THEN, SO MAYBE YOU'LL BE GROWN UP ENOUGH TO SEE THAT MOVIE, HUEY.
TEE HEE
OR MAYBE I'LL BE TOO OLD TO LIKE IT ANYMORE.
IT IS A CARTOON, AFTER ALL.

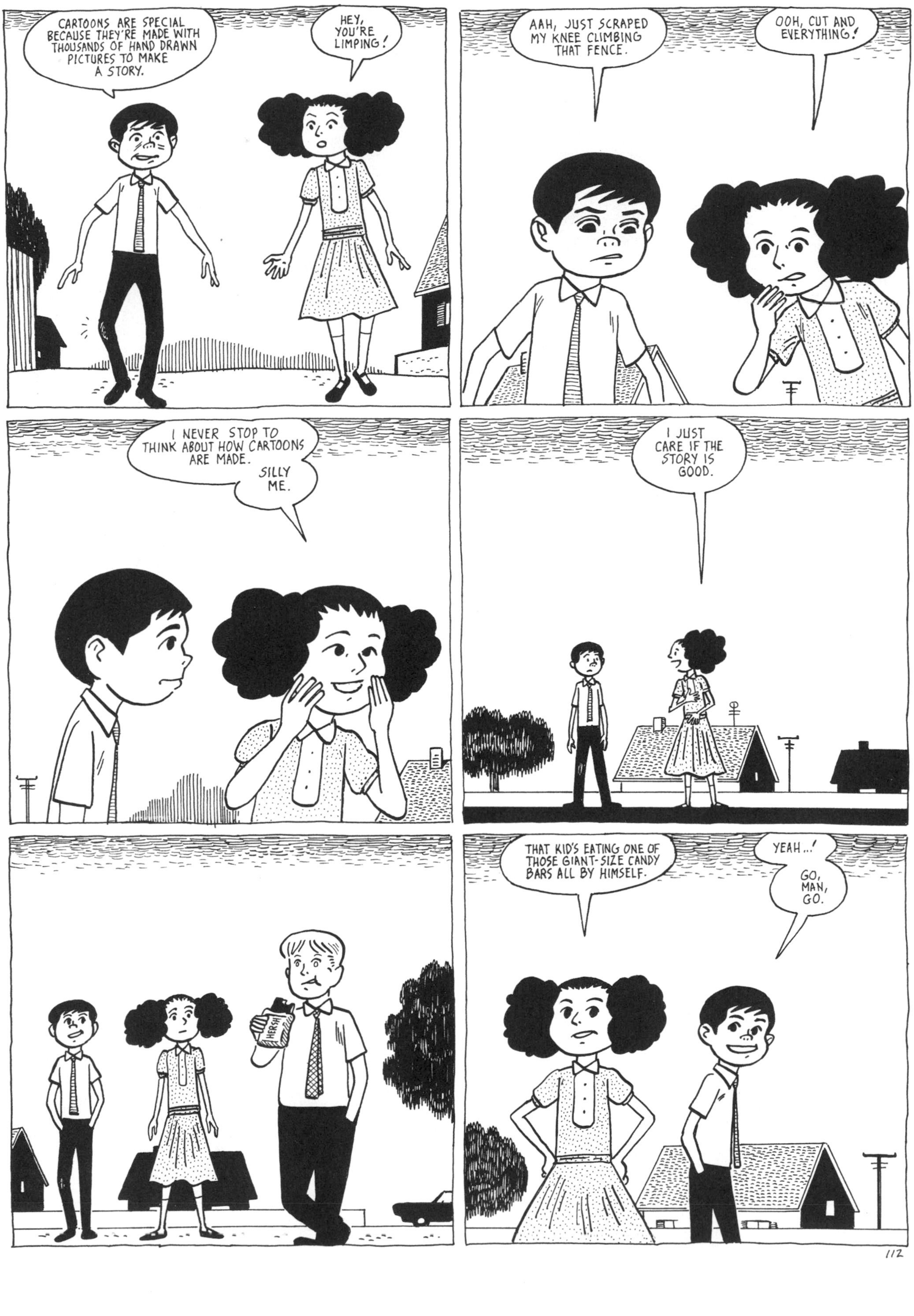
CARTOONS ARE SPECIAL BECAUSE THEY'RE MADE WITH THOUSANDS OF HAND DRAWN PICTURES TO MAKE A STORY.
HEY, YOU'RE LIMPING!
AAH, JUST SCRAPED MY KNEE CLIMBING THAT FENCE.
OOH, CUT AND EVERYTHING!
I NEVER STOP TO THINK ABOUT HOW CARTOONS ARE MADE.
SILLY ME.
I JUST CARE IF THE STORY IS GOOD.
HERSH
THAT KID'S EATING ONE OF THOSE GIANT-SIZE CANDY BARS ALL BY HIMSELF.
YEAH...!
GO, MAN, GO.

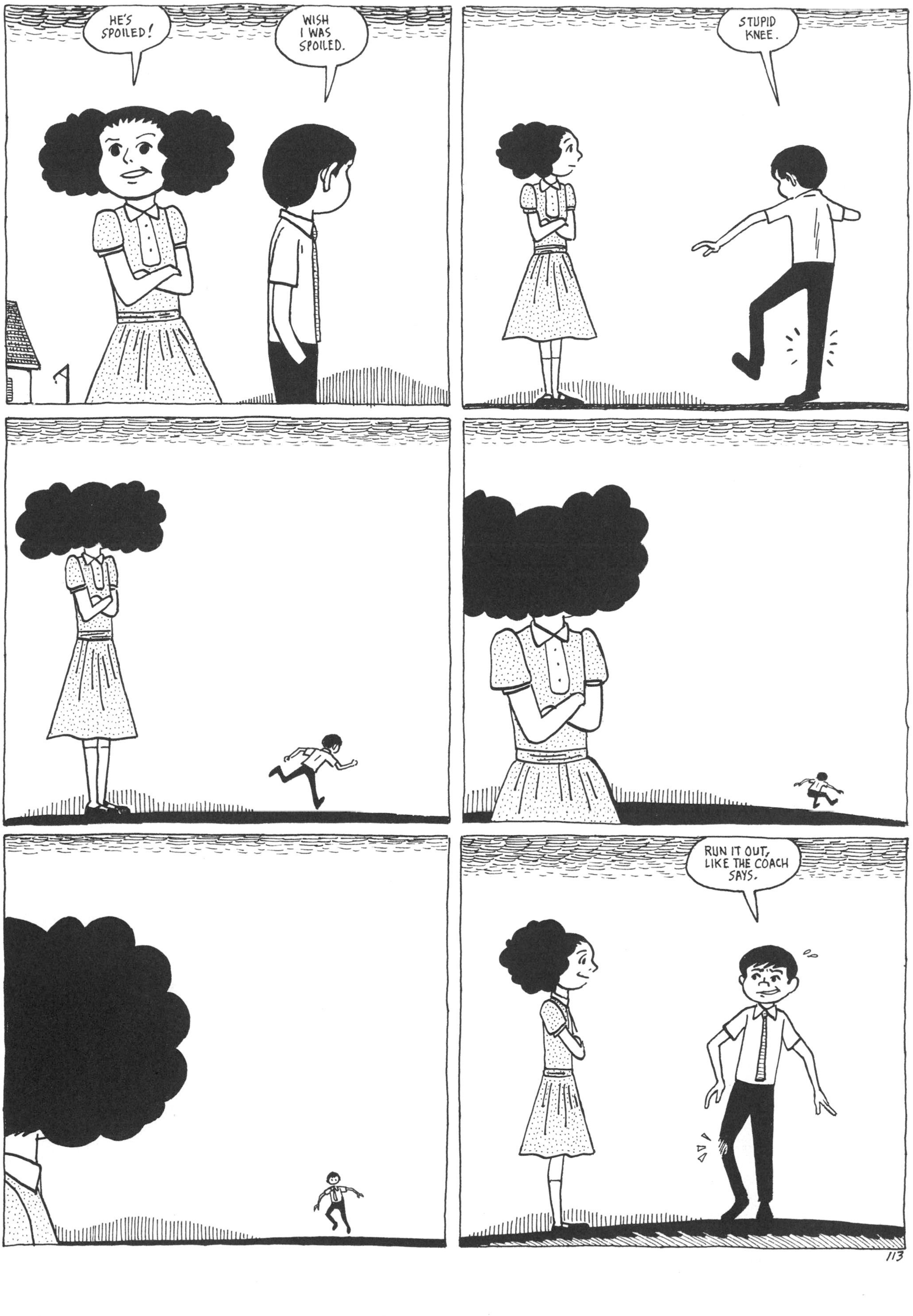
HE'S SPOILED!
WISH I WAS SPOILED.
STUPID KNEE.
RUN IT OUT, LIKE THE COACH SAYS.

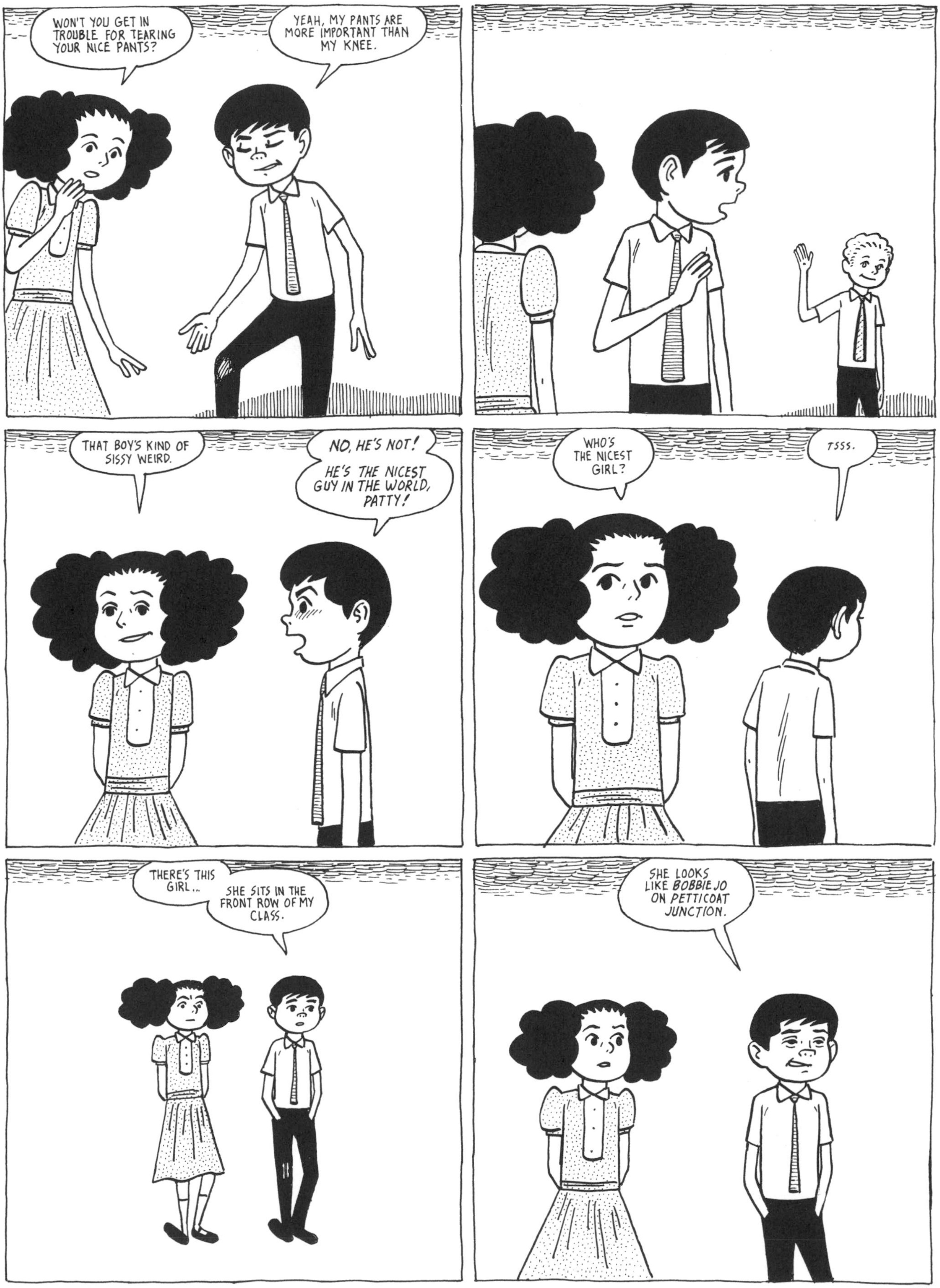
WON'T YOU GET IN TROUBLE FOR TEARING YOUR NICE PANTS?
YEAH, MY PANTS ARE MORE IMPORTANT THAN MY KNEE.
THAT BOY'S KIND OF SISSY WEIRD.
NO, HE'S NOT!
HE'S THE NICEST GUY IN THE WORLD, PATTY!
WHO'S THE NICEST GIRL?
TSSS.
THERE'S THIS GIRL...
SHE SITS IN THE FRONT ROW OF MY CLASS.
SHE LOOKS LIKE BOBBIE JO ON PETTICOAT JUNCTION.

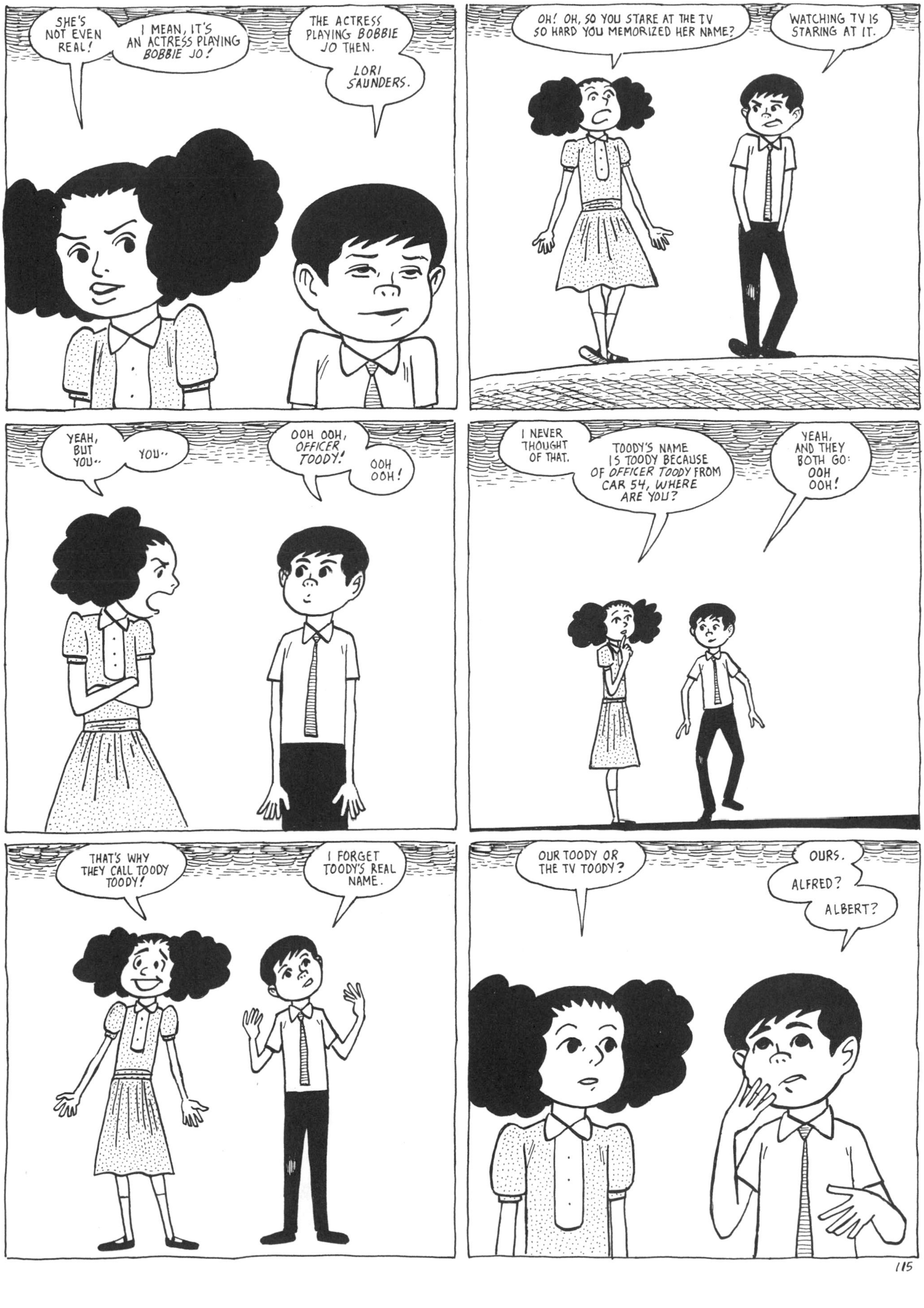
SHE'S NOT EVEN REAL!
I MEAN, IT'S AN ACTRESS PLAYING *BOBBIE JO*!
THE ACTRESS PLAYING *BOBBIE JO* THEN.
LORI SAUNDERS.
OH! OH, SO YOU STARE AT THE TV SO HARD YOU MEMORIZED HER NAME?
WATCHING TV IS STARING AT IT.
YEAH, BUT YOU..
YOU..
OOH OOH, *OFFICER TOODY!*
OOH OOH!
I NEVER THOUGHT OF THAT.
TOODY'S NAME IS TOODY BECAUSE OF *OFFICER TOODY* FROM *CAR 54, WHERE ARE YOU?*
YEAH, AND THEY BOTH GO: OOH OOH!
THAT'S WHY THEY CALL TOODY TOODY!
I FORGET TOODY'S REAL NAME.
OUR TOODY OR THE TV TOODY?
OURS.
ALFRED?
ALBERT?

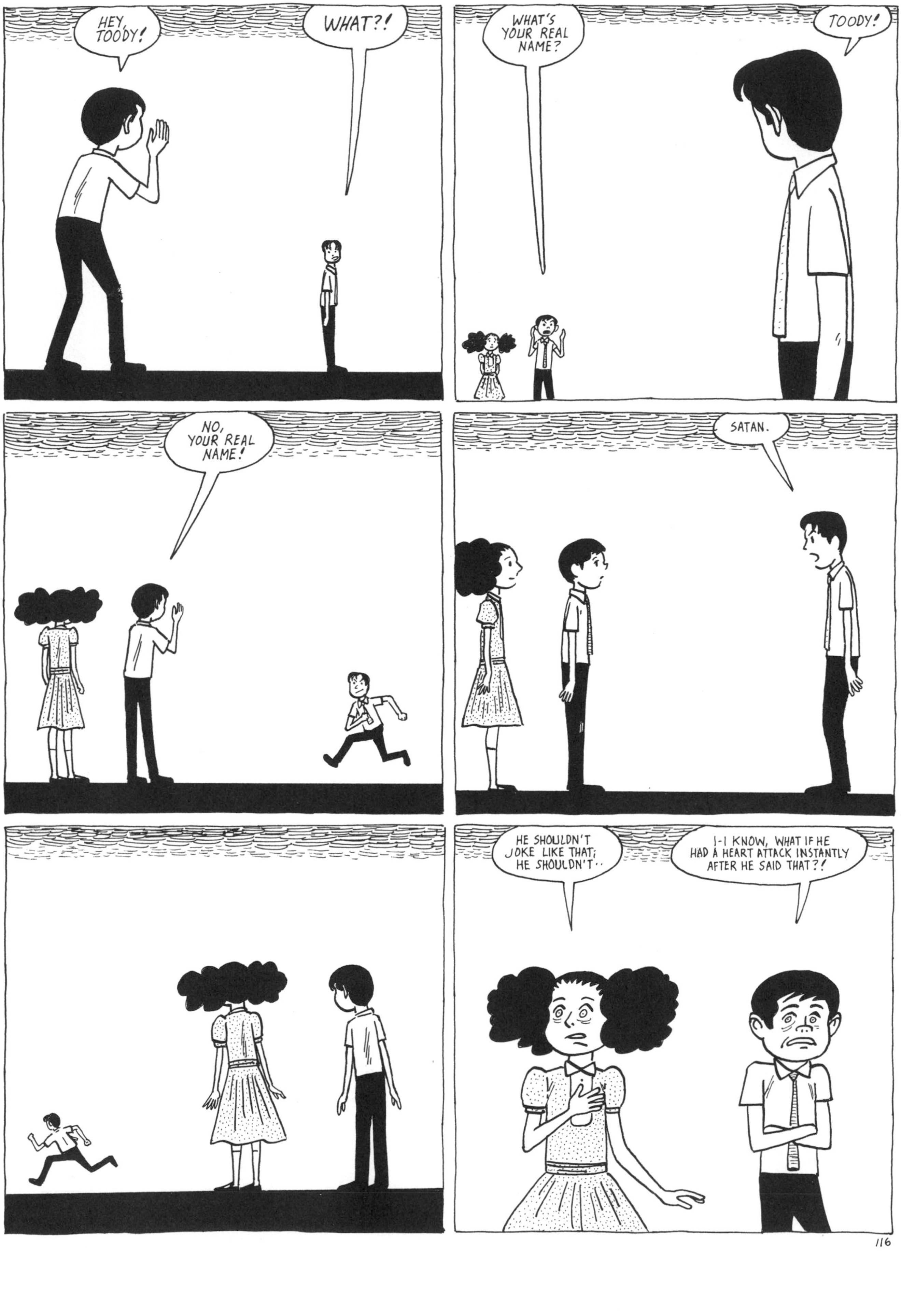
HEY, TOODY!
WHAT?!
WHAT'S YOUR REAL NAME?
TOODY!
NO, YOUR REAL NAME!
SATAN.
HE SHOULDN'T JOKE LIKE THAT; HE SHOULDN'T..
I-I KNOW, WHAT IF HE HAD A HEART ATTACK INSTANTLY AFTER HE SAID THAT?!

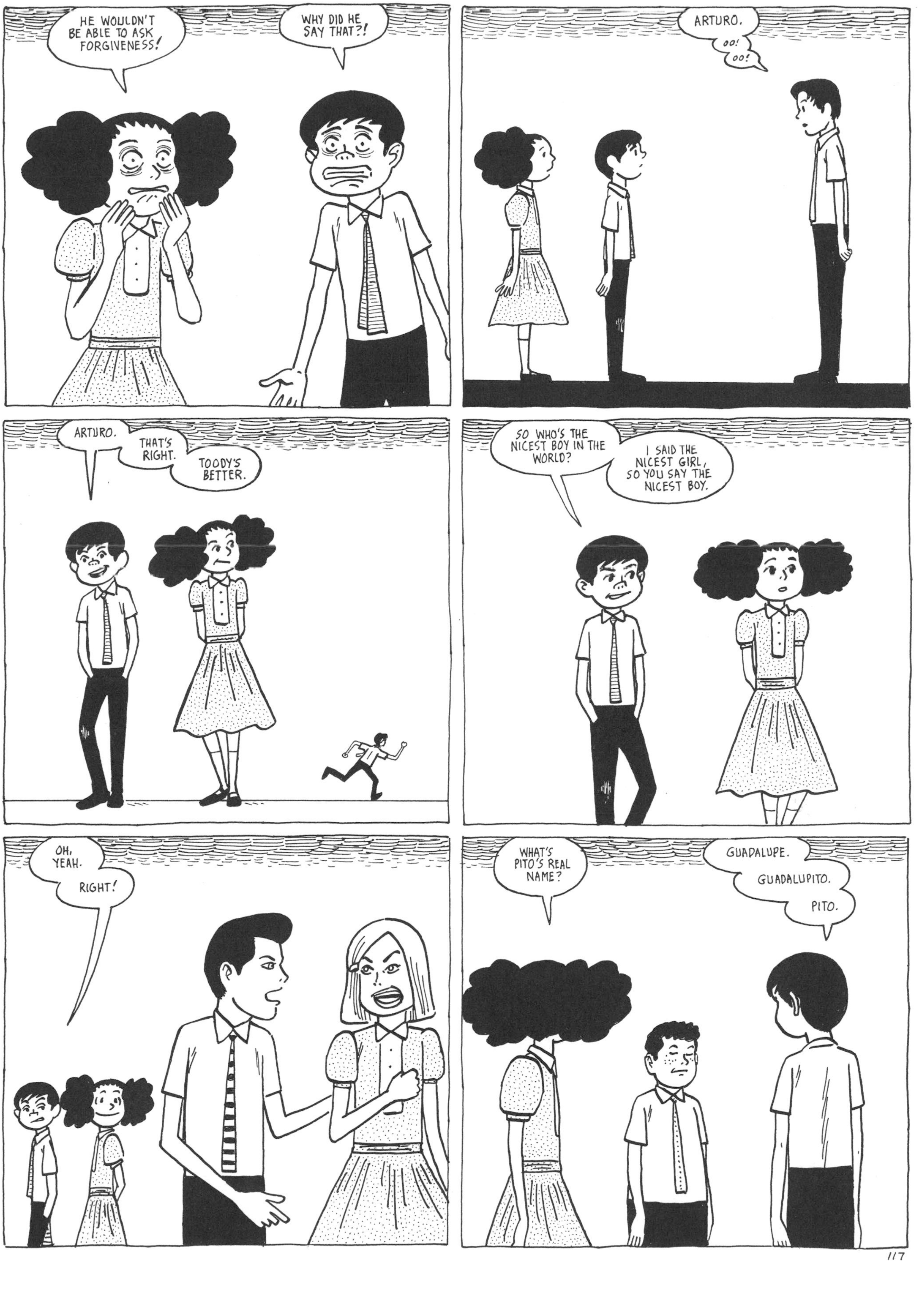
HE WOULDN'T BE ABLE TO ASK FORGIVENESS!
WHY DID HE SAY THAT?!
ARTURO.
OO! OO!
ARTURO.
THAT'S RIGHT.
TOODY'S BETTER.
SO WHO'S THE NICEST BOY IN THE WORLD?
I SAID THE NICEST GIRL, SO YOU SAY THE NICEST BOY.
OH, YEAH.
RIGHT!
WHAT'S PITO'S REAL NAME?
GUADALUPE.
GUADALUPITO.
PITO.

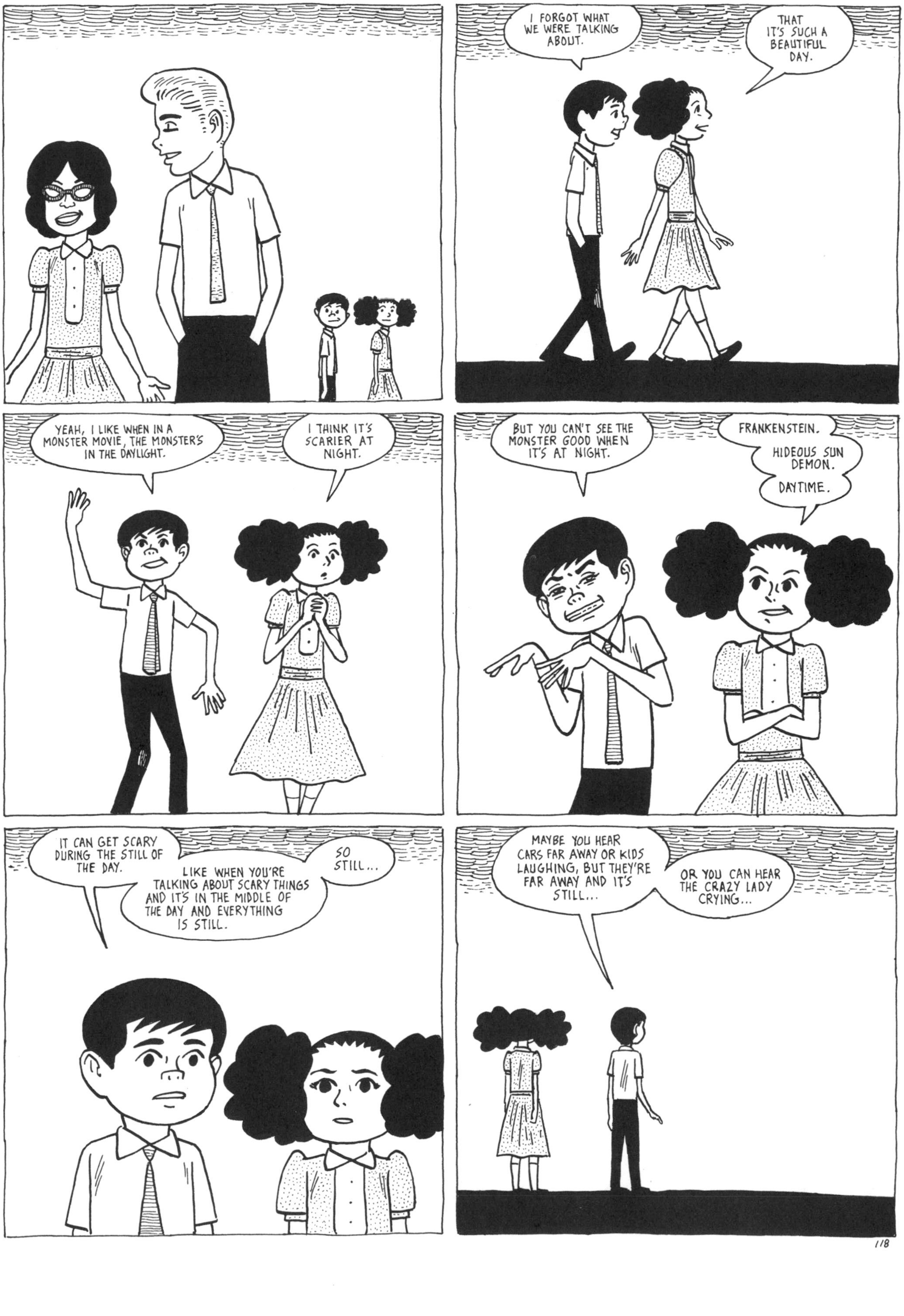
I FORGOT WHAT WE WERE TALKING ABOUT.
THAT IT'S SUCH A BEAUTIFUL DAY.
YEAH, I LIKE WHEN IN A MONSTER MOVIE, THE MONSTER'S IN THE DAYLIGHT.
I THINK IT'S SCARIER AT NIGHT.
BUT YOU CAN'T SEE THE MONSTER GOOD WHEN IT'S AT NIGHT.
FRANKENSTEIN.
HIDEOUS SUN DEMON.
DAYTIME.
IT CAN GET SCARY DURING THE STILL OF THE DAY.
LIKE WHEN YOU'RE TALKING ABOUT SCARY THINGS AND IT'S IN THE MIDDLE OF THE DAY AND EVERYTHING IS STILL.
SO STILL...
MAYBE YOU HEAR CARS FAR AWAY OR KIDS LAUGHING, BUT THEY'RE FAR AWAY AND IT'S STILL...
OR YOU CAN HEAR THE CRAZY LADY CRYING...

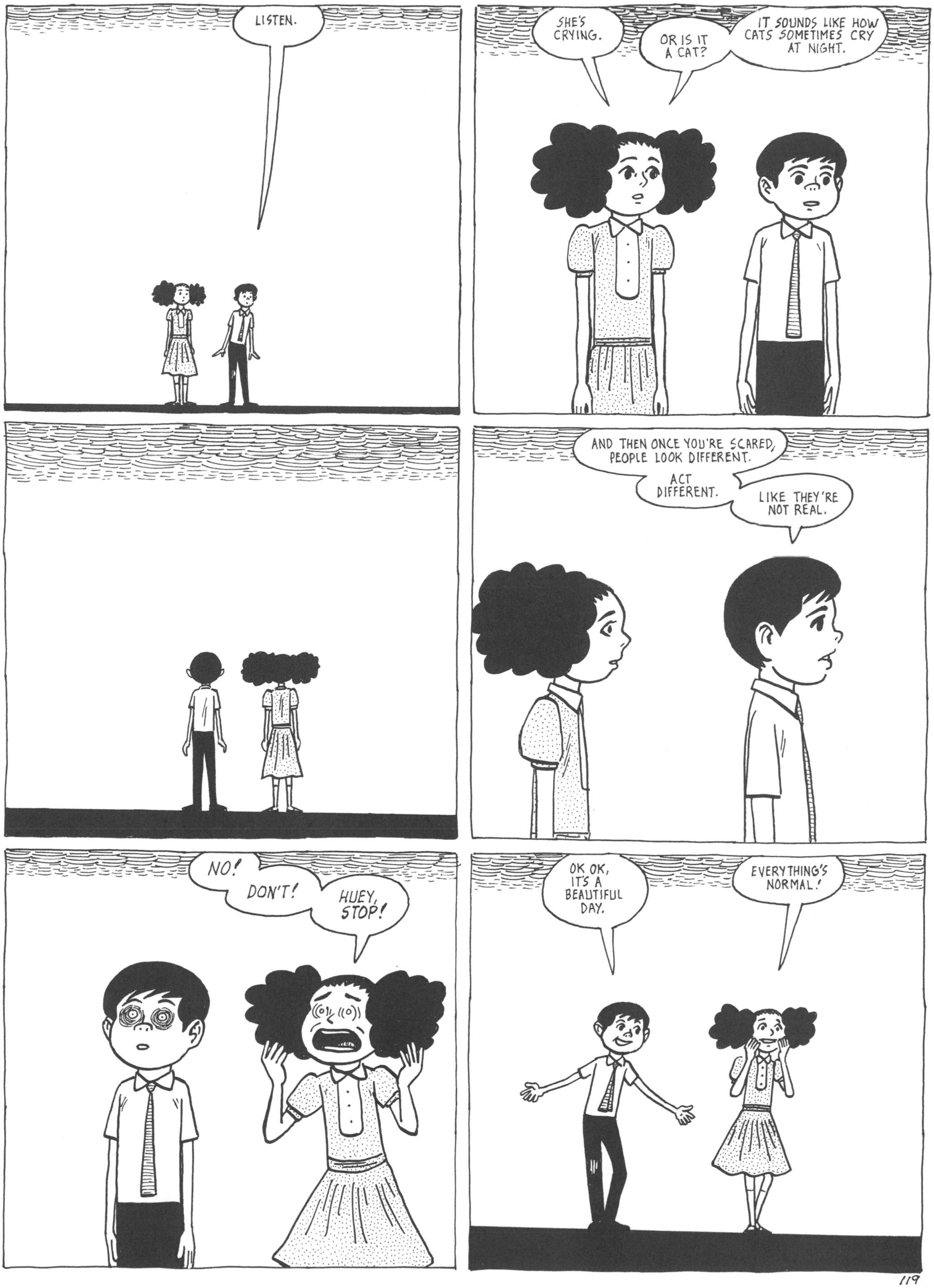
LISTEN.
SHE'S CRYING.
OR IS IT A CAT?
IT SOUNDS LIKE HOW CATS SOMETIMES CRY AT NIGHT.
AND THEN ONCE YOU'RE SCARED, PEOPLE LOOK DIFFERENT.
ACT DIFFERENT.
LIKE THEY'RE NOT REAL.
NO!
DON'T!
HUEY, STOP!
OK OK, IT'S A BEAUTIFUL DAY.
EVERYTHING'S NORMAL!

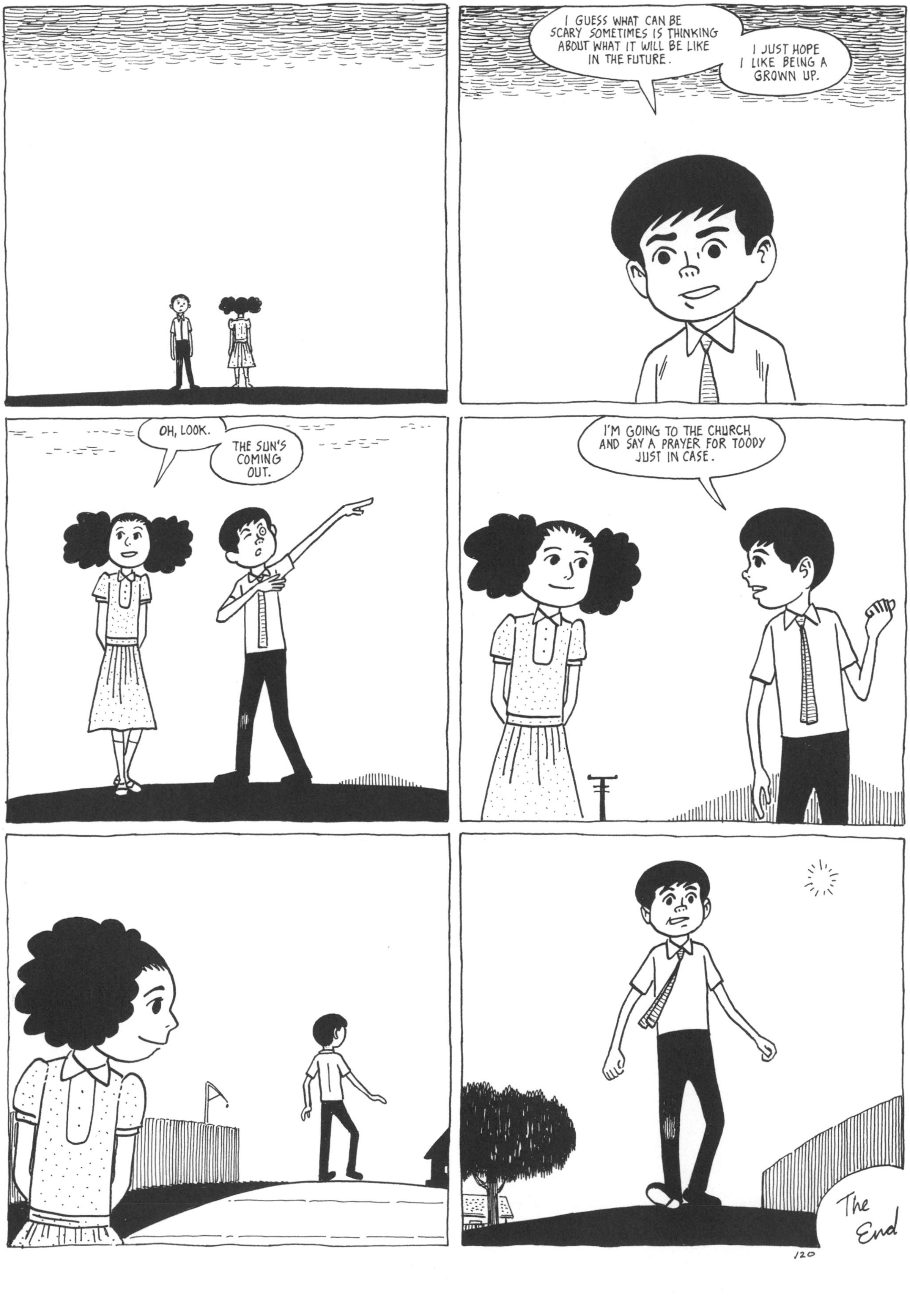
I GUESS WHAT CAN BE SCARY SOMETIMES IS THINKING ABOUT WHAT IT WILL BE LIKE IN THE FUTURE.
I JUST HOPE I LIKE BEING A GROWN UP.
OH, LOOK.
THE SUN'S COMING OUT.
I'M GOING TO THE CHURCH AND SAY A PRAYER FOR TOODY JUST IN CASE.
The End

What it Feels Like: Childhood in Gilbert Hernandez's *Marble Season*

Corey K. Creekmur, Associate Professor of English and Film Studies, University of Iowa

Every year, it seems, yet another clueless journalist writes yet another irrelevant article with the "breaking news" that "comics aren't just for kids anymore!" But does anyone still not know this? A half-century after R. Crumb's *Zap Comix* ("Fair Warning: For Adult Intellectuals Only!") relocated comics within a counter-cultural underground, or a quarter-century after *Maus*, Art Spiegelman's holocaust memoir in the form of a "funny animal comic," won a Pulitzer Prize, this is news? Ignoring the historical fact that adults have always read comics, many other touchstones might be invoked to mark the unofficial maturation of comics, but I'll choose just one. The ban on those tedious and culturally oblivious announcements should have immediately followed the 1981 appearance of the first issue of the comic book *Love & Rockets* by the artists who identified themselves as "Los Bros Hernandez." One of the defining (and, remarkably, lasting) examples of the post-underground, alternative comics renaissance of the 1980s, the black-and-white, magazine-sized *Love & Rockets* should have made it impossible for anyone to ever again dismiss comics, simply because they were comics, as merely "kid's stuff."

While they often drew upon childish—or at least adolescent—source material in their comics, Gilbert and Jaime Hernandez, the main "Bros" behind *Love & Rockets*, almost immediately combined the "adult" aspect of many earlier underground comix (in a word, sex) with an almost unprecedented artistic and narrative sophistication that demanded (and rewarded) mature readers who felt they had outgrown comic books. Indeed, in their wake—and following the emergence of key figures like Chris Ware, Joe Sacco, Alison Bechdel, and many others whose work could hardly be mistaken for children's literature—the real story persistently missed by those out-of-touch journalists is that, with rare exceptions, very few comics are for kids anymore. Once a genuine form of mass culture consumed by a large number of male and female children as well as adults, comics now address a narrowing niche market, a largely male subculture getting older all the time. Millions of people viewing recent big-budget superhero films no longer read the comics these are based on, in part because the convoluted continuities established by mainstream comics publishers haven't welcomed new readers for decades. While the recent legitimation of some comics as "graphic novels" has encouraged many readers who "don't read comics" to, well, read comics, these are largely marketed to hip adult consumers with disposable incomes, not to kids who don't yet view comics as edgy art or as investments to be sealed in plastic. On the whole, reading comics (except perhaps for the curious case of manga) is less and less a common experience of contemporary childhood. And, again, among those who effectively redirected comics away from their artistically limiting association with children were Gilbert and Jaime Hernandez, whose early work secured an especially devoted following among older readers, including the young women who by then had been virtually abandoned as an audience by mainstream American publishers.

Love & Rockets was actually the creation of three young men: Gilbert, who often signs his work as Beto, his younger brother Jaime (or Xaime), and their older brother Mario, whose contributions to the comic have been significant but less frequent. While a genuine family project as a whole, within its issues (fifty between 1982 and 1996, and ongoing in different incarnations) the comic typically divides into two ambitious, long-running, richly populated narratives. Gilbert's stories are set in the mythic Latin American town of Palomar, and often center around his formidable heroine Luba, while Jaime's stories largely take place in the Southern California barrio called Hoppers and feature the group of young women he calls "Locas," most famously the beloved (former) punk rockers Maggie and Hopey. Although both Gilbert and Jaime have written funny or sweet stories, as noted, their work often explores what are typically characterized as "adult" themes, including the vagaries of human desire and (shall we say) earthy sexuality, as well as traumatic acts of violence and social injustice that too often define the culturally diverse societies their multi-ethnic and class-divided characters inhabit.

But amidst the remarkable, decades-long unfolding of these continuing sagas, the amazingly prolific

Gilbert has also created works for kids, including the wacky series *Yeah!* (1999–2000, collected 2011), written by fellow cartoonist Peter Bagge, about an all-girl intergalactic rock band, and most recently *The Adventures of Venus* (2012), a series of short pieces about the exploits of a spunky girl soccer player (and budding cartoonist). *Marble Season* in some ways extends these works, while shifting the focus from girls to boys, and also continues the artist's steady creation of additional graphic novels apart from the Palomar stories beginning with Sloth (2006) and continuing with *Speak of the Devil* (2008) and (with brother Mario) *Citizen Rex* (2009, collected 2011). *Marble Season* is thus linked in different ways to Gilbert's larger body of work but also signals a subtle new focus: while children have appeared throughout his work, and in a few cases been his intended audience, now the experience of childhood itself seems to be his concern. (One sign of this shift is that, unlike his own previous work, but in the tradition of many previous kids' comics, *Marble Season* is set in a virtually all-kids world, with parents and teachers kept just off-stage. Parents and teachers exist in this world, but they aren't very relevant to it.)

Certainly kids have always been prominent in the work of both Hernandez brothers, even when that work hasn't been kid-appropriate. Jaime has drawn both charming and harrowing flashbacks of his main characters as children, and the sheer vital energy of kids has always been a major part of the multigenerational world of Gilbert's Palomar, and of the matriarchal Luba's life beyond Palomar in America. In addition to their regular roles within those ongoing narratives, children in *Love & Rockets* also extend the long legacy of kids in comics from Winsor McCay's dreaming Little Nemo forward. This is not just a question of shared content: if one finds echoes of the pint-sized worlds of Charles M. Schulz's *Peanuts* or John Stanley's *Little Lulu* (with its infamous "no girls allowed" boys' club invoked in *Marble Season*) within Gilbert's and Jaime's stories, their remarkably expressive drawings of little kids also acknowledge the notable stylistic influences of Hank Ketcham's *Dennis the Menace* (actually drawn for comic books by ghost artist Owen Fitzgerald) and Bob Bolling's *Little Archie* comics. (I have always found Gilbert and Jaime's ready willingness to acknowledge emphatically unhip comics among their major inspirations to

be both honest and charming.)

However, even as they echo and pay homage to such models, kids in the Hernandez brothers' work do not inhabit the nostalgic, insulated, and often all-white world of most earlier comics. At times their children are witnesses to and even perpetrators of savage cruelty; they can also be, like real kids, remarkably resilient in the face of horror or deprivation. Perhaps no other current creators of comics recognize (or vividly remember) the ways actual kids think, talk, or even stand and walk as accurately as the Hernandez brothers, and no other comics artists so delicately intertwine moments of childhood trauma with the goofy logic that otherwise sustains kids when they begin to sense that they live in an irrational world. (Lynda Barry may be their only equal in this regard.) Kids in their comics are neither sentimentalized nor sappily "innocent," and thus, as in life, they can be both scary and scared, as *Marble Season* recognizes in its brief moments depicting bullying or hints of uncertain sexuality. They are also inspiringly imaginative when they tap into that playful, adaptable ability to ignore or overcome the rational limitations adults come to sadly impose upon themselves. *Marble Season* is about, among other things, the way kids—and perhaps artists, or perhaps especially kids who become artists—think.

My claim that *Marble Season* doesn't just depict but is in some sense "about" childhood may also suggest that it's simultaneously not about much and about a whole lot. At first glance, there are very few "major events" in the story (just read Gilbert's other work if you want to see how well he can stage these when he wants to). Instead, the story is made up of the seemingly minor childhood events that might take hold as lifelong memories. (Gilbert's Palomar stories have often been compared to the "magical realist" novels of Gabriel García Márquez but I'll risk pretentiousness here and label him a *vato* Proust as well.) Perhaps saying that *Marble Season* is "about" childhood misleadingly indicates a sociological study rather than a story, but instead of either exactly, I think what Gilbert offers us in this quietly powerful work is a version of what the British cultural critic Raymond Williams famously called a "structure of feeling," a representation of the way life is lived, even or especially in the moments we might disregard as simply ordinary or everyday, within the context of a particular time and place. The focus here is therefore less on what childhood means than on what it feels like. Reading *Marble Season* induces those of us who are no longer children to remember that time in our own lives, less for its extraordinary highlights than to recover the once-common rhythms of childhood experience that are at greater risk of being forgotten. Based upon its many precise references to American popular culture, the story is set in the early 1960s, but it not only recalls, for all its readers, the past (the historical period when the story is set), but recreates that time as a present tense experience (the time the characters live in), while often quietly pointing toward the future (which is, of course, now, the time of the story's creation and our reading of it). We are motivated to simultaneously wonder what will become and what has become—in the gap between their time and ours—of Huey, his brothers, and his friends. Despite its clear, linear organization, *Marble Season* is a kind of time travel story.

Put another way, this story centers less on the series of events it narrates than the transitions (seen and not seen) between them. From the start, *Marble Season* follows the nearly imperceptible mutations within, for instance, a group dynamic in which a bully can suddenly become a quaking coward as soon as someone new enters the scene; it traces the invisible line that leads from little kids who tear up comic books to kids who read and even (someday) make comics. For what it's worth, the unstable world recreated here is much closer to my own childhood than anything I ever found in the seemingly frozen worlds of an *Archie* or *Little Lulu* comic, which were nevertheless fascinating to me precisely because they depicted kids' lives so different from my own. I never hung out in an apparently eternal Chock'lit Shoppe (whatever that was) like Archie and the gang, but I did try to destroy my G. I. Joe, seeking, like Gilbert's characters, to figure out just how a boy was supposed to play with dolls, which might be by destroying them.

Unsurprisingly, this book's title is carefully chosen. Unlike other defined temporal markers such as days, months, or years, the perceptual borders between seasons can be imprecise and vague, and their incremental transformations hard to isolate. They are also, of course, natural transitions, like the slow but dramatic physical changes of adolescent bodies, even if we try to impose cultural order and meaning upon them (as if all thirteen-year-olds are immediately teenagers on their birthdays or as if the "first day of spring" will determine that day's weather). "Marble season" is even less clearly defined than, say, "baseball season" (which has an official first day) and these imprecise, vague borders are what this work seeks to get on paper, even if that paper is ironically organized by a rigid series of bordered squares. *Marble Season* is not just a comic, like most, that signifies spatial and temporal transitions between what are in fact static panels, but it is unusually invested in the negotiation and depiction of all kinds of transitions themselves, ranging from the way a kid processes the sudden arrival and departure of new kids in the neighborhood, to the way a young boy considers his own changing body when he identifies with the mutating bodies of superheroes like the Hulk and scans the bodybuilding ads in comics, or only halfway comprehends the curious changes within a community (and in his own feelings) when the local tomboy is transformed by wearing a dress. *Marble Season* renders temporality in the way it is experienced by kids, or as it functions in our blurry memories of childhood, and this temporal flow rather than precise chronology is persistently manifested in the often elusive and elliptical transitions between the otherwise regular six-panel grid that Gilbert employs to structure the comic itself. (This technique isn't altogether new—both Hernandez brothers are widely considered masters of comics panel transitions—but seems especially important here as a means to intertwine form and content.)

I urge readers to linger on rather than speed past the silent panels that regularly punctuate this story. They aren't simple filler, but serve as their own little time capsules, moments for us as well as Gilbert's characters to pause, reflect, and take a breath before moving forward. These silent panels look and feel like what the philosopher William James called "felt time." They represent change that, at the time, doesn't feel like change, or at least like significant or momentous change, but that looks incredibly precious when it has passed, in retrospect.

If *Marble Season* encourages us to time travel by recalling and appreciating subtle change as we remember our own childhoods while we proceed—

slowly, I hope—from panel to panel, it also makes a case for the affective value of the icons and objects of American mass culture in that process. While there's no question that one of the major contributions of the Hernandez brothers to the history of American comics is their rich representation of multiethnic and multiracial communities, I sometimes think a bit too much has been made of this innovation. Despite the racial and ethnic differences that begin (as shown here) to ground the identities of young men and may eventually work to isolate them from one another, Gilbert's kids otherwise share an immersion in American mass culture. The dozens of allusions to songs, TV shows, movies, toys, and other commercial products (yeah, comics too) throughout *Marble Season* function as the *lingua franca* of childhood that allows difference to be overcome through a shared vocabulary and effective translations. The comics of the Hernandez brothers have always been densely and playfully allusive, but the many citations of popular culture in *Marble Season* seem less like hip, subcultural signifiers to reward insiders (as they often could be in *Love & Rockets*) than a catalog of the once-familiar items that would be the result of an archeological excavation of America in the early 1960s: this is the stuff you would uncover if you dug up a buried school playground or a boy's bedroom from the era. Sure, this is the ephemeral detritus of junk culture, meant to be played with until broken and discarded, or fated to be tossed out by your mother with the rest of the trash: but, as kids all know, these lowly objects might also function as magical fetishes and sacred totems, bits of fragile paper and plastic that nevertheless once sparked the imagination and now give material weight and concrete detail to otherwise elusive memories. Perhaps no one except Gilbert Hernandez vividly recalls the obscure comic book story "The Man with the Electronic Brain," written by Gardner Fox and drawn by Murphy Anderson, which appeared in DC's *Strange Adventures* no. 128 in May 1961: but Huey, at least, appreciates the story's clever gimmick, and retains the encouraging lesson (your brain can be your superpower!) it entertainingly conveyed. Mass culture, in its sheer massiveness, works that way: some of it, like the new pop group these kids call "The Beatos," attracts a vast audience and obtains lasting value, whereas some of it may

only ever resonate with one or two people, or within a few neighborhoods. Huey has been collecting the infamous Topps trading-card set Mars Attacks, which told the grisly story of Earth's near-destruction before finally blowing up Mars. Even though they were "stacked all nice and neat," his mother "just saw them as trash" and casually tosses them out. The card sets are now rare and valuable collector's items precisely because that's what happened to most of them, but *Marble Season* indicates that although as objects these and other treasures disappear from Huey's life, those cheap and lurid products of American mass culture— just kids' stuff, after all—nevertheless retain their impact, perhaps for decades. If you managed (as few did) to collect all fifty-five cards in the set, they told a linked story, not so different in structure from a series of sequential comics panels, and even though each card depicted a somewhat isolated incident, they could be "stacked all nice and neat" rather like the pages you encounter in *Marble Season* itself.

The rising status and value (literal and symbolic) of the artifacts of 1960s commercial culture is another curious transformation *Marble Season* hints at, and Huey's suspicion that the only thing he "knows how to do right is read comic books" sadly discredits his own already vivid story-creating imagination by affirming the dominant values of his society. From our critical distance, we suspect that, like his creator, Huey might someday put that unrecognized talent to good use. (There's good reason to read this work as semi-autobiographical, despite the changed names of Gilbert's characters; at the same time, it's worth noting that Gilbert Hernandez grew up with four brothers, and one sister, so creative license may also be allowed in this work about the creative imagination.) All Huey will have to do is remember and—the far more difficult task—continue to value the magic word he casually yet defiantly invokes whenever his "childish" fantasies are questioned: "pretend."

There are numerous pop culture references that may be lost on some modern readers. Gilbert Hernandez has chosen to detail these references for our edification.

Page 3   *panel 4:* The war that Huey refers to is World War II.

Page 5   *panel 1:* "Up on the Roof" is a song by the Drifters. It reached number 5 on the US pop charts in 1962.
   panel 3: The comic Junior is holding is *Strange Adventures* no. 128 (DC Comics).
   panel 5: Palisades Park was an East Coast (Bergen County, New Jersey) amusement park that eventually closed in 1971.

Page 12   *panel 3: Bozo the Clown* was an American children's TV show whose popularity peaked in the 1960s.
   panel 4: Jimmy Olsen is a character in the Superman series, played by Jack Larson in the *Adventures of Superman*, a 1950s TV show.

Page 13   *panel 1:* Lana is referring to a myth that George Reeves, the actor who played Superman in the TV series *Adventures of Superman*, mistakenly thought that he had acquired Superman's power of flight and jumped out of a window to his death. In reality, Reeves died of a gunshot wound on June 16, 1959.

Page 16   *panel 1:* Red Skull was the name used by several Marvel villains. The first two Red Skulls were Nazis and enemies of Captain America, while the third Red Skull—famous for killing Peter Parker's parents—was a Soviet and faced off against the Grand Director (a hero who impersonated Captain America after his disappearance in 1945).

Page 17   *panel 2:* Carbon paper is coated on one side with a pigment that transfers to a piece of paper underneath when pressure is applied, allowing multiple copies of a document to be written at once.

Page 20   *panel 6: It's a Mad Mad Mad Mad World* is a 1963 comedy film starring many of the greatest comedians of the day, including Mickey Rooney, Ethel Merman, Spencer Tracy, and Phil Silvers.

Page 28   *panel 5:* The comic Huey is holding is *The Incredible Hulk* no. 2 (Marvel Comics).

Page 37   *panel 2:* Curly Howard was a slapstick comedian, best known for being one of The Three Stooges. Jerry Lewis was a comedian who originally performed as a team with Dean Martin. The duo was so popular that they had their own DC Comics series. Granny, played by Irene Ryan, is a character from the 1960s TV comedy *The Beverly Hillbillies*.
   panel 2: The comic Chavo is holding is an issue of the *Fantastic Four* (Marvel Comics).

Page 39   *panels 5–6:* Huey is singing the theme song from *The Mighty Hercules* TV cartoon series (1963–1966).

Page 43   *panels 1–2:* "Thank You, Girl" is a song by the Beatles. It reached number 35 on the US pop charts in 1964.
   panel 5: Mike Nelson (played by Lloyd Bridges) is the lead character in *Sea Hunt*, a TV show that aired from 1958 to 1961.

Page 44   *panel 6:* Elasti-Girl can grow into a giant or shrink down to the size of a mouse, and wears a very short skirt. The Doom Patrol was a superhero team created by Arnold Drake, Bruno Premiani, Murray Boltinoff, and Bob Haney for DC Comics that first appeared in 1963.

Page 46   *panel 3:* Mars Attacks was a set of trading cards created by Topps in 1962.

Page 48   *panel 1:* Don Drysdale was a pitcher for the Los Angeles Dodgers baseball team in the 1950s and 1960s. He later became a well-known sportscaster.

Page 49   *panel 5: Mr. Sardonicus* was a 1960s horror film whose protagonist's face had been frozen into a horrifying grin while digging up his father's grave for a winning lottery ticket.

Page 57   *panel 2:* "You've Lost that Lovin' Feeling" is a song by The Righteous Brothers. It was number 1 on US and UK charts in 1965.

   panel 6: Lucio is singing the Hasbro jingle used in the 1960s for their G.I. Joe toy line. The tune is based on "The Army Goes Rolling Along," the official song of the US Army.

Page 59   *panel 2:* "She Loves You" is a song by the Beatles. It hit number 1 on US and UK charts in 1964.

Page 60   *panel 4: The Dick Tracy Show* always opened with the title character calling one of his associates with his two-way wrist radio to assign them a case. Go Go Gomez, one of these assistants, was a stereotyped Mexican who wore a sombrero.

Page 62   *panels 5–6:* "You Can't Hurry Love" is a song by The Supremes that topped US charts in 1966.

Page 63   *panel 1:* The comic that Huey is given is *Ghost Stories* no. 1 (Dell Comics) written by John Stanley.

Page 70   *panels 1–2:* Birdman's battle cry from 1960s TV cartoon series *Birdman and the Galaxy Trio*.
   panel 6: Project Mercury was the US's first human spaceflight program and ran from 1959 to 1963.

Page 90   *panel 3:* Buddy Austin and Mark Lewen were American heavyweight wrestlers. Austin debuted in the early 1960s and Lewen in the early 1950s.
   panel 4: Shindig! was a variety show that aired in the 1960s, hosted by Jimmy O'Neill.
   panel 5: Dick Lane was a television announcer for wrestling and roller derby on the Los Angeles channel KTLA.

Page 93   *panel 5: Creepy* was a horror magazine published by Warren Publishing.

Page 101   *panel 5:* The Howling Commandos were a fictional World War II army unit led by Sgt. Nick Fury in a comic series published by Marvel Comics.

Page 102   *panel 2:* The first Captain Marvel was originally published by Fawcett Comics in the 1940s. This was the second character to use the name.

Page 107   *panel 5: Dennis the Menace* comic books were published by Fawcett Comics from 1958 to 1980.

Page 110   *panel 3: The Hideous Sun Demon* was a 1959 film about a scientist who is exposed to radiation in his lab and then changed into a scaled demon by the sun.
   panel 5: Cinderella was released by Disney in 1950.

Page 114   *panel 6:* Bobbie Jo was a character from the 1960s TV comedy *Petticoat Junction*. She was played by Pat Woodell from 1963 to 1965 and by Lori Saunders from 1965 to 1970.

Page 115   *panels 3–4:* Officer Gunther Toody was a character on the sitcom *Car 45, Where Are You?* that aired in the 1960s and early 1970s. Toody was played by vaudeville comedian Joe E. Ross who used his characteristic "Ooh! Ooh!" exclamation in more than one role.

GILBERT HERNANDEZ was born in 1957 in Oxnard, California. In 1981, he co-self-published the first issue of *Love & Rockets* with his older brother, Mario and younger brother, Jaime. Embracing strong female lead characters and punk rock culture, this series stood out from the male dominated comics landscape of the late 1970s and early 1980s. The following year, *Love & Rockets* was picked up and republished and continued as a series by Fantagraphics Books. Gilbert Hernandez and his brother Jaime have continued *Love & Rockets* for three decades; the series is acknowledged as the creative flashpoint for the second wave of underground comics. In the ensuing years, Hernandez has been nominated for—and won—nearly every industry award, as well as the prestigious United States Artists Literature Fellowship. Hernandez currently lives in Las Vegas, Nevada with his wife, Carol, and his daughter, Natalia.

Palomar (Fantagraphics)
Heartbreak Soup (Fantagraphics)
Human Diastrophism (Fantagraphics)
Beyond Palomar (Fantagraphics)
Love & Rockets X (Fantagraphics)
Luba (Fantagraphics)
Birdland (Fantagraphics/Eros)
Girl Crazy (Dark Horse)
Yeah! (Fantagraphics) with Peter Bagge
Fear of Comics (Fantagraphics)
Grip (Vertigo)

Sloth (Vertigo)
Chance in Hell (Fantagraphics)
Love in the Shadows (Fantagraphics)
The Troublemakers (Fantagraphics)
Speak of the Devil (Dark Horse)
High Soft Lisp (Fantagraphics)
Citizen Rex (Dark Horse) with Mario Hernandez
Adventures of Venus (Fantagraphics)
Fatima: The Blood Spinners (Dark Horse)
Julio's Day (Fantagraphics)

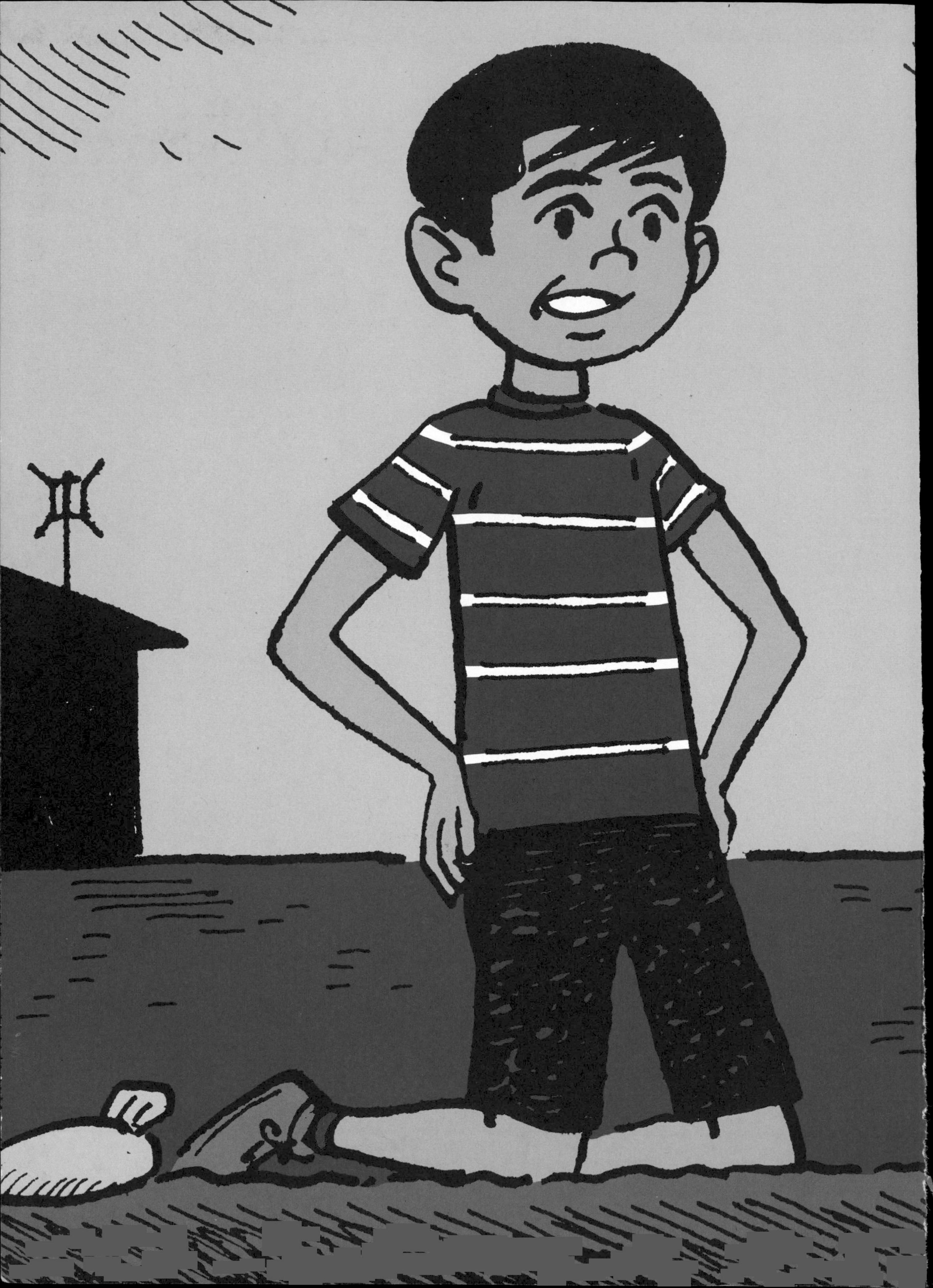